THE GREEN GHOST

THE GREEN GHOST

William Burroughs and the Ecological Mind

CHAD WEIDNER

Southern Illinois University Press
Carbondale

Southern Illinois University Press
www.siupress.com

Printed in the United States of America

19 18 17 16   4 3 2 1

Cover illustration: painting of William S. Burroughs by Alexander Adams (foreground); leaf background from Shutterstock

Library of Congress Cataloging-in-Publication Data
Names: Weidner, Chad.
Title: The green ghost : William Burroughs and the ecological mind / Chad Weidner.
Description: Carbondale : Southern Illinois University Press, 2016. | Includes bibliographical references and index.
Identifiers: LCCN 2015031333| ISBN 9780809334865 (paperback) | ISBN 9780809334872 (e-book)
Subjects: LCSH: Burroughs, William S., 1914–1997—Criticism and interpretation | Ecology in literature. | Beat generation. | Ecocriticism. | BISAC: LITERARY CRITICISM / American / General.
Classification: LCC PS3552.U75 Z925 2016 | DDC 813/.54—dc23 LC record available at http://lccn.loc.gov/2015031333

The paper used in this publication meets the minimum requirements of American National Standard for Information Sciences—Permanence of Paper for Printed Library Materials, ANSI Z39.48-1992. ∞

For W and V

CONTENTS

ACKNOWLEDGMENTS

This book could not have been written without the deep support of many institutions, colleagues, friends, and family members. My thanks go to the Flemish Community of Belgium, which provided two years of modest funding during the key formative period of this project, crucial funds without which I would never have gotten started, and to University College Roosevelt and Utrecht University, which funded research trips to scholarly conferences in Europe, Africa, and the United States. These conferences allowed me to test my ideas in front of a critical audience. I recognize my many colleagues and friends at the University College Roosevelt, including David Aiken and Hans Bloemsma. I am also grateful to Leslie Whipp, who stirred me to grip literature with both hands; Charles Peek, who embodies much of what I want to become both professionally and as a human; and Oliver Harris, who warmly invited me into his home. I am indebted to other people that have supported me in one way or another through the cultivation of this project. I thank Alexander Adams for his stunning cover art. I also express gratitude to Karl Kageff, Kristiaan Versluys, Franca Bellarsi, Bart Eeckhout, Francine, and most of all, Karolien.

A portion of chapter 3 was previously published as "Mutable Forms: The Proto-ecology of Williams Burroughs' Early Cut-ups" in *Comparative American Studies* 11.3 (2013): 314–26.

THE GREEN GHOST

1.

Introduction

The title of this book, *The Green Ghost: William Burroughs and the Ecological Mind*, is a bit ambiguous and ungraspable, much like William Burroughs himself. A remarkably complicated individual, Burroughs was at different times the son of American industry, a Harvard anthropologist, farmer, globetrotter, junkie, queer, and infamous experimental writer. But we never can completely understand him. Not totally. Every time we try to grip the author, to place him into a theoretical or historical box, he slips through our fingers, and a different Burroughs emerges. Neither the numerous biographies in existence nor the literary studies that have been carried out have successfully captured the complete essence of this most alluring and enigmatic of writers. Since the 1970s, common approaches to understanding William Burroughs involve discussions of the more sensational aspects of his incredible life and innovative writing. Researchers often deliberate key thematic issues, including homosexuality, the grotesque human body, addiction, and his legacy of literary experimentation. And while there has been a good deal of scholarship on some features of Burroughs and his writing, there are still significant gaps. In the age of environmental upheaval and increasing human awareness of ecological issues, new questions force us to reassess the writing of this extremely challenging and sometimes contradictory author. What makes this study different is its ecological focus on a number of literary texts written by William Burroughs, who remains the most slippery of authors, an eternally ethereal green ghost.

Ecocriticism is an umbrella term that encompasses many theoretical and methodological approaches to better understanding the relationship between human culture and the environment. Ecocriticism is a humanities area that examines cultural texts, such as literature or film, in the context of current environmental concerns. So I am very interested in exploring the places where there is friction between human culture and the environment, where they meet, or where they possibly overlap. Kerridge and Sammells think of ecocriticism as the study of "texts and ideas in terms of their coherence and usefulness as responses to environmental crises" (5). Lawrence Buell calls ecocriticism the "study of the relationship between literature and the environment conducted in a spirit of commitment to environmentalist praxis" (*Environmental Imagination* 430). I think Buell is too cautious here and privileges literature over other cultural texts. For the purpose of this book, *ecocriticism* can be defined as the study of the relationship between cultural texts and the environment conducted in a spirit of commitment to environmentalist praxis.

This particular study involves the examination of the relationship between humans and the environment in specific literary texts, and in this respect, this book fits the general trajectory of ecocriticism, which still emphasizes the study of literary texts. While the focus of this particular book is literary in nature, I acknowledge the need to tackle Burroughs' nonliterary creations, including collages, paintings, tapes, and films. One particular challenge of dealing with a writer like William Burroughs is finding ways to balance the polemic that is always in tension with a radical formal equivocation. Therefore, *The Green Ghost* briefly deals with a number of crucial ecological questions. What follows, then, is a brief discussion of a number of concepts that helped guide the process of researching and writing this book.

One vital concept is nature, and human language allows us to discuss the notion, at least to some extent. Henry David Thoreau wrote during a particularly striking moment in the development of American culture. The very sense of nature in the human imagination shifted, and "secularized Christianity [saw] nature as a primary revelation, displacing scripture" (Buell, *Environmental Imagination* 332). This is evident in Thoreau's own wonder for natural history: "Properly speaking there can be no history but natural history, for there is no past in the soul, but in nature" (*Writings* 86). While Thoreau was thinking about the history of the earth's geologic and biological diversity and ever-changing ecosystems, the suggestion that "there is no past in the soul, but in nature" implies a binary between the human and the nonhuman world, a separation that might exist linguistically. However, if we can accept that human language is "essentially representational" (Phillips, "Ecocriticism" 588), then we can pose the more crucial question of whether humans can ever begin to discuss the presence or absence of nature. A cynic might claim that human language is able to represent neither the passage of geological time nor the incredible diversity and variation of life on this planet. Another consideration is whether humans can even start to bridge the gap between the language of nature and our own verbal language. If one sees language as a means to an end, and not an end in itself, then language is the best means to allow human beings to begin to comprehend their existence on this planet, and literature, as an important cultural and linguistic construction, can help in accomplishing this task.

We cannot say whether nature is predictable and stable, random and chaotic, or both. Dutch environmental scholar Isabel Hoving says an "organicist approach understands nature as a self-regulating, closed, balanced system" (169). This would seem to complement the belief that if humans would only allow the earth to achieve balance, existence for plants and animals would be guaranteed, at least for a considerable time. The work of Darwin and the early geneticist Mendel would appear to support such an orderly assessment of the universe. But the existence of unpredictable natural anomalies calls such systems of natural order into serious question. If biological mutations occur randomly, then nature is not an orderly and efficient system at all; quite the contrary. Mutations are just one of the many chaotic natural phenomena that force us to reconsider the idea of systematic natural order. If one looks at the fossil record, evidence suggests that evolution provides far more paths to death than to life. While there may indeed be rules by which the universe normally operates (physics being just one example of a human discipline devoted to mapping out natural phenomena, and thereby organizing them into predictable schema), the existence of mutations and other chaotic natural occurrences shows the need to adjust our views on the seeming stability and rhythm of nature.

Heather Sullivan points to Dana Phillips, who thinks it crucial that we accept the essential chaotic rhythms of the universe: "Unbalance is where we begin; who knows where it will take us" (283). Phillips (*Truth of Ecology* 71) and Ursula Heise (*Sense of Place* 64) both reject the idea of a harmonious state of nature and see an awkward, ever-changing biological journey, going somewhere that we cannot possibly predict with accuracy. Timothy Morton (*Ecological Thought*) suggests that humans exist on one large, rather chaotic, interconnected ecological mesh, an ecological web of sorts, and that the realization of our interconnectedness with all life is what he calls "the ecological thought." However, there are problems with Morton's assessment. The inherent difficulty in defining nature leaves Morton proposing that "the ecological thought" is "a virus that infects all other areas of thinking" (2). Morton also believes that ecology is really about "love, loss, despair, and compassion. It has to do with depression and psychosis. It has to do with capitalism and what might exist after capitalism" (2). I am far less convinced on this point, since Morton is casting a very wide net indeed. He seems to accept the notion of nature as a cultural construct (11) but at the same time advises that we abandon romantic notions of nature altogether, to develop a more skeptical postmodern position. A more straightforward understanding of ecological concentrations is more helpful for framing this particular study.

In the most basic sense, ecology is the study of organisms and their interaction with the environment. European ecocritic Franca Bellarsi draws attention to T. V. Reed's chart of different ecological concentrations as helpful in separating the sometimes murky distinctions among these important concepts ("Challenges of Nature" 75). Reed ("Toward") says ecocritical studies fall under the following concentrations:

- "conservationist";
- "ecological";
- "biocentric/deep ecological";
- "ecofeminist"; and
- "environmental justice." (148–49)

To Reed, "conservationist ecocriticism" questions, "What can literature/nature writing and criticism do to enhance appreciation and improve attitudes toward the natural environment?" (148). The concentrations of the conservationist ecocritic seem clear enough. A second category for ecocritical focus exceeds purely conservationist concerns and involves what Reed calls "ecological ecocriticism," which asks how the "ecosystem idea (or metaphor) [can be] extended to a poetics of the literary system in relation to nature" (148). "Ecological ecocriticism" thus goes beyond conservationist ecocriticism in terms of attention to "particular ecosystems [and] bioregions" (148), including metaphorical representations of ecosystems in various cultural texts. An even more complex form of ecocritical focus, according to Reed, is "biocentric/deep ecological ecocriticism," which questions the central place of humans and emphasizes "the biotic sphere," often to show the limits of human thinking (148). An additional emphasis in "ecofeminist ecocriticism" interrogates cultural texts for the thought-provoking ways in which gender informs, or is informed by, ecocritical reading. Ecofeminism might ask, "How are the liberation of women and the liberation of nature linked?" (148). To go a step further, one wonders how the treatment of nature and women reflect larger cultural attitudes and practices. We can extend Reed's discussion to queer ecological issues, such as the assumed male-female heterosexual-homosexual binary that nature increasingly reveals is actually radically ambiguous. A final ecocritical focus, according to Reed, involves searching out the places in which cultural texts uncover issues of "environmental justice." Ecocritics carrying out environmental justice readings attempt to uncover the ways in which environmental despoliations disproportionately affect minorities and the underprivileged (149).

Reed's breakdown thus presents a useful outline of ecocritical concentrations as a port of entry for ecocritical studies at present. In the following chapters, I approach texts written by William Burroughs primarily from conservationist, ecological, and biocentric/deep ecological positions (148). Keeping these concentrations in mind is important because, depending on the ecological focus of a researcher, ecocritical practices also differ.

Mapping Burroughs: Four Phases

For my purposes, Burroughs' career can be broken down into four distinct phases. The initial stage included the publication of *Junkie* in 1953 and the writing of *Queer* from 1951 to 1953. Narratives from this early period involve attempts to duplicate eyewitness accounts (*Junkie*) or personal experiences and sentimental reminiscences (*Queer*). While *Junkie* provides a sense of the unconventional content found in Burroughs' future books, the narrative lacks the self-confidence and experimental importance of his later texts. *Queer* was also composed during this time, but it was not released until the mid-1980s and thus did not have nearly the cultural impact it might have had if it had been made available earlier.

Burroughs' most significant publications were written from the early 1950s until the early 1970s, and this can be called his experimental and subversive period. It was during this phase that Burroughs wrote *Naked Lunch* (1959), which still holds nearly universal controversial status. Other notable publications from this period include *The Yage Letters* (1963), which challenges notions of genre and links to crucial issues of biopiracy and ecology. The mysterious aesthetic forms in the text of *The Yage Letters* are particularly important in an ecocritical discussion of the author's writing. The cut-up years produced not only the mysterious early cut-ups present in *Minutes to Go* (1960) and *The Yage Letters* but also the ambitious and experimental *Nova* trilogy, which was recently released in its definitive form. *The Wild Boys* (1971) saw Burroughs continue to test various writing strategies incorporating cut-up and fold-in methods. The most important characteristics of the books from this time involve the practice of systematic subversion of literary conventions.

The final phases of Burroughs' writing career saw a move toward shorter, more linear narratives. From the mid-1970s until the 1980s, Burroughs recycled previously written texts. *The Burroughs File* (1984) and *The Adding Machine* (1985) were published during this time. The revisiting of previous material might appear to suggest that Burroughs was slowing down, especially given his advancing years. However, the late period demonstrated a remarkable and renewed writing energy that lasted up until his death. The final stage of Burroughs' career began with the *Red Night* trilogy (1981–87). The series was important, since it was the first large-scale project in more than a decade. Other publications during this crucial late period include *The Cat Inside* (1992), *My Education: A Book of Dreams* (1995), and *Ghost of Chance* (1995, with an earlier limited edition in 1991). In his final works, Burroughs returned to more linear narratives that focus on animals and deep apprehension about ecological destruction, yet dreams remained a vital generative force for his writing. Unsurprising is that scholars have done a great deal of groundwork in the study of the author and his literary works. While I do not intend to canvass the breadth of all scholarly production on Burroughs here, what follows is a brief look at some of the more important scholarly works until now.

Eric Mottram carried out a crucial early study that focuses entirely on Burroughs. Initially published in 1971, *William Burroughs: The Algebra of Need* was the first book-length academic examination of Burroughs' writing, which Mottram subsequently updated. Essentially, *The Algebra of Need* not only validates the existence of the novelist's writing but also calls for more research into Burroughs. Mottram claims there is great moral depth to Burroughs' fiction. *The Algebra of Need* is broad in its treatment of *Junkie*, *Naked Lunch*, and Burroughs' experimental cut-ups. The study also includes an examination of lesser-known fragments that originally appeared in small ephemeral magazines. Mottram also reveals new insights into the literary imagination of the author. For instance, in one section, Burroughs shares with Mottram what he believes is the generative force of his writing: "I am acting as a map maker, an explorer of psychic areas . . . a cosmonaut of inner space, and I see no point in exploring areas that have already been thoroughly surveyed" (Mottram 9). Such a statement justifies Burroughs' legacy of experimentalism that lasts to this day. Mottram should be recognized for studying Burroughs at a time when serious scholarly work on the author was uncommon. Even forty years after the release of *The Algebra of Need*, it remains a central study that generated much scholarship on William Burroughs.

Two other studies helped establish that Burroughs was worthy of serious study. Jennie Skerl's *William S. Burroughs* (1985) touches on the development of Burroughs' writing tactics, as well as the themes that run through his narratives. Skerl notes the shifting subjects from a hostile dystopian future to an upcoming utopia involving male communities. She could not possibly have anticipated the writer's late environmental turn. Important for Burroughs scholarship is that Skerl makes a persuasive argument for Burroughs' inclusion in the American literary canon. Her point seems to be that Burroughs' writing fits within the Beat worldview. Another relatively early, vital contribution was Robin Lydenberg's *Word Cultures: Radical Theory and Practice in William S. Burroughs' Fiction* (1987), which critically handles the author's controversial writing styles. Lydenberg examines Burroughs from post-structuralist and deconstructionist perspectives, what she terms as "radical theory." Lydenberg's book is important in that her approach set a precedent for subsequent analyses of Burroughs. She perceptively muses, "And who can anticipate in what new reincarnations William Burroughs may appear before the end of his literary career" (179). While this book is a broad study of Burroughs texts, it indeed considers the late literary manifestations from a variety of ecocritical perspectives.

Ted Morgan's *Literary Outlaw* (1988) is constructed from material gathered from interviews over a number of years. Morgan endeavors to frame Burroughs' life in terms of his efforts to become famous, as well as his relationships with various personalities. I am not convinced of Morgan's claim that Burroughs craved fame. Another gripe I have is how *Literary Outlaw* frequently shifts away from the writer to more peripheral matters. Moreover, Morgan does not really assess the novelist's writing directly. To its credit, the book does detail biographical information that relates poignant incidents in Burroughs' personal life. However, the book never considers the ways nature permeates Burroughs texts or how those texts contribute to the ways we think about ecology.

Timothy Murphy's *Wising Up the Marks* (1997) appeared just months after the writer's death. Murphy argues that Burroughs is an example of what he calls an amodern writer, which challenges the view of Burroughs as postmodern champion. Murphy discards the common view of Burroughs as revolutionary and claims the early writing on addiction was particularly unproductive and ultimately damaging to his career. This is a serious point of contention. This book challenges Murphy's view and argues that *Naked Lunch* contributes to the much more significant issue of toxic discourse. Murphy argues that the cut-up writing strategies and obsession with armed insurrection and anarchy highlight the writer's amodern status, but I am unconvinced. *Wising Up the Marks* also addresses the key issue of canonization. However, Murphy never really discusses Burroughs' views on firearms, a crucial consideration in working out the ways in which anarchist philosophy provides insight into Burroughs' own identity, or the identities with which he chooses to write. Murphy also fails to consider Burroughs' apparent support of violence to accomplish ostensibly environmental goals.

In *William Burroughs and the Secret of Fascination* (2003), Oliver Harris investigates the narratives Burroughs produced during the 1950s in a nuanced approach that challenges Murphy's dismissal of Burroughs' early period. He examines *Junkie*, *Queer*, and *Naked Lunch*. Harris carries out systematic and meticulous analyses of original manuscripts and produces intriguing insights into the many factual details and discrepancies in Burroughs texts throughout the years. Contextualizing Burroughs' writing from the 1950s both culturally and historically, Harris challenges the dominant focus on addiction. Instead, he reasons that to understand the writer fully, it is crucial to cut through the popular images and familiar mythology surrounding Burroughs as a personality. More important is to see the texts as cultural and historical artifacts. His intimate familiarity with the body of Burroughs scholarship allows Harris to place the writer, and the myth, into proper context. Finally, Harris shows that it is extremely difficult to label Burroughs, which discards any suggestion that the author was distinctly postmodern or amodern. He also emphasizes that the difficulties and contradictions inherent in the author's work are necessary aspects of the reading process. The attention to the materiality of textual production can offer exciting possibilities to exploring ecological concerns. Certainly, a grasp of the method of production is essential, even for ecocritical studies interested in other questions.

Naked Lunch @ 50: Anniversary Essays (2009) is a fresh updating of scholarship on Burroughs. Oliver Harris and Ian MacFadyen edited the collection, which is a wide-ranging survey of critical and creative perspectives on *Naked Lunch* as both lasting text and American artifact. This is the first collection devoted entirely to the examination of Burroughs' most provocative and historically significant novel. Even though many of the contributors to this collection are researchers, it is aimed at a wider audience. Aesthetically, the volume is unusually colorful and is a crucial reminder of Burroughs' interest in media beyond the text. However, the included essays discuss neither the environment nor the tensions between culture and nature as they play out in the *Naked Lunch* narrative. Significant is that even a recent collection devoted entirely to *Naked Lunch* does not find room to include ecological perspectives on the text. This fact helps justify the existence of this book.

Recent developments in Beat studies highlight the turn toward more cross-cultural and transnational perspectives. For example, *The Transnational Beat Generation* (2012), edited by Nancy M. Grace and Jennie Skerl, highlights the international contexts of much of Beat writing and culture. A number of papers delve into this theme. The book includes an inspiring interview with Anne Waldman, as well as convincing contributions by a number of academics around the world. R. J. Ellis discusses British ties to the Beat Generation and says that the British/Beat has a "hybrid identity as a transnational Atlantic" artist (160). Jaap van der Bent pushes the transnational situation of the Beats beyond English-language cultures and argues that the Beat Generation and the Vienna Group shared a common cultural and aesthetic vision, since they "are both strongly concerned with the liberation of language and consequently also of the self" (165). This suggests it is possible to stretch the idea of the Beat undertaking to other cultures from roughly the same period, as chapter 4 of this book also attempts to show.

The impetus of the European Beat Studies Network (ESBN) provides an additional forum for transnational angles into the Beats. EBSN conferences have been held in Middelburg, Netherlands; Aalborg, Denmark; and Tangier, Morocco. More conferences are planned. The EBSN has disseminated research primarily in the form of symposia but also in the form of a 2013 special issue of *Comparative American Studies*, coedited by Polina Mackay and me, which seeks to show the extent of "the Beats' international legacy, which to this day is astonishing, [and] testifies to both their transnational potential as well as to literature's potential for a global reach" (222). Important essays in this special issue include Franca Bellarsi's inspiring "'Alien Hieroglyphs of Eternity' and 'Cold Pastorals,'" in which Bellarsi argues that Keats was a central precursor to Ginsberg (262). In "The Parting of Burroughs and Kerouac," Véronique Lane highlights the recent transnational turn in Beat studies, arguing that Kerouac effectively appropriated the power of Poetic Realist cinema (277). Peggy Pacini's "Satori in Paris" examines Kerouac's search for his family name. She concludes that Kerouac was ultimately a prisoner of his own mythology (298). Given continued efforts by researchers in numerous countries, many more developments are expected in the international context of Beat scholarship.

Bearing in mind not just the book-length scholarly studies on Burroughs, but also the numerous articles, essays, and other research, one can begin to see how the author's identity has been constructed over the decades. A large amount of the scholarship on Burroughs has been biographical or sentimental in nature.[1] The author is commonly associated with the postwar period,[2] in terms of his legacy as a member of the Beat Generation, and especially as experimental writer. His creative collaborations with Brion Gysin led to wildly new artistic practices.[3] Burroughs is also widely regarded as one of America's key twentieth-century homosexual writers.[4] In addition, Burroughs is universally celebrated and vilified as one of the great writers of the drug void.[5] Moreover, Burroughs is at times considered postmodern, though I acknowledge that postmodernism remains a deeply contested term.[6] While Burroughs' identity has thus been constructed from a variety of perspectives, the William Burroughs I am concerned with is a different writer than the one commonly viewed in existing scholarship. This project is interested in Burroughs in terms of his writerly engagement with environmental discourse, his advocacy of violence to meet ideological goals, and the ways in which his texts reflect ecological concerns.

William Burroughs is often linked to his Beat companions, and although the core Beat members developed in a supportive writerly community, the three men and their writing had significant differences. Burroughs was older and initially more interested in reading than writing. In fact, he is even depicted as a literary teacher to his younger friends in *On the Road* in the form of Old Bull Lee.[7] Their crucial early publications, Ginsberg's "Howl," Kerouac's *On the Road*, and Burroughs' *Naked Lunch*, reveal similarities as well as stark contrasts. *On the Road* is swift and thoroughly American in its vernacular language and blue-collar image of America just before the Cold War. It is exuberant and celebratory, and the connections to the transcendentalist attempt to achieve higher consciousness are rather straightforward. The novel also explores the landscape of midcentury America and the people who inhabit the great inland empire.[8] *On the Road* is therefore quite different from "Howl" and *Naked Lunch*. It can be said that in their negative view of human existence in an industrialized culture, both "Howl" and *Naked Lunch* seek a place for redemption, though Ginsberg chose the long Eliot-inspired poem, while Burroughs selected a more fragmentary aesthetic form, which guided much of the writing of the rest of his career. Gregory Corso emphasizes the various narrative strategies as important distinctions, noting that "the beats I really knew, Kerouac, Ginsberg, Burroughs, they were all very diverse in their writing styles" (*Writings from Unmuzzled Ox* 123). Ann Charters insists the differences among the three can best be thought of in terms of their roles within the larger Beat Generation: Kerouac was the mythologizer, Ginsberg the prophet, and Burroughs the theorist (132). If Charters is correct, then what are the philosophical and intellectual origins of Burroughs' vision?

Green Link to Burroughs

I propose that the green anarchist leanings of transcendentalist Henry David Thoreau are the crux in establishing the real relevance of the Beat Generation, and more specifically William Burroughs, to ecocriticism. Scholars have previously connected members of the Beat Generation to ecology. Gregory Stephenson writes:

> The influence of the Beat Generation may be discerned in nearly every aspect of the counterculture: the rejection of commercial values and of conceptions of career and status . . . the pacifist-anarchist political orientation . . . the concern with ecology. (13–14)

Ginsberg too recognized that the wider legacy of the Beat Generation involved the development of environmental awareness.[9] In addition, Stephenson finds the move to a kind of transcendental primitivism provided the Beats with a belief system that, as was the case with Thoreau, was aligned against industrialist urban values: "The primitivism of Beat writing thus represents . . . a critique of urban-industrial civilization" (177). If the connection between the core Beat members and environmentalism is so obvious, then it is indeed astonishing that so little ecocritical research has been carried out on the group up to the present time.

Gary Snyder is a Beat author frequently tied to environmental thinking, and Ginsberg also believed the Beat Generation was concerned with issues of ecology. William Burroughs' renegade status can begin to place him in the realm of ecological writing as well. Barbara Rose asserts that Burroughs' position as a literary renegade makes him the hyperindividual and therefore the essential American, saying his outlaw status "suggests he is more in the mainstream of American culture than some of his readers would like to acknowledge" (89).[10] Frederick Dolan notes that Burroughs drew on the "equally nostalgic—and quintessentially American—notion of freedom as the discovery of empty space, a place of innocence outside history where the fundamentally new and original may at last emerge" (548). A significant consideration is how the Beats, and Burroughs, connect with the transcendentalist tradition.

The Beats drew on the transcendentalist legacy of individualism and spiritual enlightenment, though Burroughs' willingness to engage in direct action links him more directly to Thoreau. Thomas Newhouse argues that Kerouac in particular "held sacred the tradition of the liberated self as celebrated in the writings of Emerson, Thoreau, and especially Whitman, who joined the transcendental view with the vulgar and sensuous" ("Subcultures" 10). Vince Passaro goes further and claims, "Ginsberg and Kerouac stand within a tradition of spiritual exuberance and preacherly optimism, traceable to Ralph Waldo Emerson, Henry David Thoreau, Walt Whitman, and Mark Twain" (para. 5). However, Passaro adds, "Burroughs's influences, to put it mildly, come from deeper underground. His voices are the voices of the dark side: Edgar Allan Poe, Jack London, Stephen Crane." I do not actually disagree with him on this point, but I resist the suggestion that Burroughs was only a harbinger of darkness. But the support for direct action expressed in Thoreau's 1849 *Resistance to Civil Government* can be seen as a model for Burroughs' own green ideological leanings. Burroughs' strongest link to Thoreau is not his concern for the natural world, even though such attitudes are evident in his late publications. Instead, Burroughs' most significant connection to Thoreau may lie in his willingness to take direct action in defense of individual liberty. Thus a link can be made from Thoreau to the support for direct action by environmental writers such as Edward Abbey and, by extension, to William Burroughs.

Burroughs was a lifelong advocate of direct action to remain free from authorities, and this manifests most clearly in his uniquely American passion for firearms. Rachel Campbell-Johnston argues that guns represent a dynamic force of rhetorical power for Burroughs and says, "Guns lie at the core of Burroughs's creative vision" (W1). His fascination with firearms goes back to his youth. James Grauerholz traces Burroughs' fondness for arms to "the 1920s, when the pacification of the Western frontier was still a living memory" (Burroughs, *Word Virus* 7). The right to possess firearms is ingrained deeply in American culture and represents the archetypal nineteenth-century tool that made the conquest of the frontier possible. The author drew on the mythology of bygone America throughout his writing, so it is not surprising that he connected firearms with what he saw as fundamental issues of individuality and personal freedom. He lamented public ambivalence concerning the right to possess weapons:

> After a shooting spree, they always want to take the guns away from the people who didn't do it. I sure as hell wouldn't want to live in a society where the only people allowed guns are the police and the military. ("War Universe" 92)

In a January 1951 letter to Ginsberg, Burroughs further explains his views on firearms: "I have not only the right but the duty to carry a gun and to protect my person against any attack that might deprive my family of support" (Burroughs and Harris, *Letters* 79). Clearly, Burroughs believed firearms were intrinsically tied to individual freedom. In the context of this book, guns and violence are crucial to larger questions of direct environmental action. Can the use of violence ever be justified in environmental terms, or does the inherent violence of firearms counter the environmentalist position? It seems at first that the essential violence of firearms opposes environmental views. However, the author's attitudes about violence fit American concepts of hyperindividualism, the direct action endorsed by Thoreau and the most ardent supporters of environmentalism and green anarchism.

To begin to appreciate just how violence can actually seem to work toward the goals of environmental activism in Burroughs' writing, it is essential to understand how he believes ideological goals can be realized through direct action.[11] When asked in an interview what he thought about student riots in the late 1960s, Burroughs was unmistakable in supporting violence as a means to effect what he considered positive social change:

> There should be more riots and more violence. Young people in the West have been lied to, sold out, and betrayed. Best thing they can do is take the place apart before they are destroyed in a nuclear war. Nuclear war is inevitable if the present controllers remain in power. (qtd. in Odier 81)

The writer essentially argues, as did Thoreau, that resistance is necessary to maintain personal freedom from governmental pressures. In addition, Burroughs even suggests that violence is necessary to preemptively thwart worldwide destruction in the form of accidental or intentional nuclear annihilation. Such an endorsement of direct action in the apparent defense of humanity and the environment echoes some of the more radical calls for action from animal rights and environmentalist groups.

However, prominent ecocritical scholars have incorrectly tied radical environmental views to the American militia mentality. In his notable 2004 book *Ecocriticism*, Greg Garrard briefly addresses the influence of *The Monkey Wrench Gang* writer Edward Abbey. Garrard claims that Abbey's "enthusiasm for guns, paranoia about federal government and 'big business,' and support for violent resistance to authority risks appearing to ally environmentalists with survivalist militias" (75). Such a view at first seems equally relevant to Burroughs, since he shared Abbey's passion for firearms, suspicion of the established order, concerns about the expansive free-market philosophy of American culture, and willingness to use violence against authorities. However, Garrard is mistaken in linking an endorsement of violence in the pursuit of environmentalist aims to a militia mindset. American survivalist militias are not particularly concerned with the same issues that environmentalists consider essential, such as the unsustainable consumption of natural resources, genetic manipulation of plants and animals, overuse of chemicals, corporate environmental negligence, environmental justice, biopiracy, and animal rights issues. Militias can be considered ideologically libertarian or anarchist, but they would most certainly never support government attempts to reduce carbon emissions, much less a worldwide effort on the part of the United Nations to promote greater sustainability. Militias are much less preoccupied with the global than they are with the local. The militia attitude would therefore seem to counter many environmental views.

The combination of antigovernmental, anticapitalist, and environmentally activist views with a willingness (and desire) to use direct action against authorities is much more in line with radical green anarchism than with the militia mentality. However, Garrard is correct on one significant issue—linking paranoia to the American condition. Barbara Rose too maintains that paranoia is an essential American feature, saying, "The paranoid subject is, in the American context, the quintessential patriotic citizen" (109). Peter Knight states that a culture of suspicion has been particularly evident in the United States since World War II:

> Elevated to a principle of national policy in the McCarthy years of the Cold War, and then reappropriated as an indispensable attitude of the counterculture in the 1960s, paranoia has become one of the defining characteristics of postwar American politics and culture. (811)

Perhaps an inherent distrust of outside forces is one of the reasons why firearms still hold such an important place in the American imagination. As tricky as the issue of violence and firearms seems, it is reasonable that Burroughs would rely on the potent symbolism of firearms, both as a sentimental American and, perhaps more importantly, given his green anarchist-libertarian tendencies.

In considering how Burroughs is viewed historically, it is crucial to acknowledge not only his debt to the green anarchism of Thoreau, which is deeply philosophical, but also the importance for Burroughs of libertarianism, which focuses on individual rights. This explains his passionate individualist tendencies, his advocacy of firearm ownership, his suggestion that people should be allowed to do as they please without fear of governmental or church interference, his support of non-normative sexual practices and the personal choice to use narcotics, and so on. This individualist strain can be traced to Burroughs' youth. His family had "roots in the British origins of the first American settlers" (*Word Virus* 4). The future author grew up in St. Louis, Missouri, at a time when the concept of Manifest Destiny still resonated in the collective cultural memory of the nation. Burroughs no doubt felt just outside the situation of frontier America. At the start of the twentieth century, the wars against Native Americans and the expansion of the railroad were both relatively recent developments. In addition, as R. B. Morris maintains, Burroughs believed the time around 1910 was just before the major shifts in industrial culture had begun (109). The future writer might have sensed his unique historical position in what Leo Marx calls the "middle landscape," the place located between the frontier and the modern world (71). John Lardas further suggests that Burroughs believed "America had lost its organic roots" (26). If Lardas is correct, then the author's childhood experiences could have been the generative force for the later development of what Marx calls a "diffuse nostalgia, and a naïve, anarchic primitivism" (11) that is at times both anarchist and libertarian.

While Burroughs' ideological attitudes about violence and weapons are essential in the context of an environmental study, so too are his male-centered narratives. Women are largely absent from the communes he imagines. An intriguing contradiction is Burroughs' emphasis on radical individualism while he also shows a fascination with the role that communes and collectivist forms of direct action could play in any future society. This issue is certainly relevant to discussions of the role of individual and wider social responsibilities that a worldwide effort to combat environmental problems would involve. It is doubtful that communes as Burroughs sees them would ever support government attempts to regulate emissions. Attention to local issues first would seem to counter many environmental views. Burroughs' male-gendered stories also mirror the nineteenth-century American situation in important ways. Firearms were the most important mechanical device that allowed Americans to conquer the frontier. However, men were given the task of using guns. American folk heroes of the nineteenth century were invariably skilled shooters, but not all were necessarily law-abiding citizens. All were rugged individualists who relied on firearms as a means of forging an identity as well as ensuring self-preservation. A cursory list of such hero shooters includes Billy the Kid, Buffalo Bill, Daniel Boone, and Davy Crockett.[12] Marx points out that in the American situation, machines are consistently linked to "crude, masculine aggressiveness in contrast with the tender, feminine, and submissive attitudes traditionally attached to the landscape" (29). Mark Christopher Allister similarly reminds us that "men have traditionally been identified with the machines, from gun to plow" (2).

In his narratives, Burroughs attempts to resuscitate the myth of the American marksman, who was invariably masculine and most certainly male.

This book is also interested in the Burroughs that was drawn to the ideas of the past as a way to improve the future. As Eric Mottram asserts, "Burroughs' idea of a place to live is in the tradition of Thoreau and other American anarchists through to the present day" (156). Rose also locates the writer firmly "within the putative radical tradition of American Transcendentalism and specifically the legacy of Henry David Thoreau and Walt Whitman, who celebrated America as the place of world regeneration" (96). Burroughs identifies the West as still open to the renewal of humankind and the creation of a more perfect society, to salvage what Marx calls the potential of "America as paradise regained" (81). However, Rose believes Burroughs ultimately recognizes "his entanglement in the cultural narratives he [seeks] to undermine" (94). This is true in the final book of the *Red Night* trilogy, where the narrator seems to accept the impossibility of ever really mapping a way to a human interstellar future.

Rod Phillips sees Gary Snyder, Jack Kerouac, and Michael McClure as the Beats most obviously interested in "reconnection with the natural world" and observes that Burroughs too "demonstrated a yearning for a return to a more pastoral—and even, at times, more primitive—existence" (125). While Phillips specifically points to *The Yage Letters* as an example of Burroughs' search for primitivism, I suggest that Burroughs seeks to reconcile humanity and the natural world more widely in his texts. This manifests in both his narrative practices and the thematic content of his texts, which reveal a lifelong engagement with ecological issues. Thus the essential question of this book is, To what extent can Burroughs' texts be evaluated in an ecocritical framework? Although Burroughs is recognized for his legacy of experimentalism, what can be found in close readings of Burroughs is a vibrant, targeted, and ripe space for ecocritical dialogue. Previously, scholars touched on just the nascent.

Selection of Texts

The following chapters reread older Burroughs texts and study more recent texts, in some cases for the first time. Gary Snyder has been venerated by first-wave ecocriticism.[13] Burroughs, however, has been completely ignored in terms of the ecological value of his writing, certainly in ecocritical circles.

This is perhaps because his work does not readily fit within the nature-writing genre. However, since Burroughs' oeuvre is now complete, and since ecocriticism is expanding its range, it is time to reconsider Burroughs' narratives in a new light. Scholars have previously made an initial connection between the writer and an environmentalist political position, though no serious literary studies have established this link by examination of Burroughs' narrative strategies. The texts selected for inclusion in this study are representative samples from different periods over the long course of the author's career, not only because of the potential for environmental discourse of the texts in question but also since in many cases the narratives discussed need further research.

Naked Lunch holds a prominent position in Burroughs' wide body of work. The novel's larger cultural significance justifies, and indeed necessitates, its inclusion in any serious ecocritical analysis of Burroughs' writing. Existing studies on *Naked Lunch* emphasize the need for continued research. One contradiction is that the book has "deterred head-on critical engagement at the same time it has been *taken as read*" (Harris and MacFadyen xii; emphasis in original). *Naked Lunch* maintains that peculiar position. In 1999, Carol Loranger made an appeal for future study of *Naked Lunch*, calling for more textual than interpretive analysis. While this study is primarily interested in questions of interpretation, chapter 2 considers the form of the *Naked Lunch* text. *Naked Lunch* is a difficult text to navigate and resists any generic environmental reading. However, because of its lasting controversial status and its flash of originality, *Naked Lunch* is a rich source of material for ecocritical study, especially considering the ways in which the modern condition engenders toxicity.

Other early publications deserve additional consideration and are examined in chapter 3. *The Yage Letters* suffers from an even greater lack of critical attention than *Naked Lunch*, though the situation is slowly improving. Harris points out that although the book has been read for decades, "critical reception is almost as thin and short as the book itself" ("Not Burroughs' Final Fix," para. 11). If Burroughs is an important contributor to postwar American literature, and if *The Yage Letters* has been read for so long, what reasons can justify the shortage of research on the book? Harris points to the "peculiar hybridity of its overall contents" as one explanation. He elsewhere suggests that the absence of critical engagement stems from the book's "uncertain fictional status" (*William Burroughs* 40). Harris calls

The Yage Letters a "composite text" (Burroughs and Ginsberg, *Yage Letters: Redux* xxiv) that draws on a number of genre forms and literary traditions, including "the comic picaresque tradition, travel writing, the ethnobotanical field report, political satire, psychedelic literature, [the] epistolary narrative," and the cut-up form (xi). Each section of the book was written using different creative methods. Recently, there has been an adjustment of sorts in terms of scholarship on *The Yage Letters*. An updated and authoritative edition was published in 2006. This is certainly a welcome development. Additionally, Jennie Skerl finds that the wider body of Burroughs' writing, including *The Yage Letters*, has been the subject of increasing scholarship in recent years ("The Book, the Movie, the Legend" 169).

Finally, I also consider fascinating example cut-ups from *Minutes to Go* (Beiles et al. 1960), an early publication that demands more attention. Any serious ecocritical study needs to deal with the cut-up form, methods, and texts at least to some degree. And for that very reason, this chapter further examines example fragments of cut-ups that are far longer and from other forms of media. Avant-garde practices might help explain ways we think about ecology, but until now, environmental critics have largely overlooked the experimental. Robin Lydenberg suggests Burroughs used the cut-up technique to dispel "the illusion of the referential function of language" (*Word Cultures* 33). Micheal Sean Bolton says that not only does Burroughs' writing problematize the narrative voice, but "through the notion of the *word virus*, [Burroughs] institutes a host/parasite binary within the individual's subjectivity," which results in what can be called the "parasitic *other*" (16; emphasis in original). This leads to important other considerations, such as what fragmentary aesthetics might achieve if we have indeed lost linguistic orientation.

Another concern is whether it is even possible to find environmental meaning in what Jed Rasula calls the "holes in words and words in holes" (*Compost* 82). The recent release of the definitive edition of the *Nova* trilogy suggests the time is right to reconsider Burroughs' prolific 1960s period. While the *Nova* trilogy has received a good deal of critical attention, far less has been given to Chytilová's wildly experimental 1966 film *Sedmikrásky* (*Daisies*). Existing research commonly frames the film as feminist allegory and does not seek to ask larger questions that might touch on matters of ecology. Thus chapter 4 investigates to what degree a comparative study of the *Nova* series and *Daisies* can bring new environmental insights into radically experimental practices of the 1960s. More specifically, this chapter discusses how absurdist montage, the act of shearing, and subsequent annihilation can clarify ways in which experimental practices contribute to how we think about transnational Beat connections, as well as the third wave of ecocriticism.

Chapter 5 examines the *Red Night* trilogy, which appeared rather late in the author's career and has not received the same sustained scholarly interest as Burroughs' most provocative texts. The trilogy includes *Cities of the Red Night* (1981), *The Place of Dead Roads* (1983), and *The Western Lands* (1987). The series is important to this study because it addresses the unfulfilled potential of nature's nation. The *Red Night* trilogy deserves more attention for a number of reasons. While issues of "utopia, dystopia, and the cultural myth of the New World Eden" appear throughout Burroughs' wider writing and arouse what Barbara Rose calls an "equivocal nostalgia" (93), the *Red Night* series is remarkable in its total engagement with American myths. However, as Rose points out, the trilogy "questions how . . . narratives can resolve the failed promises of the Myth of America" (93). Therefore, it would seem that any serious study that attempts to grapple with the writer's position in relation to the bucolic myth of America past requires an examination of the *Red Night* trilogy.

The Cat Inside (1992) is a late Burroughs text that has received almost no scholarly attention. The book remains one of the author's least-known narratives, and chapter 6 is devoted to its study. The limited critical attention it has received proves brittle when challenged with a compelling ecocritical model to better identify and understand forms of human-animal relationships in literary texts. In the short and philosophical autobiographical-fictional novella, Burroughs delves into the deep connection and relationships he developed with felines late in his life. He also contemplates previous experiences with animals and mournfully reflects on his earlier mistreatment of nonhuman creatures. Moreover, Burroughs' narrative explores issues of deep ecological significance, as well as the need to develop a more biocentric attitude. Therefore, *The Cat Inside* is crucial to the completion of this study.

Perhaps the most compelling single text chosen for inclusion in *The Green Ghost* in terms of clear environmental significance is *Ghost of Chance* (1995), covered in chapter 7. The novella has received virtually no scholarly attention, but it can reveal much about the writer's late varied use of narrative strategies to convey the need for urgent ecological restoration. Because of the surprising lack of critical perspectives on the novella, and because of the rich space for ecocritical dialogue, the novella is a crucial addition to this study. This is especially true in terms of teaching the importance of not only conservation but also deeper ecological issues, such as the human place in the world and the importance of animals that have no direct utility to human beings.

The Green Ghost ultimately attempts to show that William Burroughs' writing lends itself to an environmental reading, which adds to the scholarly discussion in key ways. My study challenges the American ecocritical tradition of emphasizing nature writing. The ecocritical focus on Burroughs is unusual, since it might seem that his environmental significance is so counterintuitive. Burroughs is not a nature writer and yet, so my argument goes, he can be looked upon from an ecocritical perspective. This new angle leads to new insights on the writer and steers the study of Burroughs in a new direction entirely. This book thus seeks to accomplish two important tasks. The first is to change the critical reception of one of America's greatest literary outlaws. The second, which is equally ambitious, is to extend the range and applicability of ecocriticism to writers and genres not generally considered within the purview of nature writing. While this study looks specifically at William Burroughs, the next step would be to consider how other writers' work can benefit from new models in bringing new texts and issues within the purview of ecocriticism.

2.

Burning Bones: The Limits of Material Culture and the Toxic Human in *Naked Lunch*

> Pollution, although it's horrifying and dangerous, is maybe simply a spin-off of this new relationship to nature.
>
> —Fredric Jameson, "South Korea as Social Space"

William Burroughs' experimental early publications remain his most enigmatic and challenging ones. The main problems in attempting an ecocritical reading of the author's experimental writing are the lack of coherent narratives and recognizably relevant content. Consequently, methods of ecocritical analysis that work well for more conventional narratives seem less capable of dealing with the challenges posed by the fragmentary montage *Naked Lunch* (1959). Until now, environmental critics have overlooked *Naked Lunch* entirely. This chapter suggests that the Toxic Human, as revealed in *Naked Lunch*, is an alternative, albeit degraded, form of modern human ecological identification. Ecocriticism has to ultimately wrestle with limit cases such as Burroughs' most experimental writing.

I submit that modern notions of toxicity are heavily reliant on technological developments, historical and cultural conceptions of uncleanliness, and perhaps even notions of spiritual filth. Lawrence Buell sees toxic discourse as emerging from our contemporary situation, saying that toxic rhetoric is an "interlocked set of topoi whose force derives partly from the exigencies of an anxiously industrializing culture, partly from deep-rooted Western attitudes" ("Toxic Discourse" 639). He further asserts, "Contemporary toxic discourse effectively starts with Rachel Carson's *Silent Spring*" (645), published in 1962, though I think the clock back can be pushed back to at least the underground fiction of the period in which Burroughs' *Junkie* (1953) was produced, and possibly even further.[1]

Toxicity is a significant trope throughout Burroughs' writing, and *Junkie* traces the routine of a seemingly insignificant addict named William Lee, a character who becomes increasingly polluted through toxic exposure to narcotics. The narrative effectively conveys the horrors that accompany a junkie lifestyle. Moving geographically through the dark netherworlds of New York City, New Orleans, and Mexico City, Lee discusses his unsuccessful but earnest efforts to kick the junk habit in various rehabilitation centers. Later the tone becomes confessional, and the narrator writes about his desire to be free from both law enforcement persecution and the biological mechanism of addiction. The semiautobiographical book can be considered a cautionary tale of chemical dependence and the mental and physical consequences that result from long-lasting addiction. *Junkie* also introduces the problem of self-contamination.

Later Burroughs narratives highlight both overreliance on technology and chemicals as agents of death. *The Soft Machine* (1961) can be read as a parable of technological suicide, and issues of pollution and contaminants are central to the narrative. In the novel, the narrator attacks all forms of addiction and observes how external manipulative control machinery can physically infiltrate and seize the human body for nefarious purposes. Control in this novel can be likened to a toxin, an alien agent that takes hold of, damages, and pollutes the human body, which Burroughs calls "the soft machine." The antitechnological sentiment expressed in the book is significant, as are the ways in which the cut-up method is important to ecocriticism, as later chapters will attempt to develop. The content of *Exterminator!* (1973) involves contaminants as agents of toxic death. With numerous references to air and water pollution, the collection of short texts also discusses drugs, addiction, and paranoia of law enforcement and the state. But the book is really about deadly chemicals and the effects of such substances on insects. It further contemplates the deadly power of biological and chemical weapons and their effects on permeable human bodies. The narrator creates an inventory of various killing agents, including pyrethrum powder, arsenic, bedbug spray, phosphorous paste, cyanide dust, and nerve gas. Issues of contact with infectious diseases occur in Burroughs' later publications.

Other books by Burroughs emphasize widespread infections in advanced cultures, as well as urban matters important to ecocriticism. Although chemicals do not appear a great deal in *Blade Runner* (1979), biological contagions in a developed but crumbling civilization are discussed at length. The narrative develops around the medicine practiced by subversive underground surgeons and their allies. Doctors attempt to heal others while at the same time evading agents of a government that views them as dangerous insurgents. The physicians rely on an illicit underground network of followers to acquire scarce materials and needed tools. The smugglers helping the doctors are thus called blade runners. The narrative tracks apocalyptic events that occur in an alternative postindustrial culture, drawing heavily on the disease trope. *Cities of the Red Night* (1981) features similar concerns. The book stresses the problem of inadequate social policies and also explores the powerful social metaphor of disease. The narrative makes numerous references to an unnamed sexual disease that ravages human populations of the earth. The toxin in Burroughs' outbreak narrative is, however, not chemical, but viral. Priscilla Wald stresses that Burroughs actually saw the social conditions for the development and spread of a devastating sexually transmitted disease "as an analysis of the cultural logic of the outbreak and its accompanying narratives" (214). While Burroughs' books vary in terms of plot and thematic focus, common to each is the central issue of contamination.

Naked Lunch (1959) remains Burroughs' most important book and makes considerable use of the toxic trope. The nonlinear narrative follows William Lee and his search for narcotics in the United States and Mexico at midcentury. Lee attempts to evade the law, and much of the book is dedicated to expressing the paranoia and suffering of a chronic addict. Lee travels from New York to Tangier and then to a space called Interzone. Throughout the narrative, Lee encounters various underground characters, including drug dealers, prostitutes, and homosexuals. The book is unquestionably innovative in the context of midcentury American literature in that it provides a window into the addict's hallucinatory states and withdrawal. In the *Naked Lunch* storyline, characters morph, dreams are conveyed, and scatological routines are presented in intense and confrontational detail. *Naked Lunch* explains how both drug dealers and the government profit from addiction and suggests drugs are just one possible medium of control. The book not only presents a ruined world devoid of hope and compassion but also reveals evidence of a toxic culture.

The section titled "Hassan's Rumpus Room," for instance, describes violent acts and sexual orgies involving bizarre creatures called mugwumps, as well as boys, men, and women. But near the very beginning of the section, a few brief lines tell us much about the setting of this peculiar place:

> A vast still harbor of iridescent water. Deserted gas well flares on the smoky horizon. Stink of oil and sewage. Sick sharks swim through the black water, belch sulphur from rotting livers, ignore a bloody, broken Icarus. (*Naked Lunch: Restored* 64)

This brief selection is significant in showing points of intersection among economics, society, and the environment of the *Naked Lunch* world. This easily overlooked passage describes an ecosystem in crisis.[2] There is a lasting glow in the distance as a "[d]eserted gas well flares on the smoky horizon" (64). One may wonder why the area is no longer used, why the gas well is deserted, and why it still burns. Brownfields are sites of former industrial activity that are abandoned in a toxic state. The flaring of gas wells normally occurs when natural gas is intentionally burned off if considered too unprofitable to collect for sale. The presence of a flaring gas well can be read as showing that temporary economic gain takes precedence over long-term sustainability, at least in the world of *Naked Lunch*. Another possible explanation for the continued existence of the gas well may be simpler. The cost of cleaning up the area could be higher than any potential future value of the land, so the well remains. It may be that the well was once disabled but has reignited through accident or act of nature. Additionally, the presence of brownfields in this place may indicate the lack of an adequate political mechanism to address issues of environmental safety, as well as wider problems of environmental justice. Brownfields are "anthropogenically degraded landscapes" disproportionately situated in "poor and minority neighborhoods" (Buell, *Future* 135).

Burroughs' toxic discourse reveals the roots of present "ecosystemic distress" as the "unacknowledged allegiance to a mechanistic model of life" (Doyle, "Naked Life" 247). It would seem that faith in an industrial model has failed the *Naked Lunch* world for many who live there. However, the passage also highlights the problems of fossil fuels in this particular culture. While the air is fouled by burning off natural gas, air pollution is not the only result of gas well flaring. Water contamination is another common consequence. Therefore, it is unsurprising that one also finds evidence of fossil fuels contaminating urban septic systems, producing a "[s]tink of oil and sewage." But people and animals do exist in this hostile place.

The creatures that lurk in the hidden spaces and dirtied waters of this world are predators, and they are unhealthy: "Sick sharks swim through the black water, belch sulphur from rotting livers." Lasting exposure to their toxic environment has made the animals unhealthy. Shark bodies attempt to cleanse themselves, but they do so inadequately, it would seem. Moreover, monsters of all kinds inhabit the world of *Naked Lunch*: alligators, huge centipedes, and sharks, but also other monstrous creatures. Through the narrative, one finds drug fiends, mugwumps, murderers, pedophiles, predatory homosexuals, rapists, talking assholes, a guard wearing a "uniform of human skin" (*Naked Lunch: Restored* 49), "Arab women with bestial faces" (66), "Leopard Men [who] tear people to pieces with iron claws" (33), and cannibals eating off "noses and ears" (33). The contaminated world represented in the narrative has created an environment in which mutated monsters and violent sexual attackers are the norm, or where only monstrously hyperaggressive creatures can survive. Thus, in this ruined world, where industrial activity has polluted the land, water, and sky, the metaphorical significance of a "bloody, broken Icarus" (64) is especially fitting in suggesting how, in this place, material culture has met its material limits. Icarus here represents the pride and vanity of a naïve and youthful industrial nation soaring too high but brought back low.

An atypical passage from "The Black Meat" section of the narrative exhibits a degree of environmental mindfulness by introducing a strange, addictive, and poisonous meat into the narrative:

> Traffickers in the Black Meat, flesh of the giant aquatic black centipede—sometimes attaining a length of six feet—found in a lane of black rocks and iridescent, brown lagoons, exhibit paralyzed crustaceans in camouflage pockets of the Plaza visible only to the Meat Eaters. (45)

An initial reaction would be to pose specific questions in an attempt to seek additional meaning: What is the Black Meat? What is an aquatic centipede? The Black Meat is an illicit and highly addictive substance sold in inconspicuous areas of an urban market. But one can also find in this passage evidence of a ruined world, biological transformation, and also toxicity.

The Black Meat comes from the "giant aquatic black centipede." They reach an incredible size, "sometimes attaining a length of six feet." However, centipedes never reach six feet long in the real world. The Amazonian giant centipede reaches one foot in length, but never six (Strickman, Frances, and Debboun 255). The existence of such an enormous centipede tells the reader this is a different world, where our natural laws do not apply or at least have been altered. More clues to the possible origin of the mysterious centipede are also present in the passage. The animal is found "in a lane of black rocks and iridescent, brown lagoons" (*Naked Lunch: Restored* 45). At this point, the reader will want to learn about the uncanny environment that can produce such a miscreation. What made the rocks black and the lagoons brown? Over time, exhaust from factory smokestacks caked the rocks in a thick toxic residue. The dark lagoons were once clear pools but have long since been tainted by chemical runoff from industrial activities. The lagoon could even be radioactive. If the "black rocks and iridescent, brown lagoons" are evidence of pollution, then the huge size of the "black centipede" can possibly be explained by biological adaptation or even mutation caused by exposure to chemicals.

In such an environment, where addictive poisons and death are the norm, one might even begin to speak about the possible existence of the Toxic Human. The toxic landscape is not the only way in which *Naked Lunch* connects with issues of toxicity. The issue of addiction is also important in that drugs transform the normal human and ultimately produce what I call the Toxic Human. In "The Android and the Animal," Ursula Heise explores a concept she calls "biological otherness," which can be defined as a condition of biological difference that does not comply with usual processes of evolution (505). In *Naked Lunch*, more is accomplished than simply conveying the horrors of living in an atmosphere of death and the agony of acute drug addiction. The addict is revealed as an example of the Toxic Human, an extreme form of biological otherness, an alternative form of modern ecological identity.

What exactly is the Toxic Human? R. B. Morris comes close to outlining such a concept, suggesting that "the junk addict [is] the preeminent example of modern man at the mercy of his modern condition" (109). However, Morris stops short of further developing this idea, which can explain much about developed cultures. The modern toxic condition is a form of contemporary ecological identity that challenges stereotypical environmental views. Such views would ostensibly suggest that one should endeavor to acquire a healthy body and mind.

The addict in *Naked Lunch* is an example of the Toxic Human because of the long-term effects of chemicals on his body. The addict is regularly exposed to harmful substances. As addiction develops, ingested chemical agents gradually alter normal human biology. The addict thus exists in a state of biological transformation. In the developed world, contemporary humans come into daily contact with harmful chemicals. Given the most modern and widespread exposure to chemicals, nearly everyone can be called toxic to some extent. In the case of Burroughs' addict character in *Naked Lunch*, the addict can be described as toxic in terms of how chemicals control, consume, and contaminate the body, as well as the human imagination. In *Naked Lunch*, drugs control humans by breaking their natural will and destroying their sense of morality. At one point heroin is referred to as embalming fluid, which is the ultimate chemical triumph over the human body. A sense of the moral contamination terminal addiction causes is also conveyed: "You would lie, cheat, inform on your friends, steal, do *anything* to satisfy total need. Because you would be in a state of total sickness, total possession, and not in a position to act in any other way" (*Naked Lunch: Restored* 201; emphasis in original). While hard drugs can displace the moral center of humans, at the same time they can trap the user in a broader sense.

Heise declares that drugs can both liberate and enchain the user. On the one hand, drugs can offer therapeutic healing and open people to sensory experiences beyond the normal range of human perception. This aspect of drug use was essential to Beat Generation attempts to attain higher consciousness. However, as Heise rightly points out, drugs can also function as tools of subjugation and control. People who use drugs to escape the mechanisms of domination do so at the risk of addiction (*Sense of Place* 161). The *Naked Lunch* narrative is filled with disturbing images of losing one's own humanity to chemicals. The narrator of *Naked Lunch* attempts to express the absolute power of narcotics in disrupting normal functioning: "I had not taken a bath in a year nor changed my clothes or removed them except to stick a needle every hour in the fibrous grey wooden flesh of terminal addiction" (*Naked Lunch: Restored* 202–3). Drug use can be said to be inherently subversive in relation to the so-called control machine. While drugs temporarily allow the user to escape from a culture of control, a junkie lifestyle can also cause great damage. Greta Gaard asserts that drug dependence counters attempts to use drugs as tools of liberation, since addiction "serves the dominant culture by keeping people powerless and oppressed" (164). Thus even if narcotics work to subvert attempts at control, at the same time drug use reinforces and perpetuates the addict's conquered state.

Naked Lunch communicates not only how the junkie character is seized by addiction but also how the human body is consumed and contaminated. One instance from the narrative describes an addict in a state of physical ruin: "He is blind from shooting in the eyeball, his nose and palate eaten away sniffing H, his body a mass of scar tissue hard and dry as wood" (*Naked Lunch: Restored* 7). In another instance, we see a junkie's "abdicated flesh burning in a cold yellow halo" (9). Elsewhere, we are shown the ways addiction disrupts the normal body's ability to repair itself after injury: "No wound healed in his soft, tentative flesh" (60). In yet another passage, the narrator attempts to express the liminal state of incurable dependence: "The living and the dead, in sickness or on the nod, hooked or kicked or hooked again" (7). The power of drugs to disturb normal biology extends to more basic human drives as well: "I am forgetting sex and all sharp pleasures of the body—a grey, junk-bound ghost" (56). Other places suggest that junk works to suspend normal human function altogether.

The narrator believes that addiction is caused by a biological change in the human body and that the human body ultimately exhibits resistance against the power of addiction. Changes in the human body are clearly present in the withdrawal stages of addiction, and the narrator writes of what he considers the root causes: "[A]s soon as junk intake falls below par, the withdrawal substance floods the body" (30). It remains uncertain whether this voice belongs to Burroughs or Lee. Here Burroughs problematizes narrative voice, creating ambiguity for the reader. In other words, Burroughs shows one of the ways his narrative strategies evade simplistic readings. Even though the voice of this passage remains uncertain, the powerful experience of withdrawal symptoms is described: "For the first twenty-four hours I was literally insane and paranoid" (203). Attempts are then made to express the physical and mental discomfort of withdrawal: "There is a nightmare interlude of cellular panic, life suspended between two ways of being" (49). However, Burroughs believes a medical solution to the problem of addiction exists, which he describes as the "Apomorphine Treatment" in a section of *Naked Lunch* titled "Deposition: Testimony Concerning a Sickness." While the narrator of *Naked Lunch* discusses the procurement, use, and effects of drugs at length, it is important to note that Lee ultimately resists addiction through the presentation of such a cautionary tale about the dangers of heroin.

In *Naked Lunch*, the addict's situation articulates the struggle between humans and modernity as one example of the modern toxic condition. The Toxic Human is one of the consequences of the human struggle against modern contact with and exposure to harmful chemicals. The junkie character in *Naked Lunch* is an alternative form of ecological identity, which, while not necessarily positive, is nonetheless a legitimate depiction of one of the toxic forms of human existence in the modern world. In her introduction to the twenty-fifth anniversary edition of the book, Jennie Skerl contends that the junkie character in *Naked Lunch* "universalizes the addict experience" (ix). This is certainly true, and the addict also universalizes the experience of living in a toxic culture. A mainstream environmental message might suggest people should aim for a carbon-neutral existence while retaining a sense of wonder for nature. However, the Toxic Human, in the form of Burroughs' junkie character, is a far more realistic depiction of human existence in modern cultures. The addict is just one of the possible results of the conflict between modernity and human beings. Many individuals fit this toxic form, whether they are hooked on junk in Tangier, processed methamphetamine in the United States, or the old standbys of alcohol and tobacco. Furthermore, the modern toxic condition exceeds mere addiction.

Humans everywhere are affected by contamination from harmful substances on a daily basis, as a result of contact with sources of toxic compounds and chemical derivatives such as herbicides, food additives, leaking underground storage tanks, and nitrates from agricultural activities. Indeed, it is difficult to imagine any human life today that is not affected by this new up-close and personal relationship with chemicals. Contact with chemicals may simply be part of the modern condition. Chemicals, which are essential to the modern situation, provide humans with the ability to do masterful things but at the great risk of widespread contamination. Burroughs' addict character can be said to be *one* of the representations of contemporary ecological identification.

At the same time, the *Naked Lunch* text serves as a form of healing and advocates renewal for the contaminated. Lee names the source of his mental and physical suffering, and thus, through the narrative, begins the healing process. Lee proclaims, "Paregoric Babies of the World Unite. We have nothing to lose but Our Pushers. And THEY are NOT NECESSARY" (*Naked Lunch: Restored* 210). This passage is particularly interesting for two reasons. For much of the twentieth century, parents commonly used paregoric, an opium-based narcotic, as a pain reliever for teething babies. So it can be said that from the very moment of birth, humans are already conditioned to take drugs. What is also striking in this excerpt is the invocation of Karl Marx's call to move beyond class as the only basis for meaningful forms of human solidarity. Thus *Naked Lunch* gradually works toward ecological significance by detailing the mundane day-to-day details and struggles of an insignificant addict, from the suffering caused by such a toxic lifestyle to advocacy on behalf of the contaminated. This is where the writer's book on addiction meets environmental thinking. The source and form of toxicity do not really matter. Burroughs' message is that those who suffer because of contamination deserve healing, and in many ways this echoes the same antitoxic advocacy promoted by the most important texts in the ecocritical canon.

However, though Lee yearns for healing, *Naked Lunch* also suggests recovery is impossible to ever truly achieve in such a world. The final passages of the book provide access to the addict's subjective and shifting sense of *Umwelt* as he progresses through an endless loop of withdrawal, indignity, an angry fix, and finally despair at recognizing his toxic condition. The final passage of *Naked Lunch* announces:

> *quick* . . .
>
> white flash . . . mangled insect screams . . .
>
> I woke up with the taste of metal in my mouth back from the dead
>
> trailing the colorless death smell
> afterbirth of a withered grey monkey
> phantom twinges of amputation . . .
>
> "Taxi boys waiting for a pickup," Eduardo said and died of an overdose in Madrid . . .
>
> Powder trains burn back through pink convolutions of tumescent flesh . . . set off flash bulbs of orgasm . . . pin-point photos of arrested motion . . . smooth brown side twisted to light a cigarette . . .
>
> He stood there in a 1920 straw hat somebody gave him . . . soft mendicant words falling like dead birds in the dark street . . .

> "No . . . No more . . . *No más* . . ."
>
> A heaving sea of air hammers in the purple brown dusk tainted with rotten metal smell of sewer gas . . . young worker faces vibrating out of focus in yellow halos of carbide lanterns . . . broken pipes exposed . . .
>
> "They are rebuilding the City."
>
> Lee nodded absently . . . "Yes . . . Always . . ."
>
> Either way is a bad move to The East Wing . . .
>
> If I knew I'd be glad to tell you . . .
>
> "No good . . . *no bueno* . . . hustling myself . . ."
>
> "No glot . . . C'lom Fliday." (195–96)

Lee is absolutely controlled by his need and no longer has the natural free will of a human. The "white flash" at the beginning of the passage can be read as an indication of the onset of the psychological effects of withdrawal, and the "mangled insect screams" as a sign of Lee's uncertainty and deep apprehension. The metal taste in his mouth may have come from the iron in his own blood and reminds him he is not dead, not yet. But the Modern Man cannot avoid his toxic fate. Lee is overwhelmed by psychic terror as his condition progresses into complete heroin withdrawal. At first the subsequent lines seem rather random and disconnected asides: "trailing the colorless death smell / afterbirth of a withered grey monkey / phantom twinges of amputation." But they function to illustrate the types of fragmented thoughts that flicker through the ailing addict's mind.

Added indentation separates these lines from the main block of text. In this case, it suggests the overall significance of these lines is subordinate to that of the main textual block, but they are nonetheless essential for full understanding of the larger unit. Lee is "trailing the colorless death smell." Death is not following him, it would seem. The real futility of Lee's situation is that he himself follows death. A bizarre image follows: "afterbirth of a withered grey monkey." One wonders what other disturbing and unpleasant thoughts fill the addict's mind in the wraithlike state between consciousness and death. Admittedly, it is difficult to understand the addict unless one has shared the experience. Accordingly, Burroughs can only try to make the subjective *Umwelt* of the addict perceptible in words that can be comprehended by the reader. In an essay titled "What Is It Like to Be a Bat?" Thomas Nagel claims it is impossible to be fully capable of conceptualizing the subjective existence of other creatures "without taking up the point of view of the experiential subject" (449). While the reader cannot totally share Lee's subjective experience, ambiguous lines such as "trailing the colorless death smell" can be said to make the disjointed and inexpressible suffering through heroin withdrawal nearly comprehensible to the reader.

Subsequent lines can be interpreted as articulating the temporary elation and prolonged discomfort that follow the injection of heroin. "Powder trains burn back through pink convolutions of tumescent flesh" can be read as an attempt to communicate the throbbing sensation Lee feels as chemicals pump through his swollen arm after the injection and the untying of the elastic band. The selection of the words "powder trains" and "burn" are essential here, since the words suggest searing pain and injury. It is important to remember that although the addict initially chose a junkie lifestyle, the aspect of choice has long since been replaced by a more reticent surrender. The brief "flash bulbs of orgasm" can be read as conveying the temporary lift and elation the drugs provide Lee in the moments just after injection. Whatever pleasure is provided by the shot is short-lived, thus just a few words are sufficient to describe the totality of the high. If only a few words convey the lift, the rest of the passage can be interpreted as articulating the lengthy and disproportionate suffering outside the ephemeral euphoric state. The following lines signal a temporal shift and subtle but predictable dysphoric slide into withdrawal: ". . . pin- / point photos of arrested motion . . . smooth brown side / twisted to light a cigarette . . ." One can almost imagine the junkie coming down from his high and contemplating his impossibly trapped position, substituting his addiction to nicotine for his addiction to heroin.

The next lines are deeply ambiguous and work to further show the Toxic Human's puzzling and paradoxical existence:

> He stood there in a 1920 straw hat somebody gave him . . . soft mendicant
> words falling like dead birds in the dark street . . .
> "No . . . No more . . . *No más* . . ."

Curious is the shift from the first to the third person, from "I" throughout most of the passage to the more impersonal but not anonymous "He stood there in a 1920 straw hat." This switch may function to express the sense of disembodiment and confusion an addict experiences as withdrawal symptoms begin. The line "No . . . No more . . . *No más* . . ." suggests limits have been reached. It is possible that Lee has no heroin left in his possession and laments the forthcoming symptoms that will eventually drive him to relapse. At the same time, the line can be read to suggest the Toxic Man desires to be free of junk. Lee simultaneously wishes to have more drugs while craving deliverance from drugs. This is the unsolvable paradox of the junkie condition. Lee's entire *Umwelt* is dictated by chemicals. There is no voluntary aspect of Lee's drug use at this point—no choice. He functions nearly as a biological machine.

The final lines of the book also emphasize the urban environment in which the junkie character is situated, an environment that remains both an urban wilderness and a modern wasteland. One sees disjointed images that locate the scene in an urban space:

> A heaving sea of air hammers in the purple brown dusk tainted
> with rotten metal smell of sewer gas . . . young worker faces
> vibrating out of focus in yellow halos of carbide lanterns . . . bro-
> ken pipes exposed . . .
> "They are rebuilding the City."
> Lee nodded absently . . . "Yes . . . Always . . ."

This section highlights another paradox of the junkie universe. Even though the city around him is constantly improved and rebuilt, Lee is continually degraded and *unbuilt*. This section also recalls Ginsberg's "starry dynamo in the machinery of night" of "Howl," the awe-inspiring urban Moloch that creates the conditions under which the Toxic Human is generated (*Howl and Other Poems* 9). The word "broken" in the above selection is literally broken in half, which helps the reader visualize the image of pipes being severed by the young workers.

Further in the *Naked Lunch* passage, another line provides an additional opportunity to understand the *Umwelt* of the junkie character, but again the radical ambiguity of meaning forces the reader to question the accuracy of any observation one can possibly make: "No good . . . *no bueno* . . . hustling myself . . ." The line first seems to suggest the permanent loop of withdrawal, indignity, and reacquisition is once more repeating itself. But again, the line can also be read to suggest that when the need returns, the junkie character will yield to acts of degradation that contribute to such a harsh existence. Alternatively, "No good . . . *no bueno*" can be interpreted as Lee's own recognition that his natural will has again been circumvented by the irresistible biological power of junk, and that he is once more backsliding to an amoral position. The words "hustling myself" suggest the total relinquishment of the ego.

The final words of *Naked Lunch* suggest that humans are contaminated by a wider, cosmic pollution. "No glot . . . C'lom Fliday" at first appears to be typical Burroughs obscurity. But elsewhere in *Naked Lunch*, it is made clear that the final line represents Chinese in the context of a drug deal (121). The contrast between the comical words of the dealer and the shrinking despair of the junkie in withdrawal is powerful and highlights the plurality of meaning common in much of Burroughs' writing. Instead of saying, "I do not have any junk, so come back on Friday," the dealer fumbles over his words: "No glot . . . C'lom Fliday." Far from being amusing to the junkie, though, the clumsy words of the dealer simply imply pain, a sensation with which Lee is very familiar. The closing passage of the book thus emphasizes the futility of the junkie's position—and of all human positions. The apocalyptic scenarios played out in *Naked Lunch* are especially interesting to ecocriticism because it is already too late for recovery in this particular place. The Toxic Human was never really a choice. The Toxic Human is rather a fact and a present form of human existence. *Naked Lunch* suggests humans do not necessarily become polluted but are contaminated by their very nature, nearly in the ontological sense. Therefore, it can be said that modernity engenders both the toxic body and a sense of inevitable doom that accompanies apocalyptic thinking.

The existence of the Toxic Human means Burroughs' addict character remains relevant to environmental writing. But it is equally important to consider to what degree ecocritical methods can deal with formal literary elements of his early writing, and whether Burroughs' early experimental forms are especially suited to engaging in eschatological discourse. The narrative structures of Burroughs' early literary creations, in particular, deserve critical attention. However, they have so far escaped environmental analysis. One possible explanation may be the struggle inherent in reading Burroughs' most experimental writing in the first place. Harris points out that "one of the most distinctive features of *Naked Lunch* is the extraordinary difficulty every reader experiences in finding their way around it" ("Not Burroughs' Final Fix," para. 58). *Naked Lunch* is relentlessly disjointed, and the fragments, when placed together, create a new fractured text that causes both confusion and uncertainty in the reader. Historically, the distinctive form of the book has functioned nearly as an organism, shrinking and growing as sections were parceled out to small magazines or added and, in subsequent editions, shifted. Burroughs' fascination with the virus in his early experimental writing suggests precisely his sense of language as a parasitic organism. This shows just how writing methods can embody the text and even determines content. Our assumptions that content comes first and is the most significant element in terms of critical attention are inverted.

Most editions of the book open with "Deposition: Testimony Concerning a Sickness," an account of Burroughs' own struggles with addiction. In the testimony, Burroughs explains some of the circumstances of the book's supposed creation: "I apparently took detailed notes on [junk] sickness and delirium. I have no precise memory of writing the notes which have now been published under the title *Naked Lunch*" (*Naked Lunch: Restored* 199). However, the author later admits such an account was "an exaggeration" (211). It is known that while in Tangier, Burroughs began working on a text he called "Interzone" (Burroughs and Grauerholz x), from which much of the material for *Naked Lunch* would emerge. Harris has established that much of *Naked Lunch* originated in the earlier "Interzone" manuscript ("From Dr. Mabuse to Doc Benway"). This calls into question the common assumption that the *Naked Lunch* chapter sequence was random. At the same time, it is important to note that Burroughs did reject Ginsberg's suggestion to impart a firmer chronology to the narrative (Miles, *William Burroughs* 82). Thus the fragmented and uncertain materiality of the text contributes to the challenge of pinning the narrative down.

There are still questions surrounding the material origins of *Naked Lunch*. Harris insists that "no critical engagements with theme or theory and no textual analysis can escape the consequences of lacking an established material base" (*William Burroughs* 244). Nevertheless, the restored version edited by Grauerholz and Miles was a positive development. The book is widely available and includes editorial corrections, substantial new material, and drafts from the original manuscript. Consequently, unless important new material becomes available, *Naked Lunch: The Restored Text* can be considered a comprehensive version from which to work. However, at the same time, one can also think in terms of the possible simultaneous existence of multiple *Naked Lunches*. Furthermore, the actual experience of reading the *Naked Lunch* text is significant.

The fragmentary montage structure of *Naked Lunch* is essential to an ecocritical interpretation of other aleatory structures. Burroughs believes the fragmentary structure of the narrative is vital and emphasizes in the "Atrophied Preface," "You can cut into *Naked Lunch* at any intersection point" (*Naked Lunch: Restored* 187). Timothy Murphy recognizes the unfixed form of the book but at the same time believes it retains "a modicum of structure" in the episodic exploits of the William Lee character ("Intersection Points" 85). The fragmentary form of *Naked Lunch* allows for multiple, or even endless, interpretations. Murphy suggests one possible way to approach the form of the book is to consider it a "do-it-yourself tapestry" (88), saying that "the novel itself self-consciously encourages different ways of folding and weaving its constituent elements into intelligible large-scale structures" (88–89). Ecocritic Ursula Heise contends that fragmentary and montage writing strategies ultimately empower the reader: "The shock, surprise, and disorientation such fragments cause . . . are absorbed . . . by a mode of narration that consistently restores context, control, and orientation to the reader" (*Sense of Place* 175). The need for participatory reading is a characteristic shared by *Naked Lunch* and subsequent cut-ups. Carol Loranger insists the instability of the text is ultimately one of the most essential elements of the book's attraction: "*Naked Lunch*'s enduring appeal arises in large part from its instability, its openness to multiple and alternative readings" (para. 23). The instability and elasticity of the narrative and the unusual reading experience are two reasons the book remains so important.

3.

Mutable Forms:
The Proto-ecology of Early Cut-ups from *Minutes to Go* and *The Yage Letters*

> This is the beginning of a poetry conference.
> Linen trousers are supposed to look as if
> You slept in them. Windows sucked out of buildings
> A quarter of a mile away . . .
>
> —Tony Lopez, "Restricted Zone (slight return)"

William Burroughs' experimental early publications remain some of his most puzzling, enigmatic, and least understood. European ecocritic Franca Bellarsi reminds us of the real need for ecocritical researchers to study not only texts within the nature-writing genre but avant-garde writing as well ("Eleven Windows" 7). If Burroughs' early writing remains a mystery, and if ecocritics need to examine experimental writing, then an important consideration is what can be learned by the application of ecocritical concepts to the most radical and experimental forms of writing, such as the early cut-up. Essentially, the cut-up is a practice of violent literary sabotage by using textual fragments from an array of cultural sources to create a new text that can be subversive, as well as open up entirely new subtexts for the reader. The source message becomes commodified and fractured, which allows space for considerable critical dialogue. The inspiration for the cut-up method can be traced to the literary experiments of the Dadaists and Surrealists, though there are important methodological differences. Important is that if ecocritics are to break molds of conventional literary study, innovative models of analysis must be constantly developed and improved. Ecocriticism has to ultimately wrestle with limit cases such as Burroughs' most ambiguous early writing. I suggest that early cut-ups from *Minutes to Go* and *The Yage Letters* can be considered a move toward proto-ecological writing forms.

A number of reasons exist to examine the experimental forms that directly followed the publication of *Naked Lunch*. The deeply complex history of *The Yage Letters* (1963) makes the task of untangling the content of the book a challenge. The authenticity of mysterious letters contained in the book is questionable. *The Yage Letters* is broken down into separate sections: "In Search of Yage" (1953), "Seven Years Later" (1960), an epilogue, and appendices. "In Search of Yage" chronicles the exchange of seemingly authentic communications between Burroughs and Ginsberg. "Seven Years Later" is a short section that covers letters exchanged in 1960. The epilogue of the thin book includes a brief single note from Ginsberg to Burroughs and ends with a peculiar cut-up, "I Am Dying, Meester?" The 2006 edition of the book, *The Yage Letters: Redux*, edited by Oliver Harris, contains additional material that details the various textual transformations of the book over the years. It is noteworthy that Burroughs employs different writing strategies for each section.

At first glance, *The Yage Letters* resembles an epistolary novel. But a recent discovery raises more questions and provides good reasons for additional study. For many years, it was believed that the letters contained in the book were genuine and had been only slightly edited for eventual publication. Harris asserted in 1993, "Comparison confirms the limited extent of Burroughs' reworking" of the letters that ended up in "In Search of Yage" (Burroughs and Harris, *Letters* xxv). However, Harris has more recently revealed that many of the letters were actually fabricated, which complicates efforts to understand them. What was found is that when Burroughs arrived in New York in August 1953, the *Yage* manuscript was still "in a very rough state" (*Yage Letters: Redux* xxxv). But by the time he left for Tangier in December of the same year, the manuscript "had taken on an epistolary form." This was possibly done at Ginsberg's request, to exploit the epistolary form "to give the text a naturally loose unity" (xxxvi). Thus it is now known that a number of the letters were not real exchanges, but were fabricated to appear as such.

Yet questions remain. It is still unclear whether the content of some of the letters originated with William Burroughs the author or his shadowy double, Lee. "In Search of Yage" includes letters signed by "Bill" and "William." However, others are signed by the mysterious "Willy Lee," "W. Lee," and "William Lee." Harris has even shown that "Burroughs and his fictive persona did sometimes trade places," which complicates matters still further. For example, the letter of May 12 was originally signed with the name "Willy Lee," but in the published form it is signed by "Bill" (xxxiv). Given the mystery and questions about the authenticity of letters in "In Search of Yage," one would best avoid questions of authorial intent altogether and accept the communications as enigmatic additions to the author's prolific literary output. An important consideration is how *The Yage Letters* connects with issues of the environment. And at first glance, it may seem the book is far more visibly open to an environmental reading than *Minutes to Go* (1960).

In terms of content, communications in *The Yage Letters* include lengthy discussions of chemicals and reflections on native drug rituals. During this period, both Burroughs and Ginsberg traveled separately through South America and experimented with native drugs in an effort to understand the total range of human perception, to become what Rimbaud called becoming a seer through the "systematic derangement of the senses" (qtd. in Stephenson 64). Both Burroughs and Ginsberg were fascinated by the use of drugs in native rituals. *The Yage Letters* deals in part with the search for *ayahuasca*, the mysterious hallucinogenic brew found in South America. The vines of the plant are prepared and after ingestion are said to bestow upon users the ability to communicate across vast geographic distances. The drug can apparently also enable collective hallucinations, as well as facilitate intense encounters with both animals and the deceased. *The Yage Letters* is particularly fascinating from an ecocritical perspective in terms of the quest for the ultimate natural drug. However, *The Yage Letters* is not just about the search for the drug also called *yagé*.

The book also reveals underlying tensions between South Americans and the traveling gringo. Much of the book covers negative day-to-day interactions between the white Westerner and South Americans. Letters discuss repeated nuisances. One communication describes being pulled off a bus for being a foreigner (*Yage Letters: Redux* 48). A letter from "William" discusses detention because of a minor bureaucratic error (20). Other messages detail acts of petty larceny. A May 24 letter from Peru complains, "This is a nation of kleptomaniacs. In all my experience as a homosexual I have never been the victim of such idiotic pilferings of articles no conceivable use to anyone else" (39). "William" is conned by medicine men, who are generally described as being "the most inveterate drunk, liar and loafer in the village" (16). He is also rolled by a hustler (16). Various items begin to disappear: a watch, a jock strap, underwear, checks, glasses, and a pocketknife. The annoying events experienced by the gringo in "In Search of Yage" begin to frame the tension that exists between the West and South America. Even more revealing are letters that emphasize the commodification of South American resources and culture.

Several letters in "In Search of Yage" amplify the colonizer by mimicking Western views of the Third World and by highlighting Burroughs' own position of race and class privilege. A May 12 letter by "Bill" from Peru discusses the South American as a puzzling form of human that is "a special race part Indian, part white, part God knows what. He is not . . . an Oriental and does not belong to the West" (38). It is also suggested that South Americans "need white blood" since they understand the "Myth of the White God." Throughout *The Yage Letters*, South Americans are described in pejorative terms, as a race of dirty and diseased prostitutes and hustlers who will take advantage of the traveler from the North whenever possible.

While many of the most negative incidents discussed in the letters apparently involve Burroughs' double, Lee, both Burroughs and Lee are hustlers of sorts. Whereas hustlers generally use charm and cleverness to swindle others, the "Ugly American" simply needs the powerful dollar (xxvi). Money allows the gringo mobility and many other luxuries unavailable to the average South American at midcentury. Money also buys sex. A May 12 letter from "Bill" explains that the markets are "so full of boys they spill out onto the street, and all wise and available to the Yankee dollar" (37). A May 5 letter from "W. Lee" ponders whether he should kidnap an Auca boy for sex (35). A separate memo from "Bill" acknowledges having gone to a hotel with "a barefooted Indian," much to the amusement of hotel staff (37). Thus, even though Burroughs and Lee feel as if they are routinely taken advantage of in this non-Western place, they in turn also exploit the South American.

The issue of sex tourism is just one form of Western exploitation of the developing world as portrayed in *The Yage Letters*. More important for ecocriticism is the historic and ongoing "strategic exploitation" of South American resources by Westerners, which began in the sixteenth century (xxix). The Spanish pursuit of gold initiated the long period of Western commodification of South American natural resources. The rubber boom of the late nineteenth century "lasted over two appalling decades" and culminated in events that would now be called the ethnic cleansing of indigenous peoples (xxix). The period of the rubber boom is just one historical example where matters important to postcolonialism and environmental justice converge.

What the actions of Westerners in South America amount to can be defined as biopiracy, the exploitation of natural resources and biological material by a more technologically advanced external agent without fair compensation to local peoples. Increasing competition for natural resources has been a cause of tension between cultures for centuries, and the modern result of this tension, as shown in *The Yage Letters*, is a residual and shared distrust between the gringo and the South American. In a February 28 letter, "William" makes a dry remark about the general suspicion of Colombians, which is at the same time spot-on: "They expect trouble to come from outside in the form of a foreigner—God knows why" (19). An April 15 letter from Colombia addresses issues of biopiracy directly. "Bill" acknowledges the history of Western commodification of the region's natural resources. At the same time, the willingness of South Americans to have their resources thus exploited by foreign corporations is also obvious. He explains how, in the eyes of local inhabitants, the "White God" may come in the form of the Texas Oil Company. Locals even misinterpret Burroughs' presence as a fortuitous omen and believe he is "a representative of the Texas Oil Company" sent to survey the area for imminent development (24). The governor is confident the arrival of foreign investors will initiate a period of rapid progress, which will almost surely involve the construction of a railroad and airport (25). Thus South Americans themselves seem to buy into the short-term thinking of exchanging natural resources for what they consider to be progress, even though the practice may be harmful in the long term. "Bill" actually tries to explain to locals that salvation will most certainly not come from the Texas Oil Company, but his words are ignored (25). Letters from the same persona also discuss other environmental issues, including the decline in the rubber business and the failure of cocoa crops. However, even though the speaker seems keenly aware of many of the consequences of biopiracy in the letters, at the same time he is a drug tourist participating in the commodification of indigenous knowledge of *yagé*.

Whereas *Naked Lunch* is useful to ecocriticism in highlighting the issue of toxicity, *The Yage Letters* emphasizes friction between cultures that results in instances of biopiracy. Burroughs' other early aesthetic forms are also fascinating, though not in terms of exploring the limits of material culture or the search for a natural drug. Instead, early cut-ups provide an opportunity for ecocriticism to learn from Burroughs' methods and forms. What follows is an investigation into the ways in which aleatory writing methods can be considered emergent proto-ecological forms.

To what degree, if at all, does Burroughs' early experimental writing exhibit evidence of an emergent environmental turn? Writers constantly struggle to find suitable aesthetic forms to express the inexpressible. But the very notion of ecological death is so extreme it overwhelms the human capacity to really imagine it. Richard Kerridge argues that the idea of ecological death is simply "unrepresentable by existing forms of narrative. The possible futures it presents us with are so excessive as to break any chain of personal narrative that might link them with the experience we have now" ("Climate Change" 132). If the reality of ecological crises exceeds the ability to even imagine them, and if existing writing strategies perhaps cannot fully convey the totality of what may still come, perhaps Burroughs' early experimental forms are especially suited to engaging in eschatological discourse. But when one is confronted with his mysterious fragmentary-montage and aleatory forms, there is a problem. Tzvetan Todorov suggests that a standard narrative structure "begins with a stable situation which is disturbed by some power or force. There results a state of disequilibrium [and finally a new] equilibrium is re-established" (111). However, what becomes immediately clear is that Burroughs' *Naked Lunch*, *The Yage Letters*, and early cut-ups defy Todorov's three-part narrative model. So how can one approach such experimental literary creations? This chapter proposes that what can already begin to be seen in early cut-up experiments is a move toward proto-ecological aesthetic forms. Ecocritical concepts borrowed from the study of ecopoetry can help reveal new insights into early cut-ups and at the same time can expose some of the limits of present ecocritical approaches. In the coming pages, typical example fragments will be examined from perplexing early cut-ups.

Burroughs' experimental publications are particularly remarkable because of the peculiar methods of production and the resulting forms that materialized during the period prior to the *Nova* trilogy. The arrival of *Naked Lunch*, *The Yage Letters*, and early cut-ups demonstrated a fundamental shift from the more conventional narrative structures of *Queer* (written in the early 1950s but not published until 1985) and *Junkie* (1953). The publication of *Naked Lunch* (1959) thus marks the beginning of the author's most experimental period. In the theoretical paper of the cut-up movement by Burroughs and Brion Gysin, *The Third Mind* (1978), Burroughs is quoted as suggesting *Naked Lunch* was already a cut-up even though he was not yet aware of it (43). Richard Doyle believes the "Atrophied Preface" of *Naked Lunch* is actually "a cut-up emerging after [Burroughs'] yage experiences" (*Darwin's Pharmacy* 135). This point is up for further discussion. Robin Lydenberg has a slightly different view than Doyle and never says that sections of *Naked Lunch* were written using the cut-up method, but she does believe that Burroughs already began attacking narrative conventions in *Naked Lunch* (*Word Cultures* x). Timothy Murphy also maintains that *Naked Lunch* shows a real narrative shift that actually anticipates the cut-up form, stating, "*Naked Lunch* is not a cut-up text, but its 'mosaic' structure of routines anticipates" later cut-ups (*Wising Up* 71). *Naked Lunch* is, ideologically speaking, a *sort* of cut-up. Some may assume the cut-up writing method began with Gysin and Burroughs' experiments in Paris, but the origins go further back.

Hats Off to Tzara

The origins of the cut-up technique can be traced at least as far back as the historical avant-garde. A crucial event in the development of the cut-up method took place in Paris after the First World War. Dadaist leader Tristan Tzara offered to create an instant poem by randomly pulling words from a hat. It was more than just an act (Burroughs and Gysin 29). He also provided instructions on how to make a new form of poetry in "To Make a Dadaist Poem" (1920), which was first published in English in *Seven Dada Manifestos and Lampisteries* (39). Tzara called on writers to make chance an essential agent of the composition process: "Take a newspaper. / Take some scissors." (39). The procedure requires the poet to choose an article from a newspaper. Next, the author cuts out words from the article, places them into a bag (or a hat), and gently mixes the words. The artist pulls the words out one by one, thus creating an instant poem. Tzara explains the resulting poem "will resemble you," suggesting the randomness of the act will invariably provide some degree of truthfulness (39).

Tzara's preoccupation with cut-up forms was part of a wider aesthetic movement against the brutality of the First World War, but Brion Gysin's initiation into aleatory writing practices happened much more by chance.

While living at the Beat Hotel in Paris, Gysin was preparing a wall mount and accidentally sliced through several newspapers with a Stanley blade. This caused unusual new word combinations to appear, which Gysin found "hilariously funny and hysterically meaningful" (Gysin 57). He shared his find with Burroughs, who enthusiastically saw the results as revelatory in creating a new writing method. Gysin reports that Burroughs reached an epiphany and proclaimed, "Unfortunately, the means are at hand for disastrous success" (qtd. in Gysin 58). While Burroughs seemed to recognize the radical potential of cut-ups, Lydenberg believes "he had already served an unconscious cut-up apprenticeship in editing and rearranging the voluminous material that finally yielded the published version of *Naked Lunch*" (*Word Cultures* 44). Others discuss connections to the historical avant-garde.

Both Watson and Harris have considered the cut-up method in relation to the Exquisite Corpse practice, a Surrealist-inspired technique to collectively create a new and original text. Watson puts forward that the cut-up method "offered a verbal counterpart to the Surrealist parlor game" (279). Harris has taken this further by examining specific similarities and differences between the Exquisite Corpse as a method and the montage and cut-up practice of Burroughs and Gysin. Harris points out that while the "Exquisite Corpse required the participation of other practitioners," the cut-up was more flexible and one needed only "a sheet of typed paper and a pair of scissors" ("Cutting Up the Corpse" 90). Important differences also exist between Tzara's cut-up system and the practices of Gysin and Burroughs. Harris calls Tzara's approach "ironic" and "anti-aesthetic" but thinks Burroughs "intended" that people would follow his practice ("'Burroughs Is a Poet Too'" 30). Tzara, Gysin, and Burroughs all used aleatory methods to challenge conventional narrative practices. According to Harris, from the earliest moments of their collaboration, Gysin and Burroughs viewed the cut-up method "in relation to techniques of the historical avant-garde—collage, chance operations [and] automatism" ("Cutting Up the Corpse" 90). Burroughs and Gysin believed they were necessarily bringing the aesthetic potential of montage and collage to writing that was already at work in the visual arts. Gysin's bold declaration that writing was five decades behind painting was a call to introduce Dada and Surrealist inspiration to literature (Burroughs and Gysin 34). Gysin and Burroughs therefore owe a permanent debt of gratitude to the historical avant-garde. A significant element to the cut-up method involves rethinking the roles of the author and reader. In this sense, the cut-up form echoes the eschatology of Dada predecessors.

The foundation papers for the cut-up movement, *Minutes to Go* and *The Third Mind*, called for reconsidering the idea of the all-seeing author. According to Harris, *Minutes to Go* was "the launching manifesto of the cut-up method" ("Cutting Up the Corpse" 84). Coauthored by Sinclair Beiles, William Burroughs, Gregory Corso, and Brion Gysin, *Minutes to Go* contains the results of the early cut-up experiments and for this reason deserves additional critical attention. Harris too stresses the real necessity for more research into early cut-ups, which have been "[e]ffectively ignored by Burroughs' critics" ("Response to John Watters" 339). Harris has more recently carried out research on early cut-ups, but studies of the embryonic cut-up form remain, in the context of the wider research on Burroughs, very much the exception.

In the spirit of Tzara's original appeal—"Take a newspaper. / Take some scissors."—*Minutes to Go* encourages the reader to adopt the cut-up method: "Pick a book any book cut it up" (4). The cut-ups in *Minutes to Go* are rather diminutive compared to the extended cut-ups of the *Nova* trilogy. Early cut-ups are thus distinctive even in the broader context of Burroughs' other cut-ups; for example, each cut-up included in *Minutes to Go* is unique in terms of source material and content. Burroughs claims *Minutes to Go* "contains unedited unchanged cut-ups" (Burroughs and Gysin 29). However, the writer elsewhere admits that some degree of composition was needed: "One tries not to impose story plot or continuity artificially but you do have to compose the materials, you can't just dump down a jumble of notes and thoughts and considerations and expect people to read it" (Odier 48). David Sterritt points out that Burroughs' "cut-up spontaneity was not based on random or haphazard juxtaposition, since after cutting or folding a text . . . he would rewrite the result until it carried some degree of identifiable sense" (167). Thus it would be appropriate to say Burroughs' cut-ups were certainly not conventional, but they were not entirely random either. But the cut-up method did rely on an array of chance elements in the creation of the final product.

What is really important about *Minutes to Go* is the method it advocates. Gysin declares, "[H]ere is the system according to us" (Beiles et al. 5). Harris believes the essential feature of the cut-up technique is the practice itself, which is "to be grasped by *doing*, not as a content to be understood by interpretation" ("'Burroughs Is a Poet Too'" 35; emphasis in original). Ecocriticism holds that all cultural texts can be better understood through interpretation. However, Harris is certainly correct in pointing out that the practice of the cut-up method, the actual shearing of the text and rearrangement of the words, is essential. While *Minutes to Go* is the philosophical declaration for the cut-up method, *The Third Mind* is the theoretical document. An important concept of the cut-up method is "the negation of the omnipresent and all powerful author" (Burroughs and Gysin 18). Carol Loranger claims *The Third Mind* is a direct call for "guerrilla assault on the idea of authorial ownership" (para. 2).[1] Jeff Bryan further argues, *The Third Mind* "is partly exhortative. It is a manifesto for social change and transformation of the individual" (80). Burroughs believes "new techniques, such as cut-up, will involve much more of the total capacity of the observer. It enriches the whole aesthetic experience, extends it" (Burroughs and Gysin 6). More broadly, the cut-up form questions many conventional ideas about what literature is and what it does.

Having looked at the origins of the Gysin and Burroughs cut-up method, it is appropriate to now consider the practice. The cut-up procedure seems straightforward enough, and the method forces one to consider distinctions between human and mechanical narrative agency. Burroughs explains one way to perform the cut-up technique:

> Take a page. Like this page. Now cut down the middle and across the middle. You have four sections. . . . Now rearrange the sections placing section four with section one and section two with section three. And you have a new page. (Burroughs and Gysin 30–31)

Such a seemingly simple technique can be used to generate large amounts of cut-up text. One may look at the cut-up method as a way to destroy the conventional narrative, through the violent cannibalization of the natural text. One also has to consider the mechanical nature of the cut-up method. Gérard-Georges Lemaire observes that the cut-up technique is essentially a "mechanical method of shredding texts in a ruthless machine" (qtd. in Burroughs and Gysin 13). The cut-up method is mechanical and relies on the physical destruction of the source text. However, all writing is mechanical to some degree, in the sense that writers need technological processes to reach an audience. From the earliest woodblock printing to the typewriter, mechanical processes help people express themselves.[2]

Burroughs scholars have done considerable groundwork on the cut-up project, while others have highlighted the radical nature of the practice. Robin Lydenberg's *Word Cultures* specifically discusses the negative aesthetic of Burroughs' cut-up narratives (17). She laments the lack of scholarly engagement of the cut-up novels (55). Nevertheless, Harris observes that the "enormously fertile and innovative period of the cut-up project has enjoyed a good deal of critical attention" since Lydenberg's book ("'Burroughs Is a Poet Too'" 25). Harris is specifically referring to scholarship on the *Nova* trilogy, and not on enigmatic pre-*Nova* cut-ups, which to this day remain woefully neglected. Ted Morgan believes the cut-up experiments were difficult to sustain for the length of a book (582). If lengthy and extended cut-ups are difficult to endure, then one might better consider diminutive examples from the early period. Other Burroughs researchers highlight the radical nature of the cut-up method. Similarly to Lydenberg, Timothy Murphy believes cut-ups negate the direction of narrative control that normally runs from author to reader. Murphy adds that the concepts of montage and stream of consciousness methods already at use elsewhere simply cannot explain the true radical novelty of cut-ups (*Wising Up* 105). He further stresses that cut-ups challenge generic literary conventions and offers a procedure to abolish them altogether (106). More recently, scholars have added to the discussion.

Research has expanded beyond a singular focus on Burroughs' cut-up and hints at deep connections with the historical avant-garde. In his historical study of the development of the cut-up method, Edward Robinson expands discussion beyond Burroughs by studying the cut-up practices of not only Gysin and Burroughs but also Kathy Acker, John Giorno, Claude Pélieu, and Carl Weissner. Moreover, Robinson asserts the importance of the cut-up form to music and wider culture. Richard Doyle does not discuss the cut-up method at length, but he does make some bold propositions. Doyle maintains that cut-ups, similar to Dadaist art, allow "texts to interrupt normal consciousness" (*Darwin's Pharmacy* 186). He also argues that the cut-up method produces the "repeatable effects of manifesting the psyche through plant reagents" such as *yagé* (96). Such sentiment suggests an ancestral link between the fragmentary-montage structure of *Naked Lunch* and the cut-up form.

Ecocritical researchers have also entered the scholarly conversation on experimental writing strategies such as the cut-up method. Franca Bellarsi sees Burroughs' cut-up as a way to use language to counter existing forms of power. She believes the results of the cut-up method ultimately cause "readers to break their conditioned thought patterns" ("William S. Burroughs's Art" 52). The subversive nature of cut-ups and other experimental writing forms can even be considered a form of environmental praxis. If cut-ups make people rethink what literature is and does, then they can by extension reconsider unsustainable practices in this world. This is what Harriet Tarlo believes. She boldly asserts that experimental writing practices that use "found text" (such as the cut-up method) amount to what can be considered genuine ecological praxis:

> The freedom of citation within the poetic culture is an important part of [a] shift in consciousness. [Found poetry] *is* subversive, not just in poetic terms, but also in deeper cultural ones, and, as such, we may rightfully see it as an ecopoetic and eco-ethical practice in action. ("Recycles" 128; emphasis in original)

The environmental implications of experimental narrative forms need further consideration, and the final section of this chapter attempts to do just that. The wide range of critical voices that have already engaged with the cut-up form is a sign of genuine academic interest in Burroughs' experimental methods, but surprising gaps remain.

When examining the results of Burroughs' cut-up experiments, critics focus almost entirely on the *Nova* trilogy.[3] This is reasonable to some degree, since the *Nova* trilogy was such an extraordinarily large project. But overlooking the embryonic cut-up forms devalues the early phase in the development of Burroughs' diverse narrative practices. For those reading Burroughs, form and method are as vital as theme or content. In this sense, Burroughs' most experimental writing is a limit case of sorts, and the real difficulties he poses are impossible to avoid. But the lack of ecological perspectives on Burroughs' early writing justifies (and indeed, necessitates) more attention to the remarkable formative early period of the cut-up venture. Ecocritics too recognize the need for more study of experimental writing strategies such as the cut-up method. Harriet Tarlo makes a call for ecocritical scholarship into experimental writing practices, more specifically research into the methods authors use in the search for and reconstitution of found text. She laments the reality that "very few eco-critics engage with innovative or experimental writing" ("Radical Landscapes," para. 4). Given the general neglect of Burroughs' early cut-ups and the lack of ecocritical studies into strategies using found text, further deliberation on early cut-ups leads to a consolidation of perspectives.

Ecological Considerations of Found-Text Practices

Harriet Tarlo's "Recycles: The Eco-Ethical Poetics of Found Text in Contemporary Poetry" is one of very few investigations to specifically examine cut-up methods in an environmental context. She offers a persuasive model to analyze how environmental content is embodied in contemporary poetry through experimental writing practices. However, Tarlo's model has been restricted to the analysis of openly environmental poetry and has never been used in the examination of other experimental forms. Therefore, looking at example fragments from *Minutes to Go* and *The Yage Letters* can be useful in helping establish whether connections between ecology and the Gysin-inspired cut-up method exist, if at all. At the same time, one can also learn how applicable Tarlo's theoretical model is in finding environmental meaning in experimental writing that uses found text. The application of Tarlo's concepts to primordial cut-ups is a reasonable, but quite radical, extension of her work. Three central areas need to be kept in mind when analyzing an experimental poem to discover environmental meaning:

- "the methodology employed by poets in their use of found text";
- "the spirit of citation"; and
- "the eco-ethical significance of this practice." ("Recycles" 114)

According to Tarlo, keeping these three areas in mind will help those seeking to uncover ecological insight in found-text practices. Let's begin by looking at two striking early cut-ups written by authors not always associated with cut-up production.

Brion Gysin's "FIRST CUT-UPS" (1959) is in many ways unlike the other cut-ups found in *Minutes to Go*, being more of a collage effort, but it can be examined for environmental meaning. One of Gysin's first attempts using the cut-up technique, "FIRST CUT-UPS" offers abundant opportunities for environmental dialogue:

> It is impossible to estimate the damage. Anything put out up to now is like pulling a figure out of the air.
>
> Six distinguished British women said to us later, indicating the crowd of chic young women who were fingering samples, "If our prices weren't as good or better, they wouldn't come. Eve is eternal."
>
> (I'm going right back to the Sheraton Carlton and call the Milwaukee Braves.)
>
> Miss Hannah Pugh the slim model—a member of the Diner's Club, the American Express Credit Cards etc.—drew from a piggy bank a talent which is the very quintessence of the British Female sex.
>
> "People aren't crazy," she said. "Now that Hazard has banished my timidity I feel that I, too, can live on streams in the area where people are urged to be watchful."
>
> A huge wave rolled in from the wake of Hurricane Gracie and bowled a married couple off a jetty. The wife's body was found—the husband was missing, presumed drowned.
>
> Tomorrow the moon will be 228,400 miles from the earth and the sun almost 93,000,000 miles away. (*Minutes to Go* 6)

One can immediately see features specific to this particular cut-up. Added indentation of ribbons of text suggests the splicing together of new textual fragments. The line "It is impossible to estimate the damage" sounds strangely similar to the short apocalyptic messages Burroughs wrote over the course of the next decade. But what is essential is whether a revised system of analysis can reveal any environmental meaning from this puzzling piece.

The method of composition for "FIRST CUT-UPS" is similar to the method used by Burroughs during the same period, with some minor differences. As is seen in many of the other cut-ups from *Minutes to Go*, Gysin appropriated text found in popular print sources. Source texts for "FIRST CUT-UPS" originated in the *Paris Herald Tribune*, *London Observer*, *London Daily Mail*, and *Life* magazine advertisements (6). Gysin refers to his selection of source texts as "collage" but never explains their content, unlike Burroughs, and this is where we see a small difference. While not directly related to ecology, such methodological differences are significant in understanding not just the procedural differences but also how the reception of each cut-up can vary.

The spirit of citation of Gysin's "FIRST CUT-UPS" can be called dark and comic and reveals remnants of environmental meaning. The combination of specific lines evokes a cumulative sense of the apocalyptic: "It is impossible to estimate the damage. Anything put out up to now is like pulling a figure out of the air" suggests human death on a grand scale. The lines "A huge wave rolled in from the wake of Hurricane Gracie" and "The wife's body was found—the husband was missing, presumed drowned" imply a cumulative sense of suffering and death by natural forces. But the real comic dark ecology present here occurs in the juxtaposition of contrasting and fragmented images of death and, oddly, advertising. The gravity of death images is followed by the use of slick marketing language, which functions to provide moments of deep contrast and comic relief. "It is impossible to estimate the damage. Anything put out up to now is like pulling a figure out of the air" is immediately followed by an image of women "fingering samples" and a seeming offhand remark about great prices. Both confusing and disorienting, montage here creates tension. One layer of meaning works toward a climactic peak, but just as fast another layer prevents any real resolution. All we are really left with is the final line: "Tomorrow the moon will be 228,400 miles from the earth and the sun almost 93,000,000 miles away." This zoom out places us both before and after humanity and shows a more permanent picture of the universe beyond our own species.

Gregory Corso's experience with the cut-up method was for him personally dissatisfying, but his cut-ups are quite fascinating to study. "FRAGMENT P.B. Shelley" is a portion from "THINGS TO CUT-UP, by Gregory Corso, and offers lucid and familiar romantic images:

Vultures, who build your bowers
High in the Future's towers,
Withred hopes on hopes are spread!
Dying joys, chocked by the dead,
Will serve your beaks of prey
Many a day. (*Minutes to Go* 55)

On the surface, this section of the cut-up looks a lot like a poem. Internal rhyme is a key feature, and there is an attempt to keep line length and syllabic count well ordered. The words "bowers," "towers," "spread," "dead," "prey," and "day" are repetitive and build anticipation in the reader. The word pool for "FRAGMENT P.B. Shelley" consists of words that have loosely negative environmental significance. "Vultures," "Future's towers," "beaks for prey," "Withered hopes on hopes are spread!," and "Dying joys, choked by the dead" suggest a snowballing sense of trepidation and destruction for human beings. In other words, the word pool for "FRAGMENT P.B. Shelley" encompasses environmental apprehension in the metaphors of social collapse and human death.

The source text is related not just to method but also to the spirit of citation and remaining remnants of environmental meaning. The source text used in the creation of "FRAGMENT P.B. Shelley," I think, is Percy Shelley's "Lines," which was published posthumously in 1824. Further inspection indicates almost identical copying of the original poem, with the exception of punctuation in a few places. The source here is a single text and not multiple texts, and thus it shows yet another small methodological difference. One also notices how carefully Corso composed the cut-up to emulate the original Shelley text. But discovery of the source text only complicates matters. Is this an example of homage and glorious plagiarism? Did Corso simply cut the Shelley fragment up only to piece it back together word for word? Or was the selection of a source text and subsequent reconstitution an attempt to subvert the cut-up practice, thus subverting subversion? Given Shelley's position as romantic thinker, Corso's cut-up can be said to resurrect, to some degree, the romantic legacy of the original text. So what we can see in this particular cut-up is a powerful tribute to Shelley's dark ecological vision.

Since these early cut-ups by Gysin and Corso force us to recognize our own involvement in the creation and annihilation that surround us, a key ingredient in the post-pastoral mindset, according to ecocritic Terry Gifford,[4] they might rightly be called post-pastoral. Tarlo reminds us that post-pastoral writing "resists narrative and realist conventions in poetry in favour of evolving techniques and structures which aim to create a truer reflection of reality itself" (*Ground Aslant* 12). Even though found-text practices involve a great degree of chance recycling, such randomness does not necessarily rule out environmental consideration. The post-pastoral is situated in opposition to the sentimental pastoral. So if cut-ups are essentially antiromantic, and if they resist the pastoral mindset and yet simultaneously force us to think about issues of ecology, they might rightly be called post-pastoral aesthetic forms. Avant-garde writing such as the cut-up contests the very idea of the pastoral. And the cut-up places us directly at the center of destruction and creation. But an even more intriguing consideration than the questions posed by Gysin and Corso is what Burroughs' early cut-up attempts tell us about how we think about ecology.

"FORMED IN THE STANCE" (1959) represents one of Burroughs' earliest published cut-ups and offers immediate challenges and opportunities. Consider the following fragment:

> The beautiful disease and
> The government falls
> along the weed rooms
> flesh along the weed government/ / / /
>
> The girls eat morning
> Dying peoples to a white bone monkey
> in the Winter sun
> touching tree of the house. $$$$ (*Minutes to Go* 13)

The fragment tests conventional ways of literary reading, but the method of composition reveals ways in which the ideology of the cut-up parallels aspects of environmental praxis. The text that emerges after textual shredding and reconstitution often appears grammatically correct, though semantic meaning is missing. The lines "The beautiful disease" and "The girls eat morning" recall the striking contradictions of Dada artistic practices produced a century ago.

The method used in creating "FORMED IN THE STANCE," and the early cut-ups more generally, is helpful in trying to discover additional meaning. Tarlo defines methodology as a "series of decisions made by a writer from a spectrum of possibilities" ("Recycles" 115). Here the methodology involved the use of two source texts. One came from the *Paris Herald Tribune* and was titled "Met Performance." The selection of this source text appropriates high art, since the text discusses a performance at the Met, an icon of high culture. One can say that in "FORMED IN THE STANCE," the cut-up shreds the notion of high art and heaves it back at the reader in an undermined and modified form. What emerges from the cut-up grinder in this case is certainly not high art. The second source text was taken from the October 31, 1959, edition of the *Saturday Evening Post* (*Minutes to Go* 14) and discussed disease in human beings. What really matters is that Burroughs' selection of the second source text reveals yet a further degree of media appropriation, in this case of medical discourse from the period. The act of subversive appropriation of mainstream language is a common tactic throughout the infant stage of the cut-up.

Broadly speaking, the cut-up method forces us to consider the ways that humans make art and what constitutes art. The structured use of found text is intimately connected to "the work's ideological and philosophical stance on environment and ecology" (Tarlo, "Recycles" 115). In other words, maybe one way to avoid the fratricidal wars of the past and future is to rethink everything, including the ways we think about what art is and how it is produced. By doing this, we might finally be able to talk about what Jed Rasula calls "'biodegradable thinking,' where we can conceivably speak of what might be called an 'ecology of consciousness'" (*Compost* 43). Such a situation forces us to radically rethink the force and power of poetry to move the human imagination.

The spirit of citation of "FORMED IN THE STANCE" can be called both evasive and ironic. Readers have to accept large amounts of uncertainty, which provides the cut-up with an evasive, playful, and slippery quality. The lines "The girls eat morning / Dying peoples to a white bone monkey" cannot be read literally, even though our minds try to, so readers have to impart meaning or at least allow for the collision of contradictory concepts to flicker in the mind's eye. During these moments, the dancing images inevitably cause what Retallack calls the "ironic sprinting in place" common in found poetry (qtd. in Osman, para. 40). The use of found text in "FORMED IN THE STANCE" also problematizes the issue of authorship by recruiting the reader into coauthorship. So if the cut-up empowers readers to take action, then the subsequent consideration is whether the cut-up can even move people to environmental awareness.

"FORMED IN THE STANCE" provides opportunities to find remnants of environmental meaning as well. What becomes particularly interesting is when "FORMED IN THE STANCE" is read not as a poem, but as an extremely condensed form of short story with gaps. Such a reading is not difficult. "Dying peoples to a white bone monkey / in the Winter sun" can be read as an omen for future generations of human beings. "Dying peoples" can be understood as an image of a species in crisis—the logical conclusion of ever-increasing technological dependence and resource depletion. At a certain point, "Dying peoples" might recognize the futility of such an existence and, in a final effort to prevent the demise of the human animal, embrace a form of pantheism. "Dying peoples to a white bone monkey" can thus be read as suggesting the last generations of humans may resort to a form of monkey shamanism to save themselves from inevitable death. While the suggestion that humans may one day worship monkeys may seem exceptionally speculative, it is important to note that some present-day non-Western cultures hold the monkey up as sacred.[5] Moreover, the idea that future endangered humans will revere monkeys as a form to which they should aspire speaks, subtly, to the real destruction of primate habitats in this world. So perhaps after the scientific mindset has been cast away, near the end of the human moment, the arrival of the summer and winter solstices will once again be imbued with sacred pantheistic value. Read in this way, "FORMED IN THE STANCE" encourages present-day readers to reconsider the world in which we now live. Other cut-ups from *Minutes to Go* also deepen our understanding of the ways in which experimental found-text poems connect with issues of ecology.

"VIRUSES WERE BY ACCIDENT?" (1960) immediately poses a number of difficult problems in attempting an interpretation. This mysterious and apocalyptic piece represents another of Burroughs' earliest efforts using the cut-up method. Consider the following fragment:

> (Resevoir [*sic*] of rabies and other virus? discovered in *Brown*
> fat of vampire bats and their well known and easily
> chosen human constituent.)
> Cancer tests . . . brown blood. . live babies. . proof of virus.
> vaccine? Bio-control the London conference. . it was out sheep
> cattle and animals have wild system. . . . blood time brown
> blood. (*Minutes to Go* 15)

What is immediately clear when looking at the above fragment is the genuine challenge of suggesting, as Harris puts it, any "precise textual interpretation or aesthetic evaluation" ("'Burroughs Is a Poet Too'" 29). Harris acknowledges the genuine difficulties of analyzing the piece and even concludes, "You could say that further interpretation is simply not possible" (29). If one accepts the impossibility of effectively postulating a definite interpretation, one can look to uncover remnants of meaning instead. What follows is not simply an assessment of the limits of Tarlo's model but a real step toward developing an extension to her model.

Tarlo recommends examining the methodology employed in the creation of the poem in question first. The selection of found text is an essential part of the process. According to *Minutes to Go*, material for "VIRUSES WERE BY ACCIDENT?" comes from articles published in the *Paris Herald Tribune* (15). The source articles discuss "human cancer and animal diseases in Africa" (15). The selection of source materials is crucial here, as Burroughs deliberately chose articles discussing disease. By merging texts about disease among animals and humans, Burroughs unknowingly participates in a key discussion in ecocriticism, "namely how far we can distinguish ourselves from non-human beings" (Tarlo, "Recycles" 120). Selection here refers not only to the choice of source materials but also to the process of selecting found text, as well as the eventual rearrangement of found text into the new creative form.

Word selection often originates from what Scottish poet Dorothy Alexander calls a "word pool," which can be defined as found words with shared properties that are reused in combination for a certain effect (qtd. in Tarlo, "Recycles" 118). In "VIRUSES WERE BY ACCIDENT?" the word pool includes a combination of words that help conjure up a cumulative sense of pestilence: "rabies," "virus," "vampire bats," "Cancer," "blood," "vaccine," "Bio-control," "sheep," "cattle," "animals," and "brown blood" (*Minutes to Go* 15). Because in this case the found text is borrowed exclusively from one newspaper and is not interwoven with text written by Burroughs, one can accept the writer's contribution as an example of limited authorship. However, this does not mean Burroughs' role in the cut-up method is negligible; quite the contrary.[6] The selection of the word pool for "VIRUSES WERE BY ACCIDENT?" suggests some degree of apprehension about living in a culture and time when ecological apocalypse may not necessarily come from the sky.

A second point of analysis, according to Tarlo's model for examination of experimental ecopoetry, involves the "spirit of citation" of the found text in the new creative form ("Recycles" 119). Samples from "VIRUSES WERE BY ACCIDENT?" can be considered misanthropic and satirical forms of hostile citation. The "Resevoir" thus may be understood to be the human body itself, the "easily / chosen human constituent," which remains an appealing host and incubator for all sorts of infections. If the human body is a source and transmitter of disease, the broader message conveyed by this piece is essentially misanthropic. Alternatively, the fragment "Resevoir of rabies and other virus?" can be understood to represent a storehouse of disease, similar to the Museum of Lost Species in Burroughs' *Ghost of Chance*, a depository of deadly ailments and viruses. The "Resevoir" of disease functions as a negative representation of the human organizations that are supposed to protect the public from disease but may actually do something far more sinister. For example, the line can be read as a critique of organizations such as the Centers for Disease Control, which is a genuine reservoir of disease.[7] Moreover, developments in germ warfare since "VIRUSES WERE BY ACCIDENT?" was published in 1960 make the very suggestion of human-made pestilence slightly less absurd than it once may have seemed.[8] While it is not known for sure which source articles were used for the creation of this cut-up, the fact that the found text originates from articles that cover issues of disease suggests Burroughs appropriated the language of official media and medical discourse in order to subvert the original message.

An additional instance of hostile citation involves the fragment "Biocontrol the London conference."[9] What is immediately clear is the absence of a second-position verb. But if one sees the sentence as a simple command, the fragment takes on an unusual if not comical juxtaposition of words that create an opposite connotation to what likely was originally being communicated in the source texts. The word *biocontrol* means to use ecological methods of controlling pests that depend on "predation and parasitism" (Madan and Madan 153). Accordingly, one can consider those organizations that are meant to protect the public health as ineffective and possibly even parasitic bodies working against the public, as vermin "vampire bats."[10] The suggestion that one should "Bio-control the London conference" implies the preemptive ecological destruction of those who may one day unleash a human-made pestilence.

Read in this way, "VIRUSES WERE BY ACCIDENT?" approaches a radical position. Furthermore, the recommendation to use ecologically sound methods to destroy those who would destroy the public is an absurd notion and in this case can be considered a comical instance of Surrealist bathos. In other words, by misappropriating source texts for the purpose of subversion, Burroughs uses the cut-up process as an example of "Culture Jamming" or "Guerilla Semiotics" (Tietchen 109–10). This involves the adoption of official discourse, which is then subverted and fed back to the reader using the language that surrounds the reader, but in a more hostile, modified form (Tarlo, "Recycles" 121). Hostile citation can thus be considered one manner to express a real "sense of anger and powerlessness [that] often characterises how we feel about the global, particularly environmental, issues that face us now" (123). The appropriation of official discourse for purposes of subversion of the original message remains an important tool in environmentalist discourse at present. Thus the dainty, almost unseen question mark in the very title of Burroughs' piece "VIRUSES WERE BY ACCIDENT?" encompasses larger, even subconscious, fears of a modern manufactured plague.[11]

A final area of focus in the analysis of experimental ecopoetry, according to Tarlo, involves thinking about a text's larger "eco-ethical significance" ("Recycles" 114). In the context of "VIRUSES WERE BY ACCIDENT?" one needs to consider the source texts, which, according to Burroughs, discuss disease in different species. Oliver Harris says the methods of production remain the most important consideration in better understanding the piece: "The conclusion has to be that texts such as "VIRUSES WERE BY ACCIDENT?" remain cryptic the better to exemplify a practice that must, in order to do its work, take priority over a fully coherent thesis" ("'Burroughs Is a Poet Too'" 29). However, Burroughs also shows what Tarlo calls the "textual, material quality of [literature using found text] and, above all, the fact that it exists in a sea of other textual, material language, rather than as a separate poetic discourse existing within its own rarefied tradition" ("Recycles" 122). Tarlo's ideas about the recycling of found text are helpful in attempting to handle a most difficult piece. Until now, "VIRUSES WERE BY ACCIDENT?" has never been read as an environmental text, but Tarlo's model assists in identifying remnants of possible meaning, passing over direct expression and instead offering what Richard Kerridge calls a more "indirect statement" (143).

But complications with Tarlo's approach arise when examining an additional cut-up published in 1963. "I Am Dying, Meester?" appears in *The Yage Letters* and is an extreme example of Burroughs' early cut-ups:

> Panama clung to our bodies—Probably cut—Anything made this dream—It has consumed the customers of fossil orgasm—Ran into my old friend Jones—So badly off, forgotten, coughing in 1920 movie—Vaudeville voices hustle sick dawn breath on bed service—Idiot Mambo spattered backwards—I nearly suffocated trying on the boy's breath—That's Panama—Nitrous flesh swept out by your voice and end of receiving set—Brain eating birds patrol the low frequency brain waves.
>
> (*Yage Letters: Redux* 76)

The initial ecocritical response to the above fragment has to be paralysis. There simply does not appear to be anything to grasp on to. A worthwhile question is to what degree this cut-up can be handled by Tarlo's model.

The method Burroughs employed in locating source text for eventual reconstitution in "Meester?" is quite different from the approach he used in the creation of the "VIRUSES" piece. In *Yage Letters: Redux*, Harris says he believes "I Am Dying, Meester?" was made "by recycling fragments of 'In Search of Yage'" (xlii). Roughly 25 percent of the "660 words" contained in "Meester?" originated "mainly from the 'January 15' and 'April 15' letters" ("Not Burroughs' Final Fix," para. 33). Nevertheless, Harris acknowledges the real difficulty in knowing for certain, not simply because of the perplexing "nature of the cut-up method" but also because of the considerable amount of "internal repetition" within "Meester?" While "VIRUSES WERE BY ACCIDENT?" can be considered an example of limited authorship, Burroughs' recycling of his own words adds a different authorial dynamic to the reconstituted "Meester?" but the result confuses matters even more. The increasing challenges of tracing links to other texts to find meaning are frustrating, and the uncertainty readers have to accept is possibly dissatisfying.

If the cut-up process shreds texts, then it can be said in the case of "I Am Dying, Meester?" that the source texts have been shredded beyond recognition, at least beyond the capacity to see clear portals to other texts. In the case of "VIRUSES WERE BY ACCIDENT?" knowing a little about the source articles does help provide insight into the process of its creation. The shift in approach from "VIRUSES" to "Meester?" represents the evolution of the cut-up method. However, the increasingly complex process of selecting found text and the shredding of source text come at the cost of intelligibility in the new literary text. Lydenberg posits that Burroughs used the cut-up technique to dispel "the illusion of the referential function of language" (*Word Cultures* 33). This lack of reference is especially conspicuous in "Meester?" Therefore, the more intricate process of selecting found text for "Meester?" adds to its cryptic nature. Harris also emphasizes that an important detail in "Meester?" is the presence of more than "seventy dashes in a piece less than 700 words long," thus presenting compelling evidence of additional textual shredding. The lack of referentiality suggests the cut-up method has become even more radical in its destructive power. If "VIRUSES" is the result of textual shredding, "Meester?" is the result of textual shredding and subsequent pulverization. Although one can find the source texts for over half of the content of "Meester?" a significant amount of the reconstituted text remains unidentified.

In thinking about the spirit of citation in "Meester?" the reader is once again confronted with many of the same problems as when looking at the methods of creation, including the lack of orientation. One can certainly see a rough pool of words with vaguely negative connotations: "clung," "consumed," "badly off," "coughing," "Idiot," and "Brain eating birds." But even if a (very loose) word pool has been identified, it would be a real stretch to imply that these terms somehow express environmental significance, either individually or collectively. Indeed, without knowing more precise details about the source texts, the spirit of citation in this case remains an open problem. However, even though Tarlo's first two areas of consideration may not fully handle "Meester?" her final point of attention, the "eco-ethical significance" of the practices of manufacturing the text, can help one learn more ("Recycles" 114). If one no longer sees literature as something to be consumed and digested by the reader, then one can focus on other qualities of the text. Paradoxically, the same issues that cause problems in understanding the methods and spirit of citation can also help provide other opportunities to discover environmental value in "Meester?"

Tarlo emphasizes the need to think about how experimental writing contributes to the ways people think about ecology. If one looks beyond thematic content and considers the eco-ethical significance of the new form that emerges from the vigorous use of found text in the "Meester?" cut-up (and the early cut-ups more generally), one may better understand radically experimental texts that exhibit no outward environmental meaning. If "Meester?" is a poem, it is a radically unconventional poem. Lydenberg asserts the cut-up form "transgresses" borders "separating inside and outside, fiction and alleged fact, the private self and the words of others" (*Word Cultures* 53). "Meester?" thus violates expectations of what literature is supposed to do. Richard Kerridge maintains that "the cut-up method in particular, can bring into poetic space kinds of discourse not normally available to the personal lyric" (133). This can be taken further by suggesting that the cut-up has unique qualities that make it especially useful to engaging in eschatological discourse. Because no meaning is prepackaged for the reader, one has to search for meaning. When unsuccessful in this pursuit of clarity, readers have to impart meaning, as is the case in *Naked Lunch*. The distancing effect of the cut-up form forces us to question what Slavoj Žižek calls "our most unquestionable presuppositions" (qtd. in Kerridge 132). By making readers rethink common assumptions about what literature is and does, Burroughs' early experimental texts can teach ecocriticism about the importance of cut-ups to the issue of biopiracy. *The Yage Letters* connects the cut-up method and *ayahuasca* as radical techniques of reality transformation, which means the undoing of Western assumptions about identity. This is vital, since the method of composition may seem mechanical but is still involved in the same derangement of the senses that Burroughs learned from Amazonian shamans.

The Naked Tree

This chapter has examined unusual early cut-ups from *Minutes to Go* and *The Yage Letters* using concepts borrowed from the analysis of ecopoetry. While ecocriticism may seem better suited to dealing with issues of theme and content, Burroughs' works force readers to acknowledge the importance of method and form. In particular, Burroughs poses the important question of whether certain narrative strategies are useful in representing the unthinkable. By extension, one can even ask whether certain aesthetic forms can help "shift our human consciousness" (Cynthia Hogue qtd. in Tarlo, "Recycles" 123). I suggest the unconventionality of early cut-ups found in *Minutes to Go* and *The Yage Letters* can be considered emergent proto-ecological forms. Burroughs changed his writing strategies from *Naked Lunch* to *Minutes to Go*, *The Yage Letters*, and the even more radical subsequent cut-ups because he found existing narrative structures incapable of representing how he saw the real world, which many of his narratives show as gravitating toward irrevocable ecological ruin. Burroughs' unconventional forms allow for new ways of viewing literature and possibly the world.

Tarlo's three-part approach to the analysis of ecopoetry is helpful in recovering remnants of environmental meaning. Even though the "eco-ethical significance" of an experimental practice is perhaps still too loose a notion and does not always work with texts outside the nature-writing genre, Tarlo's approach is helpful in teaching ecocriticism to think about formal literary elements, and this is significant. At the same time, this chapter reaffirms the real difficulties of reading Burroughs in the first place. Avant-garde writing practices require participatory reading, and successful writers make readers "feel that our response is demanded and should even be translated into some kind of action" (Tarlo, "Recycles" 125). The ecological significance of Burroughs' experimental writing is found "embedded in a form that endeavours to stimulate the reader into understanding and action" (114). Burroughs' early forms are certainly not obvious examples of environmental activism. However, his experimental structures can be considered proto-ecological in their radical ambiguity, which forces readers to attempt understanding. The fragmentary-montage structure of *Naked Lunch* and early cut-ups is especially suited to expressing both increasing isolation from the natural world and the fragmentation of human consciousness in an increasingly uncertain age.

4.

A Land of Grass without Mirrors: The Dada Ecopoetics of Moving Images in William Burroughs' *Nova Express* and Věra Chytilová's *Sedmikrásky* (*Daisies*)

This film is dedicated to all those whose sole source of indignation is a trampled-on trifle. —Chytilová, *Daisies*

The American New Formalists of the late twentieth century were deeply committed to saving culture by reviving orthodox poetic practices, but Dada thinking insists the deliberate violation of aesthetic conventions is the only path to true liberation. This ideological and poetic tension can be found in a contentious 1991 essay published in the *Atlantic Monthly*. In the paper, Dana Gioia complains that poetry has all but "vanished as a cultural force in America" (94). Either consciously or subconsciously, Gioia ignored poetic practices already present in places that he preferred not to look. The New Formalists appealed for a return to formal, structured, metric verse, but their battle was more ideological and patriotic than utilitarian. Dana Gioia's understanding of poetry was actually quite limited to traditional poetic structures. His manifesto was published in the immediate pre-Internet era, so he could not fully consider the radical possibilities of intermedial convergence and what that means for aesthetics today. However, in a time of enduring economic crises and mounting environmental disorder, a crucial matter is whether orthodox aesthetic forms can ever sufficiently express the human poetic imagination.

There are real limits to what prescriptive forms can accomplish. As Herbert Eagle reminds us, an aesthetic practice that becomes well established eventually suffers "a certain loss of dynamism and of creative possibilities for the receiver, as many elements of the artwork become entirely predictable" (225). Perhaps Dana Gioia's most important contribution to poetry was in posing the provocative statement "Can poetry matter?" This contentious question stimulated debate about the form and function of poetry. I suggest that in this time of increasing environmental awareness, the answer to the question "Can poetry matter?" is a resolute yes, especially since "Dada still speaks to us" (Forcer 272). Moreover, if we see "Dada as a living spirit, as an extraordinarily rich and heterogeneous fund of ideas born out of a response to a fundamentally twentieth-century set of failures," then viewing art through an eco-Dada perspective can help us reimagine the role and purpose of art (272).

The major consideration of this chapter is whether a recent system of Dada ecopoetics can be extended to experimental aesthetics beyond strict definitions of poetry and to forms that appeared decades after the apparent end of Dada. An additional concern is to what extent a Dada theory of ecopoetics can handle some of the most fringe examples of textually based art, as well as moving images. What follows, then, is an examination of two deeply subversive experimental works from the 1960s: William Burroughs' *Nova Express* (1964) and Věra Chytilová's *Sedmikrásky* (*Daisies*, 1966).

In the 1960s, historical circumstances led to a resurgence of Dada forms, which can be seen in the work of both William Burroughs and Věra Chytilová. The rise of Dada after the First World War and the rise of Dada-inspired practices after the Second World War tell us a great deal about the ways in which humans deal with events of great social rupture. Seemingly separated by both geography and national ideology, Burroughs and Chytilová simultaneously developed radically experimental aesthetic practices that pushed the limits of both text and film. The cut-up and fold-in methods Burroughs used in creating the *Nova* trilogy blurred distinctions between texts and other forms of media. Věra Chytilová was the Czech New Wave's only female director. Not only did her fiery *Sedmikrásky* (*Daisies*) violate the doctrine of socialist realism, but more important, she applied Dada-inspired methods to the moving image. A fascinating consideration is what ecocriticism can learn by thinking more rigorously about fringe Neo-Dada forms.

A Theory of Dada Ecopoetics

In 2013, Irene Gammel and John Wrighton made a notable proposition that has potentially far-reaching consequences: Dada still matters, not just to art but also to the environmental humanities. Although the situation is changing, mainstream ecocriticism is still often associated with sentimental and neo-romanticist studies, certainly in the United States, though I recognize that ecocriticism takes multiple roads. Nevertheless, the suggestion that Dada can teach ecocritics new ways of thinking about art is uncommon and may even contribute to the third wave of ecocriticism, which Adamson and Slovic say "recognizes ethnic and national particularities and yet transcends ethnic and national boundaries" (6). Such comparative work also adds to the recent transnational turn in Beat studies. Important here is that Gammel and Wrighton offer a compelling theoretical model to analyze the complex ways environmental meaning can be found in Dada-inspired poetry. Their essay outlines a theoretical framework to identify environmentally relevant content in Dada-inspired poetry. As a case study, they examine the poetry of the captivating Baroness Elsa von Freytag-Loringhoven (1874–1927), a German who acted, modeled, wrote verse, and even experimented with sound poetry one hundred years ago.[1] Gammel and Wrighton examine her work through a model they call a "Theory of Dada Ecopoetics," which questions to what to extent the poem under study exhibits the following features:

- the "radical dismantling of nature/city boundaries";
- a "desublimated trash aesthetic";
- a "multisensorial immersive perspective";
- an "antipastoral aesthetic"; and
- a "radical ecopoetic liminality." (4)

According to Gammel and Wrighton, keeping these areas in mind will help those seeking to uncover ecological insight into Dada-inspired poetic forms.

Gammel and Wrighton should be acknowledged for opening needed space for dialogue between the avant-garde and ecocriticism, but there are limits to the scope of their study. Given the centrality of literature to ecocriticism, it makes sense that a Dada theory of ecopoetics would first emerge in literary studies. However, poetry is by no means the only aesthetic form that moves us as human beings, and I am particularly interested in pushing their concepts beyond the strict study of poetry. Gammel and Wrighton limited their examination to an artist working in the Dada era, and this is also understandable. They were focused on implementing a workable theory of Dada ecopoetics and did not have the opportunity to consider the possible wider application of their model beyond the Dada age. Indeed, it would be very interesting to see how their concepts work with fringe forms from other periods and cultures. What follows, then, is an attempt to stretch their concepts in the examination of William Burroughs' experimental *Nova Express*, in a Dada-environmental context.

The Dada Compost Grinder

In considering the critical history of the *Nova* trilogy—*The Soft Machine*, *The Ticket That Exploded*, and *Nova Express*—the most serious problem for scholars until now has been the lack of a definitive version with which to work. Remnants from the books were published in several small magazines over a number of years. Burroughs revised and rereleased the trilogy in significantly different versions, and thus until now, there has never been one reliable and definitive text. Harris insists that, given the trilogy's fragmented material history, the books demand reconsideration now: "New readers need new scholarship, the state of which has barely advanced since the 1980s, when the first serious but materially flawed academic studies appeared" (*Nova Express: Restored* xxiv). Fortunately, the trilogy's fractured publication history is much improved by the appearance of the restored 2014 edition. A second problem in the critical history of Burroughs, which remains unsettled, is the ways in which his most experimental aesthetic forms can help explain how we think about issues of ecology. Until now, with a few exceptions, environmental critics have largely overlooked the avant-garde. Surprising is that so few scholars have seriously considered the striking connections between experimental aesthetics and ecology.

The *Nova* trilogy is a direct descendant of the very idea of Dada and embraces cultural cannibalism as a form of ecoterrorism. William Burroughs and Brion Gysin carried out cut-up experiments at the Beat Hotel in Paris. Later, the *Nova* trilogy was produced by drawing on the vast amount of material contained in the Word Hoard, which formed the foundation of Burroughs' most experimental writing. Many of the source texts for the *Nova* trilogy were produced using the cut-up and fold-in methods, which recall the aleatory and aesthetically subversive practices of Dada. Source texts for *Nova Express* include fragments borrowed from "Shakespeare, Eliot, Rimbaud, and Joyce . . . newspaper reports about Polaris missiles, the Mariner II Venus probe, [and] A-bomb tests" (xv). The cut-up technique can produce large amounts of potential text in a short time. Significant is that the *Nova* trilogy's construction challenges ideas about the methods, form, and function of literature. Moreover, the extensive cut-up period that followed *Naked Lunch* not only provides opportunities to discover the proto-ecological significance deeply rooted in Burroughs' experimental writing practices, but also encourages more direct methods of extreme aesthetic sabotage, which can be called a form of ecoterrorism. Burroughs' environmental activism manifests in a method of literary sabotage inherent in the cut-up practice, which is designed to undermine and subvert present systems of thinking and writing. Harris says that Burroughs "promoted cut-up methods as a radical *cut* in literary history, the literally cutting edge of a new revolutionary movement" (*Soft Machine: Restored* xix; emphasis in original).

And this movement is not just about artistic autonomy. The revolution about which Burroughs writes concerns the power of language and, indeed, our own survival as a species. Consequently, the *Nova* trilogy attempts to recruit readers to apply cut-up practices not only to texts but also to photographs, films, tape recordings, and other forms of media to sabotage present linguistic and aesthetic structures, in effect to contaminate the public discourse with what can be considered a destabilizing virus. Apocalyptic writing practices and content can be mapped from Burroughs' early experimental writing all the way to his final diminutive and more linear novellas. After his early experimental period, Burroughs invested a great amount of energy in the *Nova* trilogy. The trilogy is crucial in demonstrating just how the apocalyptic cut-up method can effectively project a sustained image of universal death. By shredding selected source texts through the material practices of the cut-up technique, Burroughs terminates reality-based discourse in preemptive Dada destruction.

However, when thinking about the connections between Dada and Burroughs, one has to tread carefully, though Dada forms may offer a temporary escape from our steady march toward global disaster. Harris says that Burroughs "tried to distinguish his new work from high modernists and the historical avant-garde" (xxiii). This might be true, but Dada casts a long shadow. Burroughs' direct links to Dada (and Surrealism) are clearly established in his *Minutes to Go* manifesto, which outlines destructive aesthetic practices in clear terms. John Watters writes about the connections between Dada and Burroughs:

> Burroughs, while acknowledging his debt to the Dadaists, criticises vehemently the efforts of the Dadaists to bring about political change. His criticism seems to rest on two points. Firstly, that the Dadaists remained on the outside of the organs of political power and were therefore powerless, and secondly, their criticisms were too frivolous. In *Nova Express* Burroughs writes: "those dumb rubes playing around with photomontage—Like charging a regiment of tanks with a defective slingshot." In the later work *The Western Lands* he is just as abusive: "*Jeder Mann sein eigener Fussball* [*sic*]. (Every man his own football.) They deserved to lose for such vapid nonsense." (301)

It is important to note that Watters here incorrectly transcribes the original text, which says "*Jeder Mann sein eigener Futbol*" (Burroughs, *Western Lands* 14). This linguistic mixing might have been a form of Dada language play, but the mistranscription not only exposes a degree of academic imprecision but also, more important, misses the opportunity to see the Dada irreverence in the original passage. Moreover, Watters mistakenly practices the intentional fallacy, which is always troublesome.[2] The intentional fallacy is even more complicated when dealing with a writer such as Burroughs, who was so self-contradictory in his statements. In other words, here one cannot assume the speaker is the author. The fact that the passage cited by Watters itself appears in quotes in the original text also suggests the words are not by Burroughs the writer at all, but by some other speaker. While these inaccuracies need to be corrected, the larger point is that Watters neglects to contemplate the wider significance of Dada. There are no real political solutions—only aesthetic responses to calamities. The very point of Dada is that we all lose. Therefore, if industrialized society offers only industrial-scale death, perhaps Dada forms are one way out of our untenable situation.

The text of *Nova Express* uses abundant apocalyptic rhetoric in warning the reader of our dire collective environmental circumstances. The opening of the book urgently calls out with "'Last Words' in a messianic voice warning of End Times" (*Nova Express: Restored* ix). The book thus repeats the same eschatological sense of impending disaster found in the miniature cut-ups of *Minutes to Go* (1960). Perhaps unsurprising is that

Hiroshima and Nagasaki are mentioned several times in *Nova Express*. The book also suggests, as is common in later Burroughs publications, that the human moment is temporary and our chance for recovery is momentary. Moreover, *Nova Express* condemns the consumerist philosophy on which Western societies are built, including "toxic consumer capitalism" (xviii). The speaker warns that the "entire planet is being developed into terminal identity and complete surrender" (11). In *Nova Express*, it is proposed that the real problem of the disposal of toxic waste is "ultimately insoluble" (40). More broadly, the text ultimately declares the time has arrived for a broad insurgency against those in power who will destroy us. A final warning of sorts is made explicit to readers: "Listen to my last words. . . . Listen all you boards syndicates and governments of the earth" (1). Oliver Harris even goes so far as to say that *Nova Express* is in fact "a manifesto for global struggle against the 1 percent who run our planet like an alien colony" (xi).

Even though *Nova Express* is fifty years old, it is still as relevant today as it ever was. Harris asserts, "*Nova Express* is not a book from the past: it addresses our present-time disaster, our still burning planet" (xviii). And the budding anarchism present in *Nova Express* foretells much of the green anarchism found in the later *Cities* trilogy. The next consideration is what Gammel and Wrighton's recent model of a Dada ecopoetics can add to the existing scholarly discourse on *Nova Express*.

The harsh environments detailed in the *Nova* trilogy dismantle boundaries of nature and city and work toward an antipastoral aesthetic. The locations in the books are frequently toxic. The "polluted wastelands clearly develop out of *Naked Lunch*" (*Soft Machine: Restored* xxx–xxxi) but also recall the Composite City of the *Yage Letters*. The idea of toxicity is conveyed through long image lists "that depict toxic landscapes—swamps, jungles, canals, rotting cities of concrete pillars and bamboo bridges—and whirling machinery—penny arcades, Ferris wheels, pinball machines, cables cars, elevators" (xxx). Furthermore, in *Nova Express*, areas sometimes function as hybrid geographic spaces. For instance, in one section that explains an otherworldly geography, the reader sees "Yellow plains under a white hot blue sky" immediately contrasting with the spires of sophisticated "Metal cities" (*Nova Express: Restored* 71). In yet another section called "From a Land of Grass without Mirrors," the reader sees a cadet stepping "out of a jungle of rancid swamp covered with spider webs through a slat fence in a place of wooden runways and barriers" (95).

The locations described in *Nova Express*, as we see in other Burroughs texts, certainly do not represent experiences with sublime geographies and might better be called antipastoral.[3] The reader is confronted not with images of serene pastoral splendor, but instead by seedy urban "tattoo booths and sex parlors," yet on the same page also experiences the "hot winds from plains that surround the city . . . where a patient gentle crab people live" (73). Geographic disorientation continues through the entire *Nova* trilogy, and problematizes conventional zones of demarcation. Essentially, this means that the environments found in the *Nova* trilogy undo our notions of the conventional boundaries between nature and city. Moreover, an antipastoral aesthetic challenges conventional views of landscape and the more crucial concern of which geographic zones are suitable locations for aesthetic consideration. In other words, Burroughs inverts the pastoral by taking on landscapes that do not stimulate the sentimental feelings of home and hearth. In thinking more specifically about *Nova Express*, perhaps more important is that there is never any grounding, never more than fleeting suggestions of transitory spaces. The environments in *Nova Express* continually change and disorient the reader. The constant shift in settings requires great concentration from readers but at the same time makes them aware of their own need for spatial orientation. However, Dada rejects the idea of centering or anchoring. In a world gone mad, there are no locations of stability.

The presence of mysterious hybrid creatures in *Nova Express* further emphasizes the ways in which assumed boundaries of nature are undone. A number of imaginative hybrid creatures constantly inform readers that this is a different world. We are reminded by an almost never-ending list of weird creatures, including "fish People with purple fungoid gills" (111), "green newt creatures" (114), and numerous "Lemur People" (118). The presence of such strange and mysterious life forms highlights and problematizes the ways in which we think about divisions between humans and nonhumans in our own world. Burroughs further introduces the presence of a "green boy-girl" (115), which poses questions about gender identification. Moreover, we are finally confronted by the important and unsolvable question: "A Good Human animal?" (160). The question mark here reaffirms the central problem with which Dada ultimately wrestles. Are humans capable of goodness, and if so, why are we constantly confronted with potential destruction? More than that, *Nova Express* dismantles the ways we view ourselves in our own time and space, calls attention to the differences between humans and nonhuman creatures, and raises questions of gender identification and even more fundamental questions about the world in which we live.

The *Nova* trilogy is constructed from the rubbish of existing textual discourse, so the materiality of the texts can be directly linked to a trash aesthetic. The form of the books also forces us to think about the boundaries between the text and other forms of media. So essentially, what can be found in the *Nova* series is not merely the "radical dismantling of nature/city boundaries," which is important when thinking about connections to Dada. The language Burroughs uses in *Nova Express* is earthy and scatological. Scholars have recognized the slippery distinction between high and low culture in the wider work of Burroughs. Lydenberg and Skerl insist the writer "creates a new form of consciousness through a merging of high and low cultures" (11). What is significant in the use of scatological language is that language itself can be employed as primary material. The textual compost from which the *Nova* series is written forces us to consider the ways in which linguistic discourse can serve as the raw material for art. This is what Gammel and Wrighton also believe. Not only is scatological and earthy language visceral and provocative, but it "radically challenges the purified rationalism of modernism, using tropes employed by fellow Dadaists to expose interiors and challenge exteriors, and to problematize the boundaries of traditional aesthetic materials" ("Arabesque Grotesque" 9). This poses a number of important questions.

For Burroughs, language itself functions as a primary material, which recalls the Dada commodification and appropriation of everyday objects. The source texts for *Nova Express* emerged from a compost heap of recycled words and phrases, which were stripped from their original discourse and context and remained half decomposed, ready for Frankensteinian reassembly. The previous chapter discussed the proto-ecological significance of found text used in Burroughs' early cut-ups, and the organic features found in the diminutive cut-ups are extended, exponentially, in the *Nova* trilogy. I would even suggest that in the case of the *Nova* trilogy, the result is a textual ecology, an animate textual organism that reacts, contracts, and moves based on reader involvement. Furthermore, it can be said that Dada methods may inadvertently be ecological. Gammel and Wrighton proclaim, "Within the ecology of recycling and sustainability, language itself is a cultural litter to be recycled and renewed, while culture as a rich compost for poetry is subject to the ecological laws of decomposition and recomposition" (10). In essence, the textual broth of the *Nova* series accomplishes "the collage principle of combining and juxtaposing elements taken from diverse origins" (Harris, "Burroughs Is a Poet Too" 34). Remnants of cultural products are important raw material for the creation of future art. Dada ecopoetics demands that trash will inevitably become art.

Beyond merely emphasizing the aesthetic value of trash, *Nova Express* immerses the reader in a multisensorial perspective. The book demands more than just visual participation from the reader. The nonlinearity of the text makes it difficult to read, and the audience must invest not only significant energy and concentration but also greater sensory input than is required during conventional literary reading. Burroughs himself has emphasized his efforts to expand the reader's sensory experience. One must cite Burroughs' own statements carefully, since he was a constant source of contradiction. Nonetheless, in a 1965 interview published in the *Paris Review*, he justifies his writing in what would seem to be ecological terms:

> All of my work is directed against those who are bent, through stupidity or design, on blowing up the planet or rendering it uninhabitable. Like the advertising people we talked about, I'm concerned with the precise manipulation of word and image to create an action, not to go out and buy a Coca-Cola, but to create an alteration in the reader's consciousness. (Knickerbocker 49)

And the form of *Nova Express* encourages numerous different paths through the text, since the "reader's point of intersection with the text changes on every reading, [and] new combinations always keep appearing" (*Nova Express: Restored* xiv). This produces nearly infinite ways of reading *Nova Express*. Therefore, it can be said that the various points of entry into the text encourage a multisensorial experience or perhaps even a temporary change of reader consciousness. Moreover, as the previous chapter touched on, the cut-up form mimics the derangement of the senses that Burroughs learned from Amazonian shamans. Indeed, the *Nova* trilogy is incredibly ambitious in scope and strives for "phantasmagoria, which is motivated by the intense sensual derangement of yagé intoxication" (Harris, "Burroughs Is a Poet Too" 35). Such a situation not only ties Burroughs to the transcendental attempt to attain higher states of consciousness but also shows how aesthetic forms can stimulate and even expand human sensory perception.

Intermedial Convergence: The Filmic Text and Textual Imageries

Given shifting media shapes in our age, it is also worthwhile to consider the ways in which traditional media such as the book and film forms might be more elastic than convention dictates. Burroughs' *Nova* series really pushed the boundaries of the textual medium, and it is a mistake to call the series a narrative in the traditional sense. The trilogy is composed of three books—and many more forms, if one considers the various manifestations over the decades. The *Nova* books are full of text, true, but given the lack of conventional literary devices, it might be better to call the *Nova* trilogy a filmic text.

The suggestion that Burroughs wrote book-movies is not new. John Martino says the writer's use of "verbal montage via cut-up and fold-in juxtaposition, camera eye narration, cinematic directions, looping effects, and film script scenarios" (ii) results in more of a cinematic prose than conventional writing. He also asserts that in the *Nova* series, Burroughs' "writing achieves its greatest degree of fragmentation and discontinuity, and, subsequently, its closest stylistic affinity to film" (4). Others have also noted the filmic quality of the trilogy. Harris points out that "Burroughs' writing was just one in a range of experimental practices in different media that were visually-oriented" (*Soft Machine: Restored* xxxiv). The aesthetic principles of collage allow new ways to merge media. Harris wonders if the film form may be more suitable to expressing Dada concerns than the two-dimensional text: "Like the Dadaists and Surrealists before him, Burroughs found that collage-based methods effaced traditional distinctions between media" (*Ticket That Exploded: Restored* xxxvi). Also important is that to Burroughs, the text was essentially a transitional form: "His subsequent experiments with drawing, scrapbooks, tape recorders, film, photography and photomontage fed into his writing but also confirmed the limitations of texts" (xxxvii–xxxviii). In writing about the fragmentary aesthetic of *Daisies*, Herbert Eagle emphasizes how cutting can disrupt the sense of sequential space and time:

> This is quite literally a filmic world, where space can be spliced together smoothly, without gaps in time—just as pieces of a two-dimensional Dada collage on a canvas have a straightforward physical connectedness and a simultaneity of temporal experience, regardless of how puzzling the semantic connections may be. (227)

What is so interesting about Dadaism is its capacity to transgress boundaries by what Benjamin says are "pictorial—and literary—means [to create] the effects which the public today seeks in the film" (303–4). Intermedial convergence might also allow ecocriticism opportunities to expand its space of critical operation. While a Dada theory of ecopoetics is helpful in understanding the ways in which *Nova Express* works in the context of present ecological concerns, the next step is to see whether the model can be further pushed to extreme fringe aesthetic forms such as Chytilová's remarkable 1966 film, *Sedmikrásky* (*Daisies*). Thus the next consideration is whether we can push these ecocritical concepts even further, onto other forms of media, in a transcultural context.

Daisies: A Socialist, Feminist, Eco-Dadaist Manifesto

A lively addition to the Czech New Wave, *Daisies* highlights the emptiness of twentieth-century material culture. Ironically, state censors originally approved the script for *Daisies*, but the film was banned almost immediately upon its release for the depiction of excessive waste of food. Significant is that the avant-gardism of the film is revealed in its unconventional methods of composition and violation of formal conventions: "There isn't really a story to *Daisies* as much as a concept" (Der, para. 3). Essentially, *Daisies* can be called an episodic allegory filled with implied and real images of destruction, which highlight the "economic parasitism and utter lack of compassion" of material culture (Lim 57). Indeed, "consumption and destruction are the elements of the film most often remarked by film reviewers" (Lim 39). *Daisies* opens and closes with footage of bombing raids, including "houses collapsing, ships and airplanes on fire, smoke pouring from buildings, [and] bombs from afar" (Bass, para. 3). Thus from the start of the film, the audience sees destruction as a dominant thematic concern.

Daisies challenges film conventions in the same ways the *Nova* trilogy challenges literary ones. Many of the formal elements one would expect to find in a film are simply absent. Claire Clouzot believes that there is a particular barrenness to the film: "There is no involvement, no conventional chronology, no psychological development, in other words, no narration" (35). *Daisies* has no linear plot, nor do any sympathetic characters appear anywhere in the film. There is constant tension, but it does not build in a gradual and stable manner as one might expect. No new equilibrium is established, unless one considers the death of the main characters a resolution, which is entirely conceivable in a Dada-inspired film. However, what is important here is that the characters are completely flat and have no depth, so it is no surprise that their names are generic: Marie I and Marie II. The only real distinguishing feature is that one of the women has brown hair, while the other is strawberry blond. Additionally, the two protagonists of the film are really antagonists, since all they do is seek amusement through various pranks and acts of revolting gluttony. The viewer therefore has no one to root for and instead simply has to watch as the bizarre and destructive events unfold on the screen.

Daisies parallels the eschatological logic of the *Nova* trilogy, and destruction takes many forms in the film. As is the case with *Nova Express*, the non-narrative features of the film prevent any conventional reading, since *Daisies* "is the sort of film that contains whatever meaning its viewers ascribe to it" (Honeywell, para. 5). In the opening scene, the two Maries declare that the world is rotten, so they too should be rotten. This embrace of badness betrays the film's Dada inspiration.[4] It can be said that Dada is the essential philosophical and generative force for the movie. Virginie Sélavy declares that the girl's bad behavior "is a direct response to the state of the world" (para. 2), a world in which a Soviet-led invasion would soon kill dozens of unarmed civilians in Czechoslovakia and tens of thousands of riot police would confront thousands of political demonstrators in Chicago with tear gas and truncheons. Consequently, the destructive logic of *Daisies* makes perfect sense in replicating the chaos and destruction present in the real world. More than simply echoing devastation, the film embraces a theory of violent Dada aesthetics.

In *Daisies*, destructive excess takes many forms. The young women deceive numerous men to obtain free meals, booze, and other goodies, with no intention of providing sex in return. They are outrageous in public, getting rip-roaringly drunk and subsequently being kicked out of a 1920s-style club. The communist context of the culture in which the film was funded and made is also crucial in understanding just how subversive the film really is. In a culture that prided itself on work and the need for everyone to contribute his or her fair share of heavy lifting for the betterment of society, the Maries are unemployed. Nevertheless, they have an occupation, and that occupation is destruction. Near the end of the film, in a final orgy of excess, they destroy an entire banquet hall full of food, which can be assumed was meant for ranking members of the Communist Party.

Much of the existing scholarship on *Daisies* emphasizes feminist interpretations, which were important in a time of increasing gender awareness, as well as in establishing a real feminist communist aesthetic, but such interpretations overlook the complex ecological aspects of the film that are relevant now. While the two Maries always appear to be dominant and in control, the final moment of their demise highlights a serious critique of materialism. Marie I and Marie II exert complete control over would-be suitors, whom they routinely mock and emasculate. The film ridicules romantic clichés and prescribed gender roles. The two Maries appear bored with the banality of romantic gestures made by numbers of men, who appear as mere objects and not as sentient human beings. However, the Maries progress from behaving with feminist assertiveness to performing acts of disturbing symbolic aggression. In one particularly outrageous scene, as a potential suitor blathers on about his supposed love over the phone in a barely audible voice, the Maries symbolically emasculate and castrate men using shears to slice up sausages, pickles, bananas, and even hard-boiled eggs. SJ Honeywell says the feminist parable here is clear: "It doesn't take a Freudian to read meaning into the scenes where the two women devour sausages, pickles, and bananas after first slicing them into pieces with scissors" (para. 3). Others believe the formal use of "fragmentation (in sound, image, and spatio-temporality), as well as the narrative depiction of cutting and dismemberment, underscore the film's allegorical presentation of the heroines as transgressive assemblages of gender attributes" (Lim 39).[5] Consequently, it is unsurprising to suggest that thematically, the film can be read as a critique of gender boundaries, and this is why feminist readings of the film have been the most convincing to date. However, such readings deny the wider Dada decadence of the film. *Daisies* is far more subversive than simply showing a feminist mockery of patriarchal systems. The film poses larger questions about living in a materialistic culture. It directly addresses, and confuses, many assumed distinctions about the world in which we live.

Daisies dismantles gender boundaries, certainly, but it also undoes assumed boundaries between nature and the city. In the film, heavy editing and the use of montage permit sudden and inexplicable passage between the two environments. For instance, near the beginning, while the two Maries are sitting in swimsuits, one suddenly slaps the other. The recipient of the seemingly random act of violence instantly lands in a bed of daisies in the countryside. This impossible occurrence fractures distinctions between the city and nature and complicates our sense of space and time. Both Maries subsequently explore the area in the country and discover what seems to be something like the Garden of Eden, complete with what appears to be an enticing apple tree. One of the Maries plucks off not an apple, but instead a peach, and just as quickly as they had appeared in the countryside, the two Maries are instantly transported back to their urban flat, where they simply continue reflecting on both their boredom and broader existential questions. Peter Hames believes the scene in the field of daisies reveals an "abortive search for meaning in the countryside" (11). This is important if the young women are indeed searching for meaning in an empty world, which can work to remind the audience of their own material-bound existence.

At other times, the heavy use of montage overwhelms the viewer with disjointed and extraordinarily disconnected images of nature and urban settings. Chytilová inserts flickering images of nature objects into frames involving the Maries' town apartment. One sees their flat superimposed with an extreme and rapid succession of images of natural objects: leaves, grass, and butterflies. The careful technical efforts create the effect of "an animated sequence of images of leaves," which Eagle describes as follows:

> Each leaf image is optically printed on only one or a few frames of film; when the sequence is projected, our visual perception cannot register consciously the detailed image of each leaf; instead, our persistence of vision creates the effect of a rapidly, but discontinuously, changing leaf. (227)

At another point in the film, the bed in the flat is covered in what appears to be neatly trimmed turf, and large leaves are stuck to the wall. Elsewhere, numerous apples suddenly and inexplicably fall onto the apartment floor from an unknown source. The result is a weird amalgamation of urban settings with fragmented impressions of natural elements throughout the film. The "natural images are made abstract through animation" and the unexpected "combination of words and images within the same frame" is confusing, but the "principle of collage, a major source of Dada's radical collision of signs from disparate cultural and artistic orders" (Eagle 223), allows for the undoing of the divide between nature and city throughout the film. Additionally, "collage and montage [strive] to make images emphatically textual, to destroy the seeming mimicry of film by making the image more like the word" (Lim 65). Anti- or post-pastoral forms force us to reassess the spaces we inhabit. Dada aesthetics not only undo the distinctions between nature and city but also dismantle the distinctions between film and text.

Moreover, the very foundation of *Daisies* is built on an earthy, even vulgar, trash aesthetic. The overconsumption of food in the film is extreme and at times revolting. What is crucial here is that the decadence in the film reveals the wider void of material culture. It can be said that the various "happenings" in the film ultimately revolve around the leitmotif of food and even have a "scatological earthiness" (Clouzot 35). While most of the film shows the Maries carrying out obnoxious pranks, exploiting men, and generally destroying all they encounter, their actions are guided by a rabid compulsion to devour. Claire Clouzot made a significant observation in 1968, which is still relevant in thinking about the connections between material culture and the environment:

> [M]ost of the time, they are shown devouring, gorging themselves, stuffing themselves with cakes, fish, sausages, bananas, pickles and bread, going to ladies' rooms, giggling and starting again to cram, chew, masticate, swallow anything edible and within reach in their inimitable messy, egotistical, vulgar and irreverent lack of manners. Roughly, the film is a series of fluctuations between gorging and de-gorging, a come-and-go between de luxe restaurants and ladies' rooms. Our entire civilization could not be mocked more brutally. (35)

In thinking about the wider ecological significance of overindulgence in a world where hundreds of millions of people still suffer from undernourishment, the waste of food in *Daisies* becomes significant in highlighting the economic and environmental imbalance that still exists among cultures today. If one takes a utilitarian view, then the next consideration is the problem of living in cultures that are defined by waste, or the "capitalistic (or, for that matter, socialist) drive for acquisition" (36). The film confronts viewers with the implications of unsustainable living. Clouzot declares, "Gluttony and devastation are linked as an indication that consumption and destruction might not be that far apart" (36). The gluttony in *Daisies* culminates in a concluding scene in which the two Maries consume and destroy an entire banquet hall full of food.

The scene is perverse in the scope of its destruction, and the result is a level of annihilation that goes far beyond the physical destruction of just the banquet hall. The Maries leave "nothing but leftovers, trash and general destruction in their wake" (Soukup 38). Interesting is that the more abstract acts of destruction the Maries perform earlier in the film progress to a more literal form of devastation in the final scene. Eagle stresses:

> From symbolic destruction the film has moved us to concrete destruction of shocking proportions (in the spirit of a Dada happening). The destruction of so much food seems gratuitous and horribly wasteful—unless or until we think of the guests for whom it was intended. Could such a small group possibly have eaten all that food? Did they really need it? The characters' (and the director's) gesture of protest against the rich and powerful merely turns elegant conspicuous consumption into the gluttonous spectacle that it actually is. (233)

So here waste only uncovers another, deeper, perhaps even metaphysical layer of gluttony. In other words, if the two Maries waste food that would have been wasted anyway, what is the point of the artistic criticism of the practice in the first place? The viewer is thus caught in an ever-repeating cycle of consumption and waste. Spectators are likewise compelled to think about their own practices of consumption. Therefore, *Daisies* really deals with some of the same basic questions of sustainability that are still important today. Moreover, Dada forms do not really ever offer any concrete solutions to environmental problems, but they do provoke us directly with the superficiality of our own purported values. Thus it can be said that *Daisies* employs a trash aesthetic to show how a "materialistic social criticism can be turned into a poetic parable" (Clouzot 36). And in this sense, *Daisies* is still a social allegory that is just as relevant to our age as it was to the communist culture in which it was produced fifty years ago. More important is that the film is most convincing in pushing the boundaries of human sensory perception.

Daisies legitimizes a Dada theory of ecopoetics most convincingly in its capacity to force viewers to endure an overwhelming multisensorial experience, and this is accomplished through a number of techniques, including the inventive use of color. Chytilová exploits both the available technologies of her age and the relatively novel impact of striking color visuals, including rapidly changing color filters, striking monochrome, and the use of black and white. From the first few seconds of the film, it becomes clear to the spectator that their senses will be pushed beyond the normal range of a typical film viewing. *Daisies* begins with "pulsating music and images of war, destruction, and explosions rendered in a rainbow of color dyes" (Caulfield 29). Eagle says that in the film, color is intentionally "foregrounded through costuming and mise-en-scene or through the use of filters" (223). Thompson emphasizes how the visual experience of watching the film is essential to the total viewing experience: "The film switches back and forth between black & white, color, sepia tones, matching colors, off base colors, grainy stock, clear imagery, and so on and so forth" (para. 4).[6]

While the visual trickery is crucial, Chytilová also exploits the potentials of sound and heavy editing. Heavy editing and the systematic practice of montage produce an even greater multisensorial experience, and quantitative data support this. Lim asserts:

> In *Daisies*, disjunctive montage, jump cuts, unstable spatial relations, abrupt changes in color tone to fracture long takes, and a knowing use of sound bridges and matches on action in order to give the impression that the diegesis continues across temporal and spatial ellipses present the spectator with a picaresque narrative that at times seems to border on incoherence. (62)

If Lim is correct that the narrative does indeed border on incoherence, then what might quantitative data tell us about the structure of the film? Eagle says:

> *Daisies* employs a wide span of images and techniques, constantly interrupting and intersecting one kind of practice with another: painterly tableaux become animated with actions, but these actions no sooner begin than their narrativity is interrupted by a new type of formal play. (223)

Significant is that quantitative tools do exist that can help show patterns in the editing of the film and how heavy editing can assist in creating a multisensorial experience for the audience. They also show a degree of precision in the production of the film that is far from random or incoherent. Cinemetrics tools are useful for the examination of data from films for just such analysis. The idea is actually quite simple. Essentially, "Cinemetrics is an open-access interactive website designed to collect, store, and process scholarly data about films" (Tsivian 93).[7] Basically, one can measure physical characteristics of a film, such as average shot length, as well as the number of shots made in color, tonal, or black and white. Cinemetrics does not consider the content of cinematic productions, which is important, of course, but it does provide data about the physical structure of a film, which can also be helpful, especially when thinking about a nonlinear film such as *Daisies*. While Cinemetrics tools can never replace qualitative humanities scholarship, they can be quite helpful in providing additional information and especially in highlighting patterns in the structure of a film. In the case of *Daisies*, Cinemetrics provides evidence to support the contention that the film delivers a deeply multisensorial experience. When examining the data gathered from running *Daisies* through the Cinemetrics analysis program, statistics provide a picture that suggests that the use of heavy editing in the film has created a multisensorial experience.

Mohsen Nasrin's dataset for *Daisies* tells us that the film contains 736 shots in total. The shortest shot is 0.1 second in length, while the longest is 119.9 seconds in length. And it is very interesting that both the shortest and longest shots are in color. Of the 736 total shots, 502 are in color, 130 are in black and white, while 74 are tonal. An additional 30 shots consist of the film's credits. One must keep in mind that the film is just short of 76 minutes. Essentially, the data suggest that Chytilová made a number of conscious choices to employ and expand the viewing experience through technical management of spectator vision. This attempt to control and broaden the spectator's perception is an important component to a Dada theory of ecopoetics. The attempt to awaken the viewer's perception extends beyond the visual and, more specifically, to the use of sound.

The targeted and disjunctive use of nondiegetic sound adds to the multisensory experience. Given the technological limitations of the era in which the film was produced, the audio of *Daisies* exists only in mono and the Czech language. However, that does not mean the use of sound is tedious and uninteresting. Jones believes, "Creative noises [including] everything from a clock ticking to creaking upon movement, mesh well with the dialogue and various musical pieces" (para. 9). The sound in the film is often unsynchronized with the images shown, which creates a juxtaposing and distancing effect. Caulfield says the result is a sort of "image-versus-sound playfulness" (28), which is in keeping with Dada procedures. Weston goes further, arguing that the explicit use of sound is a core feature to enhance the overall sensory experience:

> The use of amplified sounds, whether they are the creaks that replicate the rickety moves of a mannequin, the trumpet calls or the Soviet cinema undertones of the film's percussive score, they all work to enhance the experience of watching. This is a sensory film, and plays with our expectations, offering up images and sound whose dislocation jars us, unveiling surprises as it goes along. (para. 5)

So it can be said that the extreme use of color and targeted use of nondiegetic sound work toward producing "sensorial overindulgence" (Wells, para. 2). This overindulgence is not only in keeping with the film's larger criticisms of debauchery and hedonism but also ultimately produces a uniquely "poetic quality, an avant-gardist's 'adventure in perception,' which saturates the film" (Hames qtd. in Caulfield 30). However, the multisensorial experience here goes beyond the use of glaring visuals and jolting sound effects. When one takes a look at the larger picture, patterns emerge.

Fringe Aesthetics as Imaginative Liminal Space

Both *Nova Express* and *Daisies* force us to acknowledge the power of liminal aesthetic forms to constantly challenge the human conceptual space in which art operates. The major concern of this chapter is whether a recent system of Dada ecopoetics is applicable to experimental aesthetics beyond firm definitions of poetry and to aesthetic forms that emerged long after the Dada era. In both *Nova Express* and *Daisies* can be found "a grotesque body which calls into question canonical representations" (Lim 68) of textually based art, as well as moving images. The desecration of literary and film conventions and the bent temporal syntax of the works under study here provide an alternative aesthetic environment that is rich for experimentation and offers new ways of understanding the world in which we live. Gammel and Wrighton emphasize that Dada forms grasp fringe forms with great force and that "the crossing of boundaries" is Dada's most important defining ecopoetic feature (15). Therefore, it can be said that liminal aesthetic spaces allow for potential cultural recovery, which becomes a much more concrete concern in the *Red Night* trilogy.

5.

The Retroactive Pastoral: Comic Dark Ecology, Deep Green Resistance, and the Romantic Plastic Indian in the *Red Night* Trilogy

You repeat three times: "Back to water. Back to fire. Back to air. Back to earth." —William Burroughs, *Cities of the Red Night*

By the early 1980s, Burroughs' writing was gradually shifting toward more readily accessible content and linear narrative structures, and both the thematic focus and the structure of those narratives reveal forms of eco-resistance in the treatment of social organization and the continued employment of fragmentary aesthetics. In the *Red Night* trilogy, an attempt is made to handle issues vital to present ecocritical discourse, including the limits of industrial culture, systems of human organization, and paths to lasting human survival. The *Red Night* series begins with *Cities of the Red Night* (1981), followed by *The Place of Dead Roads* (1983). The final book of the trilogy, *The Western Lands*, was released in 1987. While the *Nova* trilogy is a call to adopt cut-up methods, the *Red Night* trilogy proposes that other radical approaches are needed to ensure human survival. The *Red Night* series deals with issues of dismantling existing forms of social organization and implementing seemingly more workable forms of human society. The trilogy also reveals literature as a way to creatively reimagine and rewrite the past. While Burroughs' writing from the 1980s can be read in polemical terms, far more is happening in his mature writing than simply a suggestion to resist authorities. Burroughs' final trilogy is wedged between nostalgia for America's seemingly dutiful mythological past and the desire for a scientific future.

Oddly, to begin to handle such a futuristic vision for humanity as communicated in the *Red Night* trilogy, one has to return to Leo Marx's prominent study of the American pastoral, *The Machine in the Garden*, first published the same year Burroughs completed the *Nova* trilogy, to discover just how this works. Marx argues that the promise of pastoral America is evident in all its institutions. In *The Machine in the Garden*, Marx identifies two types of pastoralism in the context of American culture: "popular and sentimental" and "imaginative and complex" (5). In *The Future of Environmental Criticism*, Buell builds on Marx's insights, declaring the pastoral is not just about nature and culture and claiming the American pastoral imagination can help generate thinking conducive to issues of sustainability. Buell also reminds us that Marx's vision of the sentimental pastoral is "tacitly complicit with the advance of technoculture" (145). This is a crucial point in considering the presence of and continued need for machines and other technologies in the *Red Night* trilogy, discussed later in this chapter. Buell further believes that the complex pastoral, in contrast to the sentimental one, uses the idea of the pastoral "to politically oppositional ends" (145). This chapter thus makes two propositions. First, the *Red Night* series attempts to retrieve the popular and sentimental pastoral through a search for the failed promises of America's past. And second, *The Western Lands* endeavors to create an imaginative pastoral by revealing the potential of a complex mysticism for a future human age.

Because of the tremendous scope of the *Red Night* trilogy, the lack of critical history on the series in the context of Burroughs' wider writing, and the larger purpose of this study, what follows is best described as a preliminary incursion into the multifaceted ways the trilogy uses the past to reimagine a future for humanity. Such a complex narrative strategy of weaving diverse cultural and religious texts to create what Burroughs calls a "retroactive utopia" is important (*Cities* xiv). The extended effort to reclaim the past while evolving toward an apparent human interstellar destiny is surprisingly original and creative, but in the end, humanity remains bound to an imperfect world, overwhelmed by problems of overpopulation, corporate negligence, and an increasing number of environmental calamities. This realization and acceptance of earthbound humanity make the trilogy so remarkable to ecocriticism, since in the end we are exactly where we started. Also significant is the role that Burroughs imagines for literature in the *Red Night* series. The key to Burroughs' late trilogy is both formal and creative. The formal aspects can be linked back to the cut-up method in the systematic disruption of reader expectations and unchronological narratives that constitute the *Red Night* series. The trilogy also underlines the challenges posed by reading Burroughs. His ecological significance is not only apparent in the content of his narratives but also operative in some senses via the very medium of literature.

Cities of the Red Night, the first book in the series, is nonlinear at the outset and explores familiar issues involving both the limits of industrial culture and lasting questions of social organization. Similar to the later narrative *Ghost of Chance*, it is based on an alternative history of Libertania, a collectivist settlement of former pirates said to have existed in the late 1600s. *Cities* chronicles the adventures of a group of pirate boys who freely work together to liberate the Americas with a political system brought from Libertania. Drawing on ideas from the French and American revolutions, the *Cities* narrative proposes that human society can thrive based on community and a limited legal structure. In Libertania, people follow a legal code called the Articles and are allowed to do as they please without fear of intolerance or intrusion from the church or the central government. The narrator points out that the early attempt to create a society that values robust individual freedoms did not occur in France or America, nor anywhere else in the modernizing world: "The liberal principles embodied in the French and American revolutions and later in the liberal revolutions of 1848 had already been codified and put into practice by pirate communes a hundred years earlier" (xi).

Cities is loose in terms of narrative threads and chronology. At least three separate narrative strands work through the book. Some sections are based on apparently seventeenth-century ideas. Other parts of the novel are firmly set in the eighteenth century. Yet other episodes occur in the present day in the form of a detective story. The issue of viral disease is also a major thematic concern and presents abundant opportunities for ecocritical discussion.

Existing scholarship on *Cities of the Red Night* often involves attention to Burroughs' changing narrative methods, discussion of the potential or recovery of prior forms of human organization, and issues of disease. Jennie Skerl argues that *Cities* "shows the power of fantasy [in a satire of] contemporary Western society" (*William S. Burroughs* 89). The issue of satire and comedy in the book is crucial in attempting an initial ecocritical reading. Another critic notes that *Cities* is more comprehensible than the *Nova* trilogy. According to Paul Meisel, *Cities* is "especially convincing and absorbing because the prose was less ostentatiously surreal" than the fragmentary-montage and cut-up forms that came before (8). Robin Lydenberg has a different perspective, believing *Cities* preserves the juxtaposition that montage and cut-up practices generate (*Word Cultures* 177), as does Daniel Punday, who argues that remnants of Burroughs' "1960s experimentalism" with Gysin are clearly visible in *Cities* (36).

While *Cities* is far more linear than the cut-up novels that constitute the *Nova* trilogy, fragmentary aesthetics remain an essential narratological component to Burroughs' writing, even into the 1980s. Kendra Langeteig believes that in *Cities of the Red Night*, Burroughs' "deployment of toxic bodies (black holes, 'red hot' agents) offers ironic resistance to the laws and limitations of our knowledge system" (138). The residual fragmentation present in the *Red Night* trilogy is part of that process of challenging linguistic systems and harks back to the aleatory methods Burroughs employed twenty years earlier, also recalling the ecological significance of those practices. In fact, *Cities*—and the *Red Night* trilogy more broadly—works as a bridge from Burroughs' experimental early writing to his final, more linear narratives.

Scholarly discussion of *Cities* has also centered on the interest in creating new forms of social organization based on the potentials of past human civilizations. Timothy Murphy believes the book shows how Burroughs develops a "new historical consciousness" and fascination with the idea of communes (*Wising Up* 180), a point in considering the issue of whether existing forms of social organization are sustainable. This issue is essential to questions not only of conservation and ecology but also of environmental justice. Barbara Rose calls *Cities of the Red Night* "scandalous" in its final message and adds that the book is distinct "in the context of Burroughs's previous texts [in the] acknowledgment that there is no neutral space or ideological clean slate, an acknowledgment made explicit with some poignancy in the next two novels that conclude this last trilogy" (104). More recently, Sean Grattan says that *Cities* works to highlight a need to move away from present systems, and indeed a need for a new utopia, and at the same time stresses the book's anticapitalist drive (118). The ways in which the narrative intersects with matters of industrialization and social organization are crucial in attempting an ecocritical reading.

The Boundaries of Industrial Culture: A Dark Ecological Comedy

Cities of the Red Night proposes that industrial culture is broken, and a deadly and virulent global outbreak underlines the gravity of social rupture in this particular world. Moreover, the downfall of the industrial culture in *Cities* is manifested in the allegory of disease and in other apocalyptic events that take place as the narrative unfolds. In thinking about carrying out an ecocritical reading of *Cities*, T. V. Reed's table of ecocritical concentrations is helpful in highlighting not only conservationist concerns but also issues of ecological significance and matters of environmental justice. Those interested in conservationist issues can ask, "What can literature/nature writing and criticism do to enhance appreciation and improve attitudes towards the natural environment?" ("Toward" 148). In addition, according to Reed, examining ecological concerns in a cultural text involves studying the ways in which the idea or metaphor of the ecosystem can be analyzed for the "poetics of the literary system in relation to nature" (148). He also posits that ecocritics carrying out environmental justice readings attempt to uncover how environmental despoliations disproportionately affect minorities and the underprivileged (149). Thus an initial question ecocriticism can ask to disclose issues of conservation, ecology, and environmental justice in a passage taken from *Cities* is just how the allegory of disease is employed and what this suggests about the world of the narrative and the people who inhabit this place.

Cities chronicles the spread of an unusual sexually transmitted virus that infects the population on a massive scale. The disease is believed to have developed because of radiation originating from a meteor that crashed into Siberia thousands of years earlier (*Cities* 25), and it is assumed that the virus reemerges from its hidden place because of the radiation produced by Cold War atomic bomb testing. Thus while the virus has an extraterrestrial origin, the pestilence that erupts in the narrative can be considered anthropogenic. In the following rather typical passage from the text, a character named Dimitri discusses an outlandish view by suggesting not doing anything to prevent the spread of the outbreak, in what can be considered a form of comic dark ecology:

> "Well . . . there are those who think a selective pestilence is the most humane solution to overpopulation and the attendant impasses of

> pollution, inflation, and exhaustion of natural resources. A plague that kills the old and leaves the young, minus a reasonable percentage . . . one might be tempted to let such an epidemic run its course even if one had the power to stop it." (86)

What is immediately apparent in the above selection is that a speaker mediates the words of Dimitri, hence the presence of the quotation marks. These marks are generously employed throughout entire sections of the narrative, which makes identifying the real narrative voice extremely problematic. This intentional mediation of characters' words through another, sometimes unknown, speaker forces the reader to accept Dimitri's words secondhand and perhaps question the reliability of the narrator. Indeed, the difficulty in identifying who is speaking in *Cities* is at many times confusing and frustrating and is thus a further trace of the fragmentary forms typical of Burroughs' long experimental period. The abundant use of quotation marks throughout large sections of *Cities* might have been a further attempt by the author to complicate the narrative structure, once again violating both literary conventions and reader expectations through the employment of layers of sometimes ambiguous mediation.

More significant, however, are the ways in which the above passage can be considered an instance of what I call comic dark ecology, an extension of Timothy Morton's notions about "dark ecology" (*Ecology without Nature* 142). The combination of carefully chosen words in the passage evokes a cumulative sense of the apocalyptic. The terms "overpopulation," "pollution," "inflation," and "exhaustion of natural resources" all suggest varying degrees of human misery. The repeated use of words ending in *-tion* works to create repetition, which assists in linking the ideas together for the reader. Langeteig further proclaims that we are moving toward a culture of toxicity in the *Red Night* trilogy: "The term horror autotoxicus (the horror of becoming toxic to oneself) . . . extends in our postindustrial world to the horror of the ecosystem's toxic collapse" (140).

However, the proposition in *Cities* that human society should consider allowing the disease to run its course, thus functioning as a natural method of human population control on a massive scale, is bizarre and merits further reflection. Essentially, Timothy Morton calls the realization that humans are the perpetrators of ecological problems "dark ecology." He highlights the deep uneasiness and guilt humans feel when faced with the reality that we are the culprits of the principal problems we face. The real sense of dark ecology arises not only when we realize that we are responsible for current circumstances but also when, with a degree of shock and horror, we understand that we are the main narrators and actors in this unfolding apocalyptic narrative. Morton claims that dark ecology involves adoption of "romantic irony," the moment that people realize that they did this to themselves ("Dark Ecology"). While Morton here is referring explicitly to the larger consequences of the Anthropocene era, his ideas about dark ecology can be extended to the above passage.[1] Morton observes that the understanding that humans coexist with other people as well as nonhuman creatures is a source of uncanny anxiety and extreme guilt, given our cumulative participation in environmental crises. He further believes that humans tend to ignore and repress this apprehension, which is simply another by-product of the ecological age in which we live ("Dark Ecology"). So in the above selection, what can also be found is an attempt to confront the reader with the knowledge that apocalyptic human death can be anthropogenic in origin.

The comic element is emphasized through the subtle and ludicrous recommendations made throughout the passage. The narrative suggests that one of the most important problems facing humanity is overpopulation.[2] The real comic dark ecology of the above selection is not the creation of the circumstances in which disease can function as neutralizing agent, which is certainly dark and foreboding, but the shocking moment of realization that Morton describes ("Dark Ecology"). The character Dimitri considers the pandemic present in the narrative as a suitable method of reducing human pressure on the ecosystem. The real comic effect in the passage involves Dimitri's nonchalant suggestion that society should consider allowing the disease to run its course (*Cities* 86). What Dimitri proposes, casually and flippantly, is that the pestilence may be the best path for humanity. In fact, Dimitri says that the plague may be the most "humane" way forward (86). Also significant is that Dimitri apparently mediates the words of unidentified others, so he never has to directly propose letting the multitudes perish. The idea to let the pandemic spread is thus essentially mediated twice, both by the narrator and by Dimitri. This play with narrative voice also emphasizes the impossibility of accurately and precisely identifying whose suggestion it is to let the disease run its course in the first place.

In addition, any suggestion to allow a worldwide plague run its course involves such a magnitude of human suffering as to simply be overwhelming and farcical. In this sense, too, the passage can be considered a form of comic dark ecology. The idea to simply let the disease burn itself out is made even more outrageous by the offhand calculation of the collateral damage the pandemic will inevitably cause, as the plague "kills the old and leaves the young, minus a reasonable percentage" (86). The proposition that a proportion of otherwise young and healthy humans would succumb to the disease as a reasonable by-product of this solution to overpopulation is further evidence of comic dark ecology, since such a facetious dismissal of the countless human lives this situation would involve is inconceivable to the human mind. *Cities of the Red Night* is thick with other instances of comic dark ecology, as are Burroughs' apocalyptic narratives more broadly. This can be called satire in the tradition of Jonathan Swift's *A Modest Proposal.* The mode is comic in nature, but the function is to jolt people into awareness of the serious problems we face in order to consider alternatives to such apocalyptic scenarios. However, *Cities* also provides other opportunities for ecocritical dialogue, particularly when considering the idea of the frontier as an open space to reinvent human civilization.

In *Cities of the Red Night*, attempts are made to link the future of humanity to the potentials of the past. Important ecocritical thinkers have rightly tied the pastoral to the American experience. As Chris Coughran explains, "A series of critical interrogations—from Henry Nash Smith's *Virgin Land* through Leo Marx's *The Machine in the Garden* to Lawrence Buell's *The Environmental Imagination*—has drawn attention to what Buell calls the 'ideological multivalence' of American pastoral" (15). Coughran asserts that the "pastoral, far from being merely a usefully invoked trope, becomes the progenitor and enabler . . . of various fantasies of national or regional identity" (14). The profoundly ambiguous and mutable meaning of the American pastoral has been used as a justification for all kinds of contradictory actions: the subjugation of Native Americans and the defense of Native American cultures, the conquest of the American wilderness and the call to defend the American wilds. Does the pastoral thus lack cohesive meaning? Coughran believes the "quintessential American scene is precariously poised between nostalgia for a lost 'golden age' and an equally unquenchable longing for futurity" (16), a point also made by Marx's *Machine in the Garden* (68). In numerous ways, the *Red Night* trilogy is also wedged in what Marx calls the "middle landscape" between nostalgia for America's seemingly dutiful and righteous rural mythological past and a yearning for the inevitable technological future (152). In *Cities*, the sentimental pastoral is conjured up in an attempt to resurrect the past as a way to guarantee the future for humankind.

Cities suggests that a key to human survival is the rapid decentralization of present forms of social organization and the extensive development of anarcho-primitivist communes. This takes the form of a revolutionary campaign waged not only against mutants but also against factions of the government and the growing Industrial Revolution. In the prologue, vital contextual information is provided about the world in which the narrative takes place. We are told that the past conditions might have saved us from the present unsustainable condition. Consider the following passage, which deliberates on the potential benefits of primitivist communes to humankind:

> Imagine such a movement on a world-wide scale. Faced by the actual practice of freedom, the French and American revolutions would be forced to stand by their words. The disastrous results of uncontrolled industrialization would also be curtailed, since factory workers and slum dwellers from the cities would seek refuge in Articulated areas. Any man would have the right to settle in any area of his choosing. The land would belong to those who used it. No white-man boss, no Pukka Sahib, no Patróns, no colonists. The escalation of mass production and concentration of population in urban areas would be halted, for who would work in their factories and buy their products when he could live from the fields and the sea and the lakes and the rivers in areas of unbelievable plenty? And living from the land, he would be motivated to preserve its resources. (xiv)

Not only does the passage attempt to legitimize systematic decentralization, but it also advises that the past practice of local governance would have prevented many of the negative developments in human history. If we could just turn back the clock, it suggests, unsustainable industrialization would be stopped, slavery would be averted, and the horrors of colonization would be halted before they began. Moreover, the text implies that present rigid social hierarchies would be avoided and humanity would be much closer to reaching its full potential, since people "could live from the fields and the sea and the lakes and the rivers in areas of unbelievable plenty." Also emphasized is the idea that such rural existence would motivate people "to preserve . . . resources," thus creating a more sustainable world. In his discussion of the above passage, Murphy explains that Burroughs uses "hyperbole to utopian rather than dystopian ends, and the result is a Rousseauistic paradise, a 'plan of living' that later books will complicate" (*Wising Up* 181). Such an apparent utopia takes the form of voluntary and local forms of social organization.

Cities proposes that an anarcho-primitivist solution to the organization of government is the best way forward. This involves the creation of not only a chain of strongholds around the world but also, just as important, a simple but effective legal code that emphasizes the most robust individual freedoms conceivable:

> The Articles state, among other things: all decisions with regard to the colony to be submitted to vote by the colonists; the abolition of slavery for any reason including debt; the abolition of the death penalty; and freedom to follow any religious beliefs or practices without sanction or molestation. (xii)

We are told that "the history of the world could have been altered" if such a scenario had actually been possible (xiii). The suggestion that we return to the potentials of the past underlines the nostalgia embedded in the narrative. In a world ripped apart by disease and political chaos, an invitation to live under a simplified and mutually beneficial legal code is appealing to many in the *Cities* narrative. The tale envisions the construction of countless anarcho-primitivist settlements to provide access to freedom for the beleaguered masses fleeing from crumbling cities and desperate governments. The narrator imagines chains of communes scattered across huge expanses, including "fortified positions all through South America and the West Indies, stretching from Africa to Madagascar and Malaya and the East Indies, all offering refuge to fugitives from slavery and oppression: 'Come to us and live under the Articles'" (xiii). But the existence of legal machinery in this fictional world further complicates the attempt to retrieve the potentials of the past.

The existence of anarcho-primitivist communes depends on what Leo Marx calls "the dominant structural metaphor of the Constitution [as] a self-regulating machine" (165). This is an intriguing contradiction, and it reveals the ways in which the *Cities* narrative exposes the "sentimental pastoral" (5). The reliance on the metaphor of political machinery is complicit in acknowledging the need for legal control mechanisms and, perhaps more significantly, the need for mechanistic ways of thinking. Thus the communes as imagined in *Cities* cannot retreat entirely from the industrial imagination and are dependent on the idea of the machine as a way to repair human society. Ultimately, the narrator laments that urbanization is a real problem and that present circumstances prevent us from ever really constructing a retroactive utopia:

> There is simply no room left for "freedom from the tyranny of government" since city dwellers depend on it for food, power, water, transportation, protection, and welfare. Your right to live where you want, with companions of your choosing, under laws to which you agree, died in the eighteenth century with Captain Mission. Only a miracle or a disaster could restore it. (xv)

The attempts to write from a popular and sentimental position to retrieve an imagined rugged individualist America are creative and significant in the context of Burroughs' oeuvre. But invoking a need for minimalist government and an improved social contract is hardly new. Moreover, the attempts to revive the past to save us from our present condition are likewise rather conventional narrative concerns. But there are other links between ideals of Thoreauvian primitivism and the frontier that can help expose the ways in which the *Red Night* trilogy engages the sentimental pastoral.

Crucial links exist between the first book of the trilogy, *Cities of the Red Night*, and the subsequent narrative, *The Place of Dead Roads*. Characters in both narratives are imitations of what Marx calls the "primitivist hero" (22). Significant is that protagonists in both narratives retreat from civilization in search of a better, more basic existence, similar to Thoreau's attempts to discover a humbler and more natural human condition. Furthermore, both narratives repeat sentimental notions such as fleeing from the city, lamenting the loss of the garden, desiring Arcadian simplicity, and longing for a frontier that is open to Elysian human reinvention, which are all forms of "popular, sentimental pastoralism" (254). However, in ways *The Place of Dead Roads* goes further than *Cities of the Red Night* in complicating the sentimental pastoral. What follows is a discussion of how the second book of the *Red Night* trilogy continues to attempt to retrieve the potentials of the past while simultaneously yearning for the technological future.

The Place of Dead Roads chronicles the experiences of Kim Carsons, a masculine homosexual heroin-addicted shootist in the nineteenth-century American West. The protagonist of *Dead Roads* is most likely drawn from the nineteenth-century American frontier personality Kit Carson. Similar to the first book of the *Red Night* trilogy, *Dead Roads* explores lasting questions of social organization. It details efforts to establish self-governing communes to protect true freedom. Also significant is that the narrative details the attempts to establish forms of organized resistance to industrial culture. An important consideration worth examining is just how the narrative seeks to retrieve lost ideas about the expansion of the American nation in the nineteenth century and how such developments can inform present-day ecocriticism.

The narrative essentially works backward. *Dead Roads* begins with the killing of Kim Carsons in 1899 in Boulder, Colorado, by an unknown gun-wielding assailant who, in a dishonorable act, shot him in the back. The narrative subsequently traces Carsons' experiences prior to his death in nonchronological and patchy flashback episodes, which highlight Burroughs' continued interest in fragmentary aesthetics. The narrative incorporates contrasting themes and time travel. Carsons' purpose changes as he travels to different places and to different periods.

Researchers have previously commented on the challenges of reading the *Dead Roads* narrative because of its fragmented organization. This may be an explanation for some of its negative reviews (Lotringer 564). Given the polarizing nature of Burroughs, it is not entirely surprising that many assessments of the narrative are lukewarm to sharply negative. A scathing review by Anatole Broyard in the *New York Times* bemoans, "The only joke in 'The Place of Dead Roads' is on us. You might say that the comedy lies in people taking Mr. Burroughs seriously as a writer" (para. 3). Also in the *New York Times*, Paul Meisel says that the nonchronological structure of the narrative is unsettling and the book "slips and slides in time and place—almost unaccountably" (8). In creating *The Place of Dead Roads*, Burroughs did not employ the cut-up method of literary collage he used in his earlier novels, but there are residual fragmentary impressions that look very similar to previous cut-ups. The first half of the novel is much more stable than the second, which digresses into unstructured dialogue and sexual images. According to Meisel, "The result is a watery realism on the one hand and a now tiresome imitation of the Joycean approach on the other" (8).

Negative assessments aside, *Dead Roads* emphasizes a continued interest in dealing with lasting questions of human organization and the potential of communal living. The book ponders the creation of a better society, yet again, through the development of local systems of governance, the construction of communes, and the direct action of eco-guerrillas. Introduced in *Dead Roads* is a group of anarchist/libertarian characters called the Johnson Family, insurgents that are determined to fight the growth of central government and industrial civilization by building a chain of self-ruling communes (*Dead Roads* front matter). According to the narrator of *Dead Roads*, the term "Johnson family" was actually an early twentieth-century expression to distinguish between "good bums and thieves" (front matter). In the narrative, the Johnsons' seemingly honorable attitude is explained to the reader: "A Johnson honors his obligations. His word is good and he is a good man to do business with. A Johnson minds his own business. He is not a snoopy, self-righteous, trouble-making person." The family is rugged and independent. Johnsons are decent and helpful people and will assist others when needed: "A Johnson will not stand by while someone is drowning or trapped under a burning car." The Johnson Family "upholds States' Rights and opposes any further encroachment of Washington bureaucrats" (158).

Murphy rightly reminds us that the discussion of state rights versus federal control locates *Dead Roads* firmly in the nineteenth-century United States, whereas the *Cities* narrative was primarily situated in the revolutionary circumstances a century earlier (*Wising Up* 185). The enlargement of federal government and the increased economic power of industrial culture from the temporal position of *Cities* to *Dead Roads* is an essential matter in the attempts to subvert the systems of governance in the second book of the trilogy.

Deep Green Resistance

Dead Roads intersects with issues of environmental discourse in significant ways, especially in terms of the development of organized forms of resistance to industrial culture. The book attacks the Industrial Revolution, contemplates the idea of small communes as an alternative method of social organization, and suggests that forms of collectivism are keys to the future for humanity. But the narrative also advocates violence as necessary in the pursuit of a more environmentally just civilization. *Dead Roads* declares that tactics similar to those endorsed by the radical Deep Green Resistance movement are required to save ourselves from certain ecological death.[3] The insurgency documented in the *Dead Roads* narrative takes the form of the Johnson Family, which, under the leadership, planning, and support of Kim

Carsons, works to dismantle the infrastructure of industrial culture and undermine the control of the federal government. This is also the guiding philosophy behind the Deep Green Resistance movement—that a forced shift toward more local and sustainable forms of existence will provide humankind better chances for long-term survival. Derrick Jensen argues that since "we know in our bones, if not our heads, that [industrial] culture will not undergo any sort of voluntary transformation to a sane and sustainable way of living," it is up to a worldwide eco-guerrilla movement to take apart the industrial machine (12).

Whereas in *Cities*, the effort by pirates to fight against authorities and the rising Industrial Revolution takes place in the open, based in part on the revolutionary philosophy defined in the Articles, the power and range of federal government and industrial culture in *Dead Roads* force the insurgency deeper underground:

> As soon as Kim started organizing the Johnson Family, he realized how basically subversive such an organization would appear to the people who run America. So the Johnson Family must not appear to these people as an organized unit. The Johnson Family must go underground. (130)

What is clear from this passage is that the activism rooted in *Dead Roads* takes a much different form than the activism present in *Cities*. By adopting similar strategies to those of other radicalized ideological groups such as the Weather Underground, Earth First!, and the Animal Liberation Front, the Johnson Family functions largely hidden in the *Dead Roads* narrative, until opportunities emerge that it can exploit.

The ultimate aims of the Johnson Family insurrection in *Dead Roads* are quite similar to the goals of the Deep Green Resistance movement:

> We will endeavor to halt the Industrial Revolution before it is too late, to regulate populations at a reasonable point . . . to decentralize, to conserve resources. The Industrial Revolution is primarily a virus revolution, dedicated to controlled proliferation of identical objects and persons. (98)

Certainly, the attempt "to halt the Industrial Revolution before it is too late" (98) parallels the primary goal of the Deep Green Resistance movement. Significant is that the forms of resistance exhibited in *Dead Roads* are more organized than the brazen rebellion detailed in *Cities*. The objective of the Johnson Family is world revolution against centralized government, organized religion, and industrial institutions intent on controlling the earth and its natural resources. The ecological significance of the presence of the Johnson Family in the narrative lies in the awareness of the role that forms of Deep Green Resistance can play in the violent overthrow of industrial culture. Also significant are the ways in which communes can assist in generating social conditions that are more conducive to issues of sustainability and population control than urban existence. While *Dead Roads* does not fully deal with lasting questions of social organization, it certainly poses the question and forces us to think about alternative paths to the future. But there are problems with Kim Carsons' plan for global insurrection.

The attempted takeover of the US government and the industrial infrastructure would ultimately be ineffective and incredibly damaging. War against the technological, economic, and military capacities of the American government and the most powerful corporations, even in the context of the nineteenth century, is an utterly unachievable goal. This issue is relevant not only to *Dead Roads* but also to the beliefs of the Deep Green Resistance movement. More important, the scale of carnage that would be involved in the rebellion against existing society is so great as to make the suggestion moot. The eco-guerrilla war against civilization proposed in *Dead Roads* is therefore futile. Even if the insurgency chronicled in the book were even moderately successful, the social upheaval caused by the guerrilla campaign would negatively affect the most vulnerable members of human society and raises serious questions of environmental justice. Therefore, the suggestion that true freedom can be found in casting off civilization for simple commune life is not what it first appears to be. Since the leader of the guerrilla insurgency is killed in the first pages of the book, it can be said that here the eco-insurgency has failed and may even be a sardonic play on the very idea of revolution. While *Cities* stresses problems of our own making, *Dead Roads* too highlights the problems of living in the modern world.

Another problem in the *Dead Roads* narrative involves a contradiction within the movement. In *Cities*, it is suggested that as long as one follows the code of the Articles, one can lead a life of liberty and true freedom. An important consideration when thinking about the communes as they exist in *Dead Roads* is, just how free are they? Kim Carsons is clearly the self-appointed leader of the movement. However, any underground insurgency that is capable of dismantling industrial culture would require incredibly deep and complex levels of organization that exceed the capacity of any single individual. If we follow the goals of the insurrection to their logical conclusion, eventually a large number of underground leaders would have to emerge. The narrative never explicitly clarifies how such leaders would be put in place, much less how they would govern. There is every reason to believe that any governing structure that would eventually develop would in some ways replicate present structures, which could conceivably be worse than the existing government the insurgency seeks to replace. This is yet another striking example of the ways in which, in order to create a more perfect society, it is necessary to re-create the machinery of government to save the garden. Contradictions in the narrative reveal the problems of expressing polemical intentions through the literary form.

The lengthy discussion of firearms and other technologies is an additional feature of *Dead Roads* that displays an effort to retrieve the sentimental pastoral. One could simply dismiss such considerations as a possible biographical slip, where Burroughs' own fascination with firearms seeps into the narrative. However, such biographical speculation misses the opportunity to better understand the presence of firearms and other machines in *Dead Roads* as further attempts to retrieve Marx's sentimental pastoral (5). Indeed, firearms are discussed in detail and function as an archetypal form of American individuality and independence in the narrative. In a crucial passage of *Dead Roads*, the revolutionary leader of the Johnson Family, Kim Carsons, reveals that he has devised a complex plan for the approaching insurgency, which depends on technological developments to reach the goals of decentralized, self-ruling communes:

> Soon Kim will have enough money to implement the first stage of his plan—Big Picture, he calls it—his plan for a Johnson Family takeover. He will set up base in New York. He will organize the Johnsons in Civilian Defense Units. . . . He will buy a chemical company with research facilities where he will develop sophisticated biologic and chemical agents. He will start a small-arms factory. (104–5)

On the surface, *Dead Roads* appears to emulate a desire to return to rural conditions, much as the previous book *Cities of the Red Night*. However, in *Dead Roads*, it is significant that firearms remain a potent symbol of masculinity, strength, and technological power. These developments emphasize the continued importance of technology to even those who claim to resist industrial civilization.[4]

The need for machines and other forms of advanced technology to complete the revolution in *Dead Roads* exposes the ways in which this world is similar to, and different from, the world depicted in *Cities*. Both narratives are fixed in the "middle landscape" (Marx 71), where once again the sentimental pastoral is revealed (5). Whereas in *Cities* the mechanistic mindset shows connections to the need for scientific thinking, in *Dead Roads* the sentimental pastoral takes a different form. The above passage divulges the real contradiction between the stated goals of the Johnson Family insurgency and the reality of setting up the communes. How can one possibly "endeavor to halt the Industrial Revolution before it is too late" (*Dead Roads* 98) while relying on the very systems of the Industrial Revolution, including dependence on machines and technology in the creation of a so-called better society? Such a contradiction shows how Kim Carsons and his comrades need to hold on to certain machines, while also developing other technologically advanced armaments. Thus even as they crave a simpler existence, they rely a great deal on the powerful image of the machine in the pursuit of their retroactive utopia. In other words, because Kim Carsons and the Johnson Family require machines and technology to carry out their insurgency, they are complicit with the industrialist thinking the communes were originally set up to oppose. Even as they strive for existence outside of the modern world, their actions dictate the need to hold on to the machine to maintain the garden. But in the end, neither *Cities* nor *Dead Roads* is capable of fully restoring the potentials of America past. Rose emphasizes that ultimately "there is no neutral space or ideological clean slate" (104). The resurrection of America past will never happen. The clock cannot be unwound. The creation of an ideal society that balances the integrity of nature and the benefits of civilization can exist only in the human mind.

In many ways, however, the final book of the trilogy is more creative in linking to the pastoral imagination. *The Western Lands* completes the *Red Night* trilogy and appears to accept the genuine difficulties of ever really escaping our present circumstances. In *Western Lands*, it is suggested that the best alternative to our present condition involves forsaking the idea of the commune. Inspired by the *Egyptian Book of the Dead*, *Western Lands* explores the spirit world through dreams, the contemplation of talismanic magic, and various superstitions. Further, the novel delves deep into ancient history and can be understood as an attempt to move beyond Judeo-Christian theology. The first two books of the trilogy argue that the retrieval of political solutions from the past holds the key to the future for humanity. But *Western Lands* suggests that a complex shift in human consciousness may be the only way to allow humans to escape from a ruined planet. The narrative proposes that it is possible to resolve the interminable distance between the ancient Egyptian other and the Amerindian by drawing on and consolidating elements from both cultures' mythologies to create a cosmic mysticism for the future. This can save humanity from what the narrator sees as its present broken condition.

The critical response to *Western Lands* was generally more positive than that to *Dead Roads*. In the *New York Times*, Jonathan Baumbach writes a positive evaluation of the novel, calling it "remarkable" and proclaiming it "a comic meditation on death in the guise of a novel" (para. 7). Murphy reminds us that *Western Lands* "differs markedly from the other two volumes in its approach to the problem of revolutionary subjectivity" (*Wising Up* 174). Robin Lydenberg further asserts, "Earlier novels often intone a nostalgic litany of farewells to the past or telegraph urgent messages of an apocalyptic or utopian future" ("El Hombre Invisible" 235). However, in the last book of the trilogy, "[i]t is finally clear that 'There is no transport out. There isn't any important assignment, there is only an aimless itinerary of dead-end excursions'" (235). She raises the crucial question of whether the *Red Night* trilogy exhibits a defeatist position. Is the *Red Night* series ultimately bound by the weight of the failed promise of America past, and how does spirituality help us understand the complex subjects discussed in the trilogy?

The next section deliberates these issues and how *Western Lands* reveals what Marx calls the "imaginative and complex" pastoral (5). Burroughs' attempt to create a more complex pastoral by weaving together the diverse religious texts of Native Americans and ancient Egyptians is bold, though in the end the endeavor is perhaps too ambitious. Consideration of plastic shamanism is essential to understanding the ways in which *Western Lands* connects with native mysticism, as well as reflecting both the sentimental and imaginative pastoral.

The Romantic Plastic Indian

Plastic shamanism can be defined as the commodification of native beliefs, ceremonies, or artifacts, often for commercial purposes (Aldred). It likely developed as a seemingly harmless extension of sentimental views of aboriginal inhabitants, but in the extreme, it can be terribly damaging to Native American cultures. Some who can be referred to as plastic shamans claim to share Native American insights or even ancestry. Beat writers, including Gary Snyder, have occasionally been accused of exhibiting a superficial view of Amerindians. Leslie Silko once bemoaned Snyder's apparent "cultural arrogance in presuming to write from a standpoint of superior knowledge concerning Indian worldviews and spirituality" (qtd. in Hobson 1). Such criticism of Snyder fails to recognize his earnest attempts to connect with and understand native cultures; however, the extremes of plastic shamanism are incontrovertibly destructive. Often Western cultures display false images of the Native American living in total harmony with nature and conveniently neglect to show the real impact of all humans, including Native Americans, on the environment. Evidence of the belief that Native Americans are somehow stewards of the earth can be found throughout North America and, increasingly, world cultures. Online and throughout industrialized cultures, stores can be found that specialize in selling false relics of native cultures. Leo Marx would certainly declare such commodification of native cultures to be an example of superficial identification with native tribes, as well as an effort to retrieve the sentimental pastoral.

The ethical implications of profiting from another culture's spiritual ceremonies are no doubt dubious, but what can be called mild plastic shamanism represents an attempt to maintain and preserve native concepts after those cultures have been largely decimated. In addition, such false identification still shows that Amerindian culture captivates the contemporary white imagination. While present-day Native American tribes decry plastic shamanism as the plundering of ancient spiritual beliefs, certainly a valid point, such commodification may at the same time also signify an earnest endeavor to retroactively regenerate indigenous cultures. This is a contradiction, however; as Lisa Aldred points out, the "fetishization of Native American spirituality not only masks the social oppression of real Indian peoples but also perpetuates it" (330). Plastic shamanism reflects the extremes of exploitation of Native American spiritual traditions. However, it can also serve to restore the sentimental pastoral.

Amerindian culture was a source of magnetic fascination for the Beat Generation and for Burroughs, and it shows in their attempts to duplicate rituals including the ingestion of herbs and other drugs in order to find paths to the spirit world. Native Americans in pre-Columbian America used peyote in religious ceremonies for millennia. Beat writers tried to link such mystical enlightenment to their literary productions. In fact, some of the most influential poems of the Beat Generation canon were produced, at least in part, while the writers were under the influence of native drugs. For instance, peyote helped shape both Ginsberg's "Howl" (1956) and Michael McClure's "Peyote Poem" (1958). In *Junky*, Burroughs describes the experience of using peyote:

> Everything I saw looked like a peyote plant. Our faces swelled under the eyes and our lips got thicker through some glandular action of the drug. We actually looked like Indians. The others claimed they felt primitive and were laying [*sic*] around on the grass and acting the way they figured Indians act. (*Junky: Definitive* 144)

Such an attempt to imitate the way "they figured Indians act" and feel is openly ironic and at the same time illustrates the inability to ever really transform oneself. Thus Beat efforts to mimic Native American rituals may have been a subconscious effort to temporarily transform into or find an ecological cultural link to the Indian other.[5]

Burroughs' narratives often blend concepts borrowed from native cultures with his own ideas about the function of time. This is shown in a chapter in a later edition of *The Soft Machine* titled "The Mayan Caper," where the narrator describes time travel as a means to manipulate the past to change the recorded historical media tape that dictates our current conditions. This represents yet another attempt to change the present by first retreating to, and then altering events that took place in, the past. More thought-provoking is that while indigenous peoples appear infrequently in Burroughs' wider writing, the indigenous other remains an important generative and creative force in his narratives. The efforts to reach out to the indigenous other, perhaps to find cultural belonging, are significant.

In the context of Burroughs' wider corpus, efforts to retrieve the reverent mysticism of ancient civilizations are not uncommon. In *The Yage Letters*, Burroughs details attempts at the anthropological study of various tribes, as well as the commodification of indigenous knowledge of local drugs. Also noteworthy are the descriptions of the sexual possession of South American Indians. A crucial connection to native cultures in *The Yage Letters* is the documented quest for the *yagé* drug. The text seeks to intersect with the natural, ideological, and mystical heritage of the native.

An additional concern is whether the efforts to get close to the Indian both sexually and through the derangement of the senses that *yagé* provided represent a legitimate and genuine development to restore the pastoral, or whether such efforts to engage native beliefs simply mirror the somewhat superficial charm some of the Beats felt toward black culture in the 1950s. The search for and commodification of *yagé* also highlights what can be called an attempt to retrieve the sentimental pastoral (Marx 5). The experiments with the drug at the same time emphasize an earnest attempt to experience a mystical connection with native spirit worlds. In other words, the use of *yagé* in *The Yage Letters* is a further instance of making an effort to retrieve the mystical insight of sacred native traditions and to bring humans closer to nature, as understood to the twentieth-century white imagination. Thus the issue of *yagé* in *The Yage Letters* reveals both the "sentimental" and "complex pastoral" (Marx 5). This interest in connecting with the mystical knowledge of the ancients is also expressed in *Western Lands*.

The consideration of different faiths is crucial in understanding the larger quest to reclaim the past for the future of humanity as revealed in the final book of the trilogy. *Western Lands* evaluates monotheistic faiths and contemplates different attitudes concerning spirituality. Distinctions are made between "One-God religions," including Judaism, Christianity, and Islam, and what are called multigod religions (70). We are told the "One-God Universe" is a present limitation to human thinking (113) and that the worship of a single deity is in effect a spiritual impasse:

> One God concept set out to crush a biologic revolution that could have broken down the lines established between the species, thus precipitating unimaginable chaos, horror, joy and terror, unknown fears and ecstasies, while vertigos of extreme experience, of immeasurable gain and loss, hideous dead ends. (112)

At the same time, the narrator argues that the worship of a single deity limits humanity to an essentially two-dimensional existence: "The OGU is a pre-recorded universe of which He is the recorder. It's a flat, thermodynamic universe, since it has no friction by definition" (113). *Western Lands* condemns monotheism as doomed, since the One-God Universe is slowly "running down like an old clock" (113). Additionally, the narrative is critical of other beliefs.

A leading character of *Western Lands*, named Joe the Dead, rejects religion in a wide sense. The narrator explains, "Over the centuries and tens of centuries, Joe had served many men—many Gods, for men are but the representatives of Gods. He has served many, and respected none" (28). Joe is unwavering in his rejection of existing faiths:

> I don't believe in the Christian God or Allah or any of that second-rate lot, in their sleazy heavens of pearls and gold with their houris, gods for slaves and servants, with lying promises . . . the Slave Gods. (193)

In *Western Lands*, the speaker addresses Catholicism, Coptic Christianity, Hinduism, Islam, and Judaism. The narrative discusses the absurd idea of bringing a pig into a mosque and how such an occurrence would be interpreted in the context of Islam (21). Christianity is also a frequent target of scorn:

> I spit on the Christian God. When the White God arrived with the Spaniards, the Indians brought down fruit and corncakes and chocolate. The White Christian God proceeded to cut their hands off. He was not responsible for the Christian conquistadors? Yes, he was. Any God is responsible for his worshipers. (165)

The narrator thus links Christianity to the extermination of Native Americans. While acts of moral failure committed in the name of Christianity are explained at length, criticism is also extended to other ancient faiths.

In addition to examining and criticizing monotheism in *Western Lands*, the speaker reveals an initial attraction to another spiritual road involving ancient Egyptian mysticism: "I first encountered this concept [of ancient Egyptian mysticism] in Norman Mailer's *Ancient Evenings*, and saw that it corresponded precisely with my own mythology, developed over a period of many years, since birth in fact" (5). However, Egyptian mythology did not totally agree with the views of the storyteller, or there would have been no need to try to build a better faith, as happens later in the book. The speaker of *Western Lands* is particularly taken by the Egyptian concept of "many degrees of immortality" (7), as well as the idea of "Total Death. Soul Death. It's what the Egyptians called the Second and Final Death" (9). But *Western Lands* also challenges what is considered common thinking about the ancient religion:

> It is of course assumed by Western savants that the Egyptian animal Gods are the fantasies of a primitive and backward people, who did not have the advantage of the glorious gains of the Industrial Revolution, a revolution in which a standardized human product overthrows himself and replaces his own kind with machines (they are so much more efficient). (112)

While critical of industrial culture, at the same time the narrator does not shy away from questioning features of ancient Egyptian beliefs, contending that their trust in the physicality of spirituality was misguided and that the mummification of human bodies was simply foolish. In the speaker's view, the Egyptians' obsession with the flesh links their beliefs to Christian reliance on the body as a source of holy power: "Both believe in the resurrection of the body. That's what mummies are all about" (195). The narrative proposes that the very problem with connecting the spirit to the human body is the temporary state of human physicality.

Western Lands asserts that the forces of scientific thinking and industrialization have perpetrated a great deception on human societies, once again emphasizing the urgent need for human renewal. As in the later novella *Ghost of Chance*, *Western Lands* criticizes the scientific mindset, which in the speaker's view is the root of present-day social and environmental problems:

> Joe the Dead belongs to a secret breed of outlaws known as the NOs, natural outlaws dedicated to breaking the so-called natural laws of the universe foisted upon us by physicists, chemists, mathematicians, biologists and, above all, the monumental fraud of cause and effect. (30)

While this narrative contains a different form of struggle against industrial culture than the tactics of Deep Green Resistance in *Dead Roads*, there is a concerted effort to highlight issues of ecology. This effort is exemplified in a tight passage that touches on issues of conservation and environmental justice and also reveals the presence of the romantic plastic Indian:

> No one but Joe and his team knew that a basic aim of his research was to sabotage the proposed highway through the Amazon basin. Coca-Cola, McDonald's and Hiltons waiting offstage. He knows that if the highway goes through, it will mean the destruction of the last great rainforest on the planet. . . . The motels and souvenir shops and hamburger joints, drunken Indians, polluted rivers, the gritty bite of diesel fumes. (37)

The passage works toward conservationist concerns by expressing the need to protect the biodiversity of regions in lesser-developed nations, a concern also articulated in *The Yage Letters*. In *Western Lands*, Joe and his team actively work to prevent the development of Western economic interests in the Amazon region. The origins of Joe's apprehension can be found in the nineteenth century, when Western economic interests began a campaign to exploit the region's biodiversity and less-developed legal and regulatory machinery. A first-wave ecocritical reading would focus on the consequences of such developments and how they can teach us to appreciate the continued need for biodiversity. In the above passage, the point of the proposed highway, according to the speaker, is not to provide economic opportunities for people living in and around the Amazon. Instead, the problems of development are attributed to large, multinational corporations that have shown a long history of exploitative practices. These organizations, including "Coca-Cola, McDonald's and Hiltons" simply wait for their turn to occupy the region. Joe understands that "if the highway goes through, it will mean the destruction of the last great rainforest on the planet." While a conservationist reading of the above passage is rather straightforward, the passage also exhibits considerations of environmental justice, a hallmark of more recent developments in ecocriticism.

The above selection highlights environmental justice issues that are inevitably linked to Western corporations operating in developing nations. T. V. Reed reminds us that "environmental problems cannot be solved without addressing the drastic political and economic inequalities existing within and between nation states" ("Toxic Colonialism" 26). In this sense, the passage highlights decolonizing environmentalism, which not only defends rich pockets of biodiversity but also is essential in protecting indigenous cultures that inhabit such regions. The passage emphasizes the ultimate results of Western exploitation of indigenous cultures. The souvenir shops the narrator describes will no doubt participate in the practice of plastic shamanism, the deliberate commodification of indigenous beliefs for sale. But the passage is even more powerful, since it connects plastic shamanism to Western development of "hamburger joints," a powerful image of American economic imperialism. The most damaging aspect of the rise of the romantic plastic Indian is the move toward cultural and species homogeneity, a lack of cultural and biological diversity that can ultimately have severe consequences for humankind.

This is best depicted in the passage as the stereotypical and bigoted view of "drunken Indians" who have lost their cultural identity, which is for sale in an artificial and inauthentic form in nearby souvenir shops. The final result of Western economic development in South America, as implied in the passage, is a sequence of increasingly negative consequences. This ranges from the loss of the rich cultural and ecological biodiversity of the region before development to forms of plastic shamanism and the resulting demoralization and marginalization of indigenous peoples. The final negative consequences of development are predictably described in clearly environmental terms: "polluted rivers [and] the gritty bite of diesel fumes." Reed declares that "decolonial environmentalisms . . . articulate the links between oppressed humans and exploited Nature via objectification, commoditization, and degradation" ("Toxic Colonialism" 38). Burroughs articulates these developments by revealing the shallow romantic plastic Indian. Western corporations exploit the Amazon not just for rubber but for its unique biodiversity, which enriches pharmaceutical companies. Ultimately, the Westerner is confronted not by the remnants of the diversity of indigenous cultures, as marketed and sold. Instead, the Westerner is confronted by images of "drunken Indians," which no doubt awaken nostalgia for the romantic plastic Indian, which is permanently for sale but only ever truly existed in the white imagination.

While on one hand, *Western Lands* is highly critical of the commodification of indigenous knowledge and the rich lands these peoples inhabit, the narrative is simultaneously and subtly complicit in the perpetuation of the romantic plastic Indian in the course of trying to develop a new mysticism for the space age. The narrator tells us in *Western Lands* that "[a]ll the old answers have failed: the Church, the State" (115). A final confrontation between orthodoxy and commoners clamoring for a new society is imagined; the speaker believes it will involve "a confrontation between the old tired way, Church and State, rule of the unfit for the unfit, biologic suicide" (117). We are told that perhaps by reinventing ourselves yet again, we can avoid destruction of the planet. The first two books of the *Red Night* trilogy attempted to retrieve the potential of America past. Now it is proposed that we reinvent human civilization neither through an improved social contract nor through the creation of self-governing communes. After weighing different approaches to spiritual enlightenment, the final book of the trilogy concludes that to save ourselves from certain death, we must endeavor to abandon present civilization by inventing a new faith for a future era that involves aspects of various ancient cultures as well as space.

The narrator considers various theological and philosophical positions: "Any dogma must postulate the way, certain steps that will lead to the salvation which the dogma promises. The Christian Heaven of pearly gates and singing angels, the Moslem paradise of eternal whores and plenty of water" (241). By confronting the paragons of science and religion, the narrator appears to propose that we are at the end of time and such a revelation requires a fundamental reconsideration of spiritual beliefs. Lynn White Jr. claims:

> What we do about ecology depends on our ideas of the man-nature relationship. More science and more technology are not going to get us out of the present ecologic crisis until we find a new religion, or rethink our old one. (12)

This is precisely what is advocated in *Western Lands*. However, the narrative does not totally abandon the past. In fact, the past remains a crucial link to the future.

The speaker is confident that humans can still escape from a ruined planet by building a better faith. The narrative suggests an "immortality blueprint" has yet to be discovered that can still save humans from painful soul death (151). The narrator declares, "The Western Lands cannot have disappeared without leaving a blueprint behind" (195). While it is apparent that the speaker lacks specific knowledge about ancient Egyptian religious beliefs, he imagines how their mysticism can be reinvented for the present time: "The visions, the glimpses of the Western Lands, exist in space, not time, a different medium and a different light, with no temporal coordinates or recurrences. The medium bears some relation to holograms" (242). A bold leap from ancient Egypt to native cultures of Central and North America is then made: "In present-day Egypt, or in the areas of the Mayan and Aztec ruins, one encounters truncated history, where the present-day reality has lost all connection with historical past, to create a solid time-block" (202). This is where Burroughs attempts to generate what Leo Marx calls the "imaginative and complex" pastoral (5). Burroughs accomplishes this by creatively extracting elements from both ancient Egyptian and Native American mythologies and mixing them to create a cosmic mysticism for the future age.

Western Lands argues that bringing together two ancient forms of mysticism can save humanity from its present broken condition. The narrator boldly declares, "We can make our own Western Lands" (164). The suggestion that we move into a new realm echoes traditional Mayan and Hopi folklore. The effort to create a map to the next world emulates aspects of certain Native American faith systems. According to some Native American folklore, humans now inhabit the Fourth World (Aldred 334), but we are soon to be presented with a choice to either remain on the earth—and in the Fourth World—or be given passage into the next world, the Fifth World (Johnson 112), which will permit humans to escape a ruined planet.[6] Kelli Lyon Johnson explains that the work of Joy Harjo is especially relevant to discussions of ecology and spirituality in the present context: "For the fifth world, the next world, no map yet exists. The absence of the map, for Harjo, is a sign of hope: the new world has not yet been mapped—that is, poisoned, littered, destroyed" (112). Harjo further asserts that to reach the next world, as the narrator of *Western Lands* also suggests, "You must make your own map" (112). An attempt is made to challenge the Egyptian reliance on the physical world, and eventually the speaker decides that an improved theology should bring people into a new realm altogether, thus bypassing the physical world entirely. An unnamed character in *Western Lands* ponders:

> "But how can we make [the next world] solid? . . . We don't. That is precisely the error of the mummies. They made spirit solid. When you do this, it ceases to be spirit. We will make ourselves less solid." (165)

By making ourselves less solid, it is believed, humans will no longer need the destroyed physical world.

Western Lands proposes that by moving to the next realm, which involves outer space, humanity can finally escape environmental devastation. Legend shows that the Fifth World will be attractive, but various Native American groups disagree whether the next world is ultimately a positive or negative terminus. This is the point where the modified version of the mysticism contemplated in *Western Lands* digresses from native beliefs, since the narrator considers the Fifth World to be space itself. In his view, the movement to the Fifth World is an expected and necessary evolutionary step for human beings, as Burroughs himself has elsewhere argued: "Man is an artifact designed for space travel. He is not designed to remain in his present biologic state any more than a tadpole is designed to remain a tadpole" (*Adding Machine* 85). In *Cities*, Burroughs also posits that we need to tear "a hole in the fabric of reality" (26) to reach our evolutionary destiny: "I propose to remove the temporal limits, shifting our experimental theater into past time in order to circumvent the whole tedious problem of overpopulation" (21). In the *Red Night* trilogy more broadly, it is suggested that humans can evade environmental problems and overpopulation by colonizing space. Thus although the West cannot be resettled, the narrator believes that a place still exists where we can regenerate the human race. What is effectively proposed in *Western Lands* is therefore not so different from the attempt to resurrect the myth of America past in *Cities* and *Dead Roads*.

According to Native American beliefs, an event called the Great Purification will befall humanity, thus reproducing the eschatology common to many faiths (Geertz 269). Such an apocalyptic view is presented in the *Red Night* trilogy. In *Western Lands*, it is thought that the Great Purification will take the form of nuclear annihilation. Such a scenario would provide ample stimulus for humans to leave a dying planet, to flee from the "billions of radioactive corpses unfit even for fertilizer" (*Cities* 21). *Western Lands* proposes that existing social structures are losing cohesive power and are a mark of the real need to radically change our condition: "Political structures are increasingly incompatible with space conditions. They are inexorably cutting our lifelines to space, by imposing a uniformity of environment that precludes evolutionary mutations" (192). Near the end of *Western Lands*, the narrator proclaims his ultimate role is to rouse humanity to reach its biological destiny in space: "I WORK FOR THE BLACK HOLE, WHERE ALL NATURAL LAWS ARE INVALID" (243). The narrative thus attempts to dodge earthly environmental catastrophe and mortality by selectively drawing from elements of different faiths, buffet style. The narrator seeks to avoid the physical death required by one-god religions and the reliance on the physical body of Christian and Egyptian spirituality. At the same time, it is hoped that the promise of the potential of what Native Americans call the Fifth World can be achieved.

The Half-Finished Totem Pole

This chapter suggests the *Red Night* trilogy endeavors to accomplish two aims. The first is to resurrect the failed promises of America past. The second aim is even more daring: to grasp the potential of a complex mysticism for a future human age. Langeteig maintains, "The survival lesson that emerges from the *Red Night* trilogy emphasizes the need for evolution as well as revolution in order to escape from the plagued pages of the body's and the planet's history" (168). By merging Egyptian notions of spiritual multiplicity, elements borrowed from Native American cultures, and the involvement of space as a site of mystical retreat, the trilogy attempts to create a cosmic shamanism for the intergalactic future. Such a complex narrative strategy of weaving diverse religious texts to create what Burroughs calls a "retroactive Utopia" (*Cities* xiv) is significant in the wider context of his writing. The extended effort to reclaim the past while evolving toward an apparent human interstellar destiny is extraordinarily creative, but in the end, humanity remains bound to an imperfect world, overwhelmed by familiar problems of overpopulation and increasing pollution.

A larger question the trilogy poses is whether it is possible to ever really escape to a place of redemption. By emphasizing the need for humans to keep their machines as well as their need to construct the romantic plastic Indian, the series reveals sentimental and imaginative renderings of the pastoral. The *Red Night* trilogy is a powerful meditation on mortality in the form of disease and nuclear peril, as well as the eternal hope for an existence that transcends mere flesh and a devastated world. But America past is never fully restored, nor is the construction of a faith for the space age complete. Thus it is perhaps fitting that near the end of Burroughs' life, he subsisted on the edge of the old frontier in a modest home, built from a house kit bought from a Sears catalog.

In the search to build a better faith, Burroughs is ultimately bound by the limits of the textual medium: "The old writer couldn't write anymore because he had reached the end of words, of what can be done with words" (258). In his late period, after a career of experimentation with a variety of writing strategies as well as other forms of media, perhaps Burroughs realized the limits of the textual medium and, more broadly, the limits of art. This is essential in understanding Burroughs' project. If literature indeed has limits, then an important consideration is whether literature is ever capable of fully expressing the phenomenal human imagination.

6.

Terrestrial Creatures: Problematizing the Animal and Empathizing the Human in *The Cat Inside*

> [H]e and the Cat looked at each other across an impassable barrier of silence which has been set between man and beast from the creation of the world. —Mary Freeman, *Understudies*

In the period after the *Red Night* series, Burroughs wrote on issues involving the plight of nonhuman creatures as well as broader ecological concerns. This change is especially evident in Burroughs' late narratives, *The Cat Inside* and *Ghost of Chance*. However, scholars have so far totally overlooked this late shift in focus, instead choosing to continue concentrating on earlier, more provocative books. Any cursory glance at the existing scholarship on Burroughs' writing verifies a clear lack of critical engagement with these slender yet crucial narratives that can help establish scholarship on his late works, as well as teach ecocriticism about the need to continue testing ecocritical models.

In the following pages, I seek to rectify the scholarship on *The Cat Inside* by challenging Kelly Anspaugh's essay "The Black Cat Inside: Burroughs as Unredeemed Confessant," published in *Genre* in 2001. Anspaugh's provocative article argues, among other things, that Burroughs remained unredeemed and that his lack of redemptive qualities is somehow revealed in the narratives of *Junky* and *The Cat Inside*, two texts that nearly span his whole oeuvre. Through the application of Randy Malamud's criteria for one form of an "ecocritical aesthetic" (43), this chapter offers a very different view.

Anspaugh rightfully identifies *The Cat Inside* as a text worthy of study. He also correctly reminds us that Burroughs' narratives do not always portray benevolent coexistence between humans and animals; at times they do the reverse. Occasionally, Burroughs' narratives expose the real tensions and even primitive violence that exists between humans and other animal species. This tension can be seen from the start of Burroughs' oeuvre, where it takes the form of conflict between humans and nonhuman creatures in *Junky*, a text that Anspaugh also addresses. In this passage from *Junky*, the narrator describes how he transfers and transmits the pain of his own drug withdrawal to a blameless feline:

> The end of the month. I was out of junk and sick. Waiting for Old Ike to show with a morphine script. A junky spends half his life waiting. There was a cat in the house which we had been feeding, an ugly-looking gray cat. I picked the animal up and held it on my lap, petting it. When it tried to jump down I tightened my hold. The cat began to mew, looking for a way to escape. I brought my face down to touch the cat's cold nose with mine, and the cat scratched at my face. It was a halfassed scratch, and didn't even land. But it was all I needed. I held the cat out at arm's length, slapping it back and forth across the face with my free hand. The cat screamed and clawed me, then started spraying piss all over my pants. I went on hitting the cat, my hands bloody from scratches. The animal twisted loose and ran into the closet, where I could hear it groaning and whimpering with terror. "Now I'll finish the bastard off," I said, picking up a heavy painted cane. Sweat was running down my face. I was trembling with excitement. I licked my lips and started toward the closet, alert to block any escape attempt. At this point my old lady intervened, and I put down the cane. The cat scrambled out of the closet and ran down the stairs. (*Junky: Definitive* 102–3)

The passage is alarming and effective because of the use of verbs of capture and violence, as well as the first person. The narrator picks up the animal, tightening his grip on the cat. More than just capturing the creature, the speaker slaps and hits the cat, his hands bloodied from the futile feline attempts to defend itself. The scene from *Junky* is an especially convincing example of the ways in which Burroughs' narratives occasionally show acts of unnecessary human violence against nonhuman creatures. The use of the first person in this section helps in projecting a powerfully anthropocentric view.

The use of the third person would arguably have much less impact on the reader. While a typical reader may not readily identify with the narrator's extreme violence, or is even repulsed at the thought of smashing the spine of such a small helpless creature, the use of the first person nonetheless forces the reader to participate, reluctantly and indirectly, in the figurative wounding of the fictive cat. The abundance of the personal pronoun "I" throughout the passage also suggests the narrator is immersed in himself and his own pain, and thus cannot easily show empathy for the pain of other creatures. Only the intervention of the narrator's wife prevents him from killing the cat altogether. The only reason the narrator has for his shocking actions is the fact that he "was out of junk and sick." Therefore, in *Junky*, one sees a figure in need for recovery from addiction and from pain. The speaker even needs spiritual redemption.

The contrast between the events as presented in *Junky* and the more psychic happenings in *The Cat Inside* are astonishing. *Junkie: Confessions of an Unredeemed Drug Addict*, was first published in 1953, nearly four decades before the release of *The Cat Inside*.[1] More important than the lengthy temporal distance between the two publications is the completely different subject matter. *Junky* depicts an addict's lifestyle and his endless hunger for the needle, as well as the damage his addiction causes. Far from displaying a biocentric position, the chronicle reveals a completely self-interested narrator who is aware only of his own needs. While a haunting account of addiction, *Junky* contains important social commentary for the period in which it was produced. *The Cat Inside*, on the other hand, does not describe illicit ways to acquire money for drugs or recount the abuse of animals prompted by drug withdrawal. Instead, *The Cat Inside* focuses on everyday interactions with cats, as well as the common conversations the speaker has with elderly women about the relative quality of competing brands of cat food in supermarkets in Lawrence, Kansas. The work also touches on more personal and emotional interactions with nonhuman creatures.

Malamud's Model for Tracing Animal Ethics in a Literary Text

Randy Malamud's 2003 *Poetic Animals and Animal Souls* is one of the more significant works over the last twenty-five years to explore the relationship between humans and animals in literary texts. The work offers a compelling theoretical model to analyze the connections between humans and animals in poetry. The application of Malamud's concepts to other forms of literature is a reasonable and logical extension of his work. In the following pages, William Burroughs' *The Cat Inside* is examined to determine just how closely the novella meets Malamud's criteria on a point-by-point basis. Such an examination will help establish whether *The Cat Inside* exhibits an advanced sense of awareness of animal considerations and indeed even empathy for nonhuman creatures. Therefore, I posit that *The Cat Inside* shows a special awareness of animals in a literary text and establishes the relevance of the writer's later work to contemporary environmental literary scholarship. But even if Malamud can help untangle the ways *The Cat Inside* bridges and problematizes the human and the animal, Burroughs' creative use of chimera creatures and dream visions with fantastic animal hybrids still lies beyond existing critical models.

According to Malamud's model, a literary text revealing what he calls "an ecocritical aesthetic" should, in the spirit of environmental praxis, attempt to do the following:

> - "seeing animals without hurting them . . . literally, *or* spiritually, metaphysically";
> - "seeing them in *their* contexts";
> - "teaching about animals";
> - "advocating respect for them"; and
> - "*knowing* them, richly, but also incompletely." (44–45; emphasis in original)

Malamud believes the observance of the above points allows for scholarly evaluation of texts that can help establish a model for the ecocritical analysis of animality. He believes his model exceeds the occasional sentimental explorations of animals that are common today, even within ecocritical circles.

A first point of study is to examine a literary text for evidence of resistance to the hurting or capturing of animals, not only physically but also spiritually, metaphorically, or metaphysically. By not harming animals, texts can teach an appreciation for the richness of animals artistically and culturally, and not just physically (44). Several sections of Burroughs' text are relevant to this condition. In *The Cat Inside*, the speaker describes the real pain that animals feel. The issue of the mistreatment of nonhuman creatures is also investigated at length. One particularly poignant example of empathy involves a childhood event that was engraved in the narrator's memory.

The narrator tells how a personal experience at a childhood summer camp helped crystallize his understanding of both animals and human beings. At this point, fiction possibly overlaps with autobiography.[2] The incident involves the premature death of a badger at the hands of a camp counselor at the Los Alamos Ranch School.[3] In the scene, the actions of a cruel human being result in the distressing and untimely demise of a young badger.

A badger—curious, lively, and inexperienced—suddenly appears in front of the children (*Cat Inside* 14). The camp counselor rushes to retrieve his Colt .45 from his saddlebag and shoots at the animal, missing badly. The counselor, however, is determined to kill the animal and finally shoots into the badger's stomach. The speaker laments, "I can see the stricken animal, the sad shrinking face, rolling down the slope, bleeding, dying" (14). The badger obviously posed no threat to the safety of the camp. The camp counselor's reaction is exaggerated at best. At worst, the killing represents the senseless slaughter of a possibly sentient creature. By documenting the incident, and by unfolding it for the reader, the narrative teaches about the genuine injuries and hurt that animals experience because of human actions. The narrator implores the reader to identify with the tragedy: "Contact *that*. Identify with *that*. Feel *that*" (15; emphasis in original).

Another essential point here is that Burroughs asks the reader to identify not only with the death of the animal but also with the murderous human that lies within all of us. This is an especially challenging tactic. The text moreover denounces the killing of a creature solely because of its membership in a specific nonhuman animal species. As Cary Wolfe emphasizes, humans need to reconsider the notion that "it is all right to systematically exploit and kill nonhuman animals simply because of their species" (8). The narrator of *The Cat Inside* goes on to imply that the kind of people who find pleasure in abusing and killing animals are likely to be the same sort of people who extend aggression to vulnerable people such as queers. Later in *The Cat Inside*, the speaker relates how cats have been historically neglected and abused. Malamud's focus on resisting the physical and metaphorical harming of animals highlights aspects of the text that are particularly effective.

The Cat Inside also directly addresses controversial cultural practices in which humans actively observe and participate in the death of animals as a form of ritual entertainment. The narrator approaches an activist ideological position by condemning the British fox-hunting ritual (58). It is argued that such forms of animal death rituals that occur for human amusement are ethically wrong, since "you see . . . the pain and fear of the final death" (70).[4] This recognition of animal suffering marks the literary as a way to generate empathy. It is important to note that *The Cat Inside* appears to contain some degree of autobiographical writing, and this typically Burroughsian play with ambiguity between author and narrator continues to make his writing difficult and challenging to read, because one can never be sure who is really speaking. But Anspaugh nevertheless generally assumes the author is speaker, which may be the reason his reading of *The Cat Inside* is so moralistic and disapproving.

Elsewhere in the novella, the narrator deals with his previous disposition toward animals in a confessional style. Over time, from *Junky* to *The Cat Inside*, Burroughs would seem to have redeemed himself radically, contrary to Anspaugh's contention. If Anspaugh is correct, then here Burroughs may be writing about his own prior mistreatment of cats, such as "[t]he white cat in Mexico City: I slapped it across the face with a book . . . I was literally hurting myself and I didn't know it" (48). Again, this reflection on the violent mistreatment of nonhuman creatures parallels Malamud's code well, since the incident described involves teaching the reader about the physical and emotional pain animals suffer. What is particularly distinctive here is the comment that the narrator was literally in pain. This could mean that the speaker's actions suggest that he was himself suffering and his lashing out at other creatures was simply a manifestation of his own pain. By acknowledging previous transgressions, and by identifying with the suffering of animals, *The Cat Inside* effectively teaches about animal lives and emotions.[5] Such recognition of animal pain reveals compassion and even empathy.

Apart from condemning earlier misdeeds against felines, the narrator of the novella also unexpectedly attacks the conduct of the Humane Society of the United States. A late section of *The Cat Inside* discusses the Humane Society, where lost and stray animals are often taken when they do not have a home or have become separated from their human owners. In the United States, animals are routinely kept in these shelters for a short period so that their owners can come to retrieve their lost pets. However, if the dogs and cats are not reclaimed, they are systematically killed, though the preferred euphemism is "put to sleep." The narrator relates a specific incident in which the Humane Society apprehends one of his cherished cat companions. Consequently, the underlying values and core principles of the social institution of the Humane Society are considered. Ultimately, current practices in the United States of capturing, detaining, and finally killing animals are presented as immoral. In the view of the narrator, the captured animals can sense their imminent death (85). An analogy is even drawn between the Humane Society and a concentration camp: "We arrive at an animal shelter. The place is a death camp" (85).

Such criticism necessitates the reconsideration of cultural values. The narrative forces the reader to consider the reasons why such objectionable methods of animal extermination occur in modern, so-called developed societies. If one assumes that animals have a natural right to live, then the intentional killing of animals, in this case captured animals at an animal shelter, amounts to the slaying of possibly sentient creatures. The narrator questions the act of euthanizing stray animals and points out that lesser-developed societies have a more ethically consistent and compassionate response to the problem of large numbers of stray and lost animals: "Turn to backward countries that don't have Humane Societies for a simple alternative. In Tangier stray cats fend for themselves" (87). A better and more compassionate approach would be to sterilize and release feral cats, the narrator suggests.

In a later incident from *The Cat Inside*, Ed, one of the narrator's cats, wanders from his home. The local authorities subsequently seize the cat as an illegal stray animal. The seizing of the animal creates a bizarre situation whereby it is illegal to exist as an animal outside the context of being a direct human possession. The speaker quotes the Kansas animal control officer: "'It's illegal to allow your cat to run free . . . It's the law'" (85). It says a great deal about the assumed human sense of supremacy and dominion over animal species when all animals, not just those that are potentially dangerous, are deemed subordinate to the rule of human beings.

One more incident in the narrative centers on another encounter with animal control officials and exposes resistance to the capture and confinement of other creatures. At the edge of the speaker's property near a grove of trees, one of his feline friends, Ruski, is caught in an animal trap. The narrator writes about his own ignorance of the practice: "I didn't know about animal traps. . . . Close. Very close" (88). He reflects on the possibility that animal control authorities could have caught and euthanized his cat and describes measures he subsequently takes to make sure all of his cats have proper identifying tags. The speaker of *The Cat Inside* therefore seeks to protect his animal companions from capture, and he strongly disapproves of the practices of animal control authorities.

While certain sections of *The Cat Inside* would seem to try to persuade readers to think about animals outside the contexts of violence or confinement, other aspects of the narrative encourage an artistic view of nonhuman creatures. According to Malamud, "seeing animals without hurting them" also requires valuing "the richness of seeing [animals] artistically [and] culturally" (44). The narrative fulfills this not only by the protagonist's description of his relationship with cats but also in the attempts to use writing as a means to mediate among the author, the narrator, and the human and nonhuman spheres. The nature of the text thus allows for a creative artistic exploration of animality. The narrator promotes respect for other life forms in one particular incident in which he introduces the mythical figure of Bigfoot. When asked what should happen if such creatures were ever to be found, a local screams, "'Kill Them!'" (16). This incident highlights the human arrogance toward nonhuman animals in that even mythical creatures are the recipients of cruel human violence. More important, though, the scene also allows the reader to imagine fantastic and artistic animals. Burroughs' refusal to distinguish between common and imagined animals has an effect on the reader.

In much of Burroughs' late writing, the thematic focus is on environmental endangerment, and at times his narratives castigate all of modern civilization, including human beings. Such sweeping moments of judgment in *The Cat Inside,* where the apparent evil of certain animal species such as dogs and insects is suggested, reveal that the leap to true animal altruism has not been completely made. The speaker still prefers certain kinds of animals, and reviles others, simply because of their species. This departure reveals the limits of the narrator's own (human) view and shows how people often rely on their own subjectivity. In other ways, though, *The Cat Inside* encourages a positive view of the aesthetic richness of animals.

The narrator conveys the aesthetic beauty of various animal species with descriptions that go far beyond simply naming different breeds or uncommon varieties of cats. He beholds the beauty and importance of other creatures and writes of "[f]lying foxes, bush babies, the gliding lemurs with enormous yellow eyes that live in trees and are helpless on the ground, ringtailed lemurs and mouse lemurs, sables, raccoons, minx, otters, skunks and sandfoxes" (4). Admiration for these animals is apparent in the very language Burroughs chooses to employ. The dense asyndetic enumeration works like a Whitmanesque catalog passage: the very naming of the animals is an expression of pure delight.

A second condition for what Malamud considers a fully developed sense of animal ethics in a literary text requires a much higher standard of behavior than merely seeing animals without harming them physically or metaphysically. He proposes that one needs to learn to appreciate animals "in their own contexts [and] not in our contexts" (44). This is a difficult task, indeed, since it requires humans to escape their own limited view. This second point of observation involves a clear move toward a more biocentric position. As Lawrence Buell argues, such a biocentric position counters anthropomorphic thinking (*Future* 134). Burroughs' work reflects the difficulty involved in moving from one viewpoint to the other. Linda Vance asserts that humans need to avoid anthropomorphic thinking to truly connect with animal concerns:

> Crafting narratives that will give voice to animals and make humans care about them in appropriate ways is no easy task. We want to avoid anthropomorphizing animals even though that has proven itself an effective tactic for mobilizing public sympathy toward them. We need to be faithful to their stories, not our own. The goal is not to make us care more about animals because they are like us, but to care about them because they are themselves. (185)

But *The Cat Inside* is not free from anthropomorphizing tendencies. A shift to a more biocentric position would require learning to appreciate the fundamental otherness of cats (and other nonhuman animals), which is something the speaker is never really able to do and therefore is bound by the limits of subjective human thinking.

The narrator frequently displays an uncertain attitude concerning the appreciation of animals in their own contexts. He seems unable to value animals in their own state on a consistent basis. This is a troublesome issue, since he actively exhibits (and at times almost flaunts) a patently anthropomorphic vision of the universe throughout the narrative. For instance, the central figure named his cat companions after people from his past—a questionable move for someone who desires to understand animals on their own terms. Lawrence Buell suggests that such projection of human characteristics onto nonhuman creatures can be called "homocentrism" (*Future* 134). Homocentrism is the belief that objects and animals are valuable only to the extent to which they contribute directly to human beings or to human qualities. It also suggests that humans are the only creatures with intrinsic value, since humans are the only creatures that are sufficiently sentient.

While much of *The Cat Inside* is bound to human perspectives, the narrative nonetheless challenges anthropocentric and homocentric views by describing and exploring the physical and psychological anguish of cats. While anthropomorphic thinking can actually arise from anthropocentric or homocentric perspectives, it can also work toward promoting a biocentric standpoint, thus creating a perplexing contradiction. If the purpose of a given text is to move the audience to a more ethical position in relation to animals, or even to ideological action on behalf of the environment, then the use of anthropomorphic writing as a technique is not nearly as inconsistent as it would first appear.[6]

Anthropomorphic writing can work toward conservationist objectives, as it can create a linguistic and conceptual bridge to the human mind. As Onno Dag Oerlemans points out, anthropomorphizing may actually work to affirm human connections with animals, since such tendencies can reveal shared interests (12). In *The Cat Inside* as well as other later Burroughs publications, a common thematic concern is the voicing of anxieties about animal extinction and environmental destruction. Anthropomorphic writing is especially suited to evoking sympathy from readers by communicating issues of moral significance. This is possibly why anthropomorphic writing has been used so successfully for so many centuries to articulate concerns about animals.

In *The Cat Inside*, the practice of anthropomorphic writing is not the straightforward application of human characteristics to nonhuman creatures. Here, anthropomorphic writing is more subtle and even inadvertent. For example, the distinction between the narrator's cat companions and human characters from Burroughs' own past is blurred. At one point in the text, the speaker picks up Ruski, one of his cats. He holds the cat but feels the presence and hears the words of Kiki, a former human companion and lover of Burroughs who has long been dead. In the narrator's mind, there is no sharp distinction between memories and emotions involving people from Burroughs' past and his pets. In this case, anthropomorphic thinking works to cement the emotions the writer feels about former human friends and his feline companions. The narrator tries to identify with animals by humanizing them. Marc Bekoff argues that anthropomorphic thinking is completely natural, since it involves the language with which we are familiar (123). Bekoff also suggests that anthropomorphism works as a mechanism to make animals more accessible to humans. Anthropomorphizing, as such, can function to evoke compassion for nonhuman creatures.

As *The Cat Inside* shows, the protagonist depends on other animals a great deal and even melds them together with humans from his past to satisfy his emotional needs. At the same time, his actions work to affirm a positive view of animals. The speaker wants to evoke the reader's empathy. Lawrence Buell recognizes that, given the impossibility for humans to ever truly escape their own human subjectivity, a certain degree of homocentric thinking is natural and not necessarily evidence of dishonesty or inauthenticity. He points out that while biocentrism is a quality for which biocentrists and ecocentrists seek to strive, zero-degree anthropocentrism might be neither feasible nor desirable (*Future* 134). He argues, "It is entirely possible without hypocrisy to maintain biocentric values in principle" while conceding human considerations (134). The narrator of *The Cat Inside* displays a position that acknowledges both animal and human concerns, which is a move toward a biocentric position.

A third condition for a highly developed sense of animal ethics involves the open support of animals in literature. Specifically, Malamud suggests that one should teach "about animals' habits, their lives, their emotions, their natures, as much as can be done from our limited and biased perspective" (44). In *The Cat Inside*, the narrator touches on his cats' instinctual urges after observing what many humans may consider a ghastly event, one of his cats hunting and killing a small rabbit. The feline subsequently drags the rabbit's dead body under the porch, where it consumes the remains. Humans typically recoil at the grisly sight of a cat ripping apart a small rabbit, but the narrator appreciates the instinctual drive that impels the act.

While the narrator does not cringe at the gruesome death of the rabbit, as one might expect, he demonstrates a possible shift in position. This move from "homocentrism toward biocentrism" is analogous to the move Buell argues occurred in Henry David Thoreau's thinking over the course of his writing career (*Environmental Imagination* 138). The speaker of the story still acknowledges that cats are animals that retain instinctual urges. By recognizing and embracing this fact, he tries to understand the animal on its own terms. Never mind that the cat was well fed and did not need the added nourishment the rabbit meat provided. The mother cat only did what comes naturally for its species. Cats kill mice. Cats kill rabbits. The speaker observes her state of extreme contentment "out on the porch licking the blood off her paws" (*Cat Inside* 27). He accepts the killing as a normal animal occurrence, even if to human eyes it may be seen as an unnecessary act. The later reflection on the rabbit kill is appreciative, almost wistful. The next morning, the cat's small kittens greedily consume what rabbit remains are left. The narrator makes an attempt to capture the event in terms of the female cat's maternal role, saying, "She takes her role as huntress . . . very sincerely. The little cats romp about, pouncing on grasshoppers" (28). He does not discipline the cat or try to prevent it from eating the rabbit, nor does he (this time) attach human values to the event.

Instead, an attempt is made to view the event with an appreciation of the cat's perspective, in an effort to understand its natural urges. The narrator conveys the notion that instinct should be respected. As observes in "Walking," "The seeds of instinct are preserved under the thick hides of cattle and horses" (para. 39). Why should it be any different for the animals that occupy our backyards and homes? Domesticated animals are still animals nonetheless. This suggests that animals should be allowed to maintain a sense of the feral. Even more intriguing issues arise. For example, humans often consider those animals that are especially close to them as being somehow fundamentally different from the creatures that roam wild and fend for themselves. Here the narrator breaks out of the tendency to graft his own values onto domesticated animals, particularly tame animals.

However, the incident of the rabbit kill also suggests a point where the narrator's thinking runs up against its own limits. A proposition is made that cats should be allowed to kill rabbits because it is normal for creatures to retain natural animal qualities. If this is true, then why should humans not be allowed to kill animals because of those same raw impulses? This contradiction is never resolved in the novella, and there is no convincing explanation, except to suggest that humans really are somehow different from other animals and should thus be held to higher ethical standards. If this is true, then the human capacity to be moral involves higher standards of behavior.

In other places in *The Cat Inside*, the narrative falls back on nostalgia. Such emotionally driven writing shows that the narrator is keenly aware of, and tries to connect with, animal emotions. The frequency of such writing can appear repetitive or even possibly self-absorbed.[7] An abundant amount of romanticizing is evident in the novella, some of which borders on sentimentalism. One of the more compelling incidents in the text involves a situation in which one of the narrator's favorite cats wanders away from home and fails to return. A hastily written flyer reports, "ED IS MISSING. LOVED ALBINO CAT WHITE ALL OVER. EYES ARE WHITE AND PINKISH. WEARING FLEA COLLAR. REWARD. CALL 841-3905" (*Cat Inside* 42). Pet owners commonly post flyers on bulletin boards at local supermarkets or on telephone poles downtown. Many people who pass by likely take no notice of such small tragedies. In this case, the narrator's attempt to reclaim his feline is ultimately unsuccessful. The futility and sadness of the occurrence convey the sense of desperation animal lovers share at the loss of one of their creature companions. The narrator defends the power of his own emotions about the loss: "And why shouldn't the loss of a cat be as poignant and heartfelt as any loss? Small deaths are the saddest" (45). He goes on to describe the personal depth of the loss he experienced:

> I used to put cans of cat food on the windowsill. . . . Ed would get up on the sill and knock the cans down into the sink. A terrible clatter would wake me up. . . . Well, I can put the cans up there now. And at this moment I feel a sharp pang of loss. (43)

The speaker holds out some feeble hope of a reunion with the animal: "I have put the cat food cans back onto the window, still hoping he will come back and knock them over." The protagonist realizes that the cat is gone and keeps the cat's food dish in the front room. The anguish of the loss is thus articulated for the reader. By being drawn into using what is at times excessively emotional imagery, in the attempt to deal with personal loss, the narrator is caught in a sentimental snare. As such, some of the melancholic writing risks appearing conventional in tugging at the emotional strings of the reader for dramatic effect. While such personal reflections work to demonstrate connections with animals, the sheer amount of gushing sentiment in *The Cat Inside* can appear repetitive. This is not to suggest that the narrator was somehow being dishonest in his feelings toward the animals—on the contrary. Emotion is employed to elicit notions of empathy and responsibility from readers. In such copious amounts, though, the outpourings of feeling ultimately risk appearing self-interested and somewhat flat. Additionally, the narrator's anthropomorphizing demonstrates the imperfect human understanding of animals. While the narrator of *The Cat Inside* attempts to comprehend creatures, even on their own terms, in the end he falls short of truly understanding the pets for which he cares so deeply. Although he is unsuccessful in fully connecting with cats (an exceedingly difficult task to begin with), it is significant that he puts a great deal of energy into searching out opportunities to connect with animal emotions and to describe the experience through the vehicle of literature.

In other places in the text, the narrator attempts to teach the reader about animals through the transference and interpretation of dream visions. He details a recurring dream he had as a young person. The speaker explains that he was drawn to a mystical, unidentifiable animal creature in his early visions: "I recall a recurrent sensation of cuddling some creature against my chest. It is quite small, about the size of the cat" (3). In the ecocritical context, the unidentifiable animal is relevant in that it can represent a great number of animal species, including both humans and cats. The narrator further believes his relationship with cats transcends that of pet and owner and that his bond with specific cats borders on the supernatural. He suggests a connection with cats that moves beyond empathy and approaches symbiosis. He explains, "Cats started as psychic companions . . . and never deviated from this function" (8). The speaker sees his role as that of protector and feels compelled to look after the fragile, hybrid creatures that appear to him in his dreams. He comments, "I am cast in the role of Guardian" (3). The narrator, as agent, neither harms nor constrains animals in *The Cat Inside*, but identifies himself as self-proclaimed protector and guardian of his feline companions. He describes his role in the dream visions as a steward of fellow creatures.

The dream episodes also reveal a breakdown in the apparent human-animal dichotomy. The narrator seeks to discover the ways in which humans and animals connect and share experiences. Imagined creatures are invoked. One such depiction involves an animal that shares physical characteristics with various creatures:

> His face is something between a bat and a cat and a monkey . . . the ears fuzzy and bat-like. . . . Easy to imagine a Bat Cat, its leathery black wings glistening, sharp little teeth, glowing green eyes. His whole being radiates a pure, wild sweetness, flitting through the night woods with little melodious cries, on some cryptic errand. (60)

Interestingly, while much of Burroughs' broader writing may be difficult to penetrate, the descriptions of animal dreams are lucid and sharp. The speaker explains how his "cat dreams are vivid and frequent" (5). In his imaginings, he interacts with the hybrid cat-human creatures, which rely on him completely. As a guardian, the narrator feels compelled to provide safety for these unknown hybrid animals (7). He describes a general feeling of anxiety and inadequacy in his role of provider and protector and demonstrates an almost maternal insecurity. In his dreams, he is at a loss as to how to look after the animals properly. He laments, "I encountered a dream cat with a very long neck and a body like a human fetus." Although insecure in his responsibilities, the speaker feels a need to provide for and protect the creature, and even attempts to sense the dream cat's desires. In another vision, he describes an unknown animal that totally trusts him: "I wonder what it is . . . a squirrel? . . . not quite" (3).

This idea of unidentifiable animals trusting the narrator occurs frequently in his dreams. At some level, such frequently occurring dreams would seem to suggest a psychological connection with animals. His dreams fit into his broader position toward animals in that he believes dreams provide vital insights. Indeed, the importance of dreaming to Burroughs and his writing is crucial in two ways. First, dream episodes show the writer's creativity in using dream imagery in his writing. Second, the dream episodes are significant in stressing his vision of life, which exceeds the materialistic universe. He universalizes his own experiences throughout the text, and his dream episodes also work to that end. However, the narrator never really questions the validity of those visions and suggests that they are somehow applicable to the wider world.

The narrator further believes that cats have powerful emotions and attempts to identify with them as well as he can. For example, at one point he writes about "that one time I ever slapped Ruski for attacking one of the kittens. The way he looked at me, the shock and hurt . . . I had to make amends" (34). In another scene, the speaker describes a moment when he was sleepy and annoyed and subsequently slapped his cat Kiki for being too clingy: "Kiki sat there with a tear in the corner of his eye" (34). His later apology speaks to the attempt to empathize with the cat's pain. Elsewhere in *The Cat Inside*, the narrator tries to understand other animal emotions as well. These episodes underline not just the ways in which the speaker identifies with cat emotions, but also the ways in which the aesthetic beauty of animal emotions can be expressed in literary form.

The speaker further describes an aesthetic appreciation of cat anger that borders on empathy: "A cat's rage is beautiful, burning with a pure cat flame, all its hair standing up and crackling blue sparks, eyes blazing and sputtering" (63). At another point, the narrator explains how he knows when to tread carefully around his cats, comparing their rage to that of a nervous horse (71). This attempt at recognizing animal emotions echoes what ecocritical theorists consider a vital component to understanding the connection between humans and animals. Elizabeth Atwood Lawrence suggests that empathy is vital to human-animal interactions (52). Marc Bekoff agrees and further believes that empathy is a basic ingredient to developing an advanced sense of morality (87–88). A further consideration is whether Malamud's model can convincingly reveal further connections between the narrative and what Malamud calls an "ecocritical aesthetic" (45).

Malamud's fourth point goes further than merely teaching others about animal natures and involves "advocating respect for animals, on their own terms—not because of what they can do for us or what they mean to us" (45). The domestication of animals was a practical arrangement. Humans first chose to domesticate wild dogs for logical reasons. Together they formed a mutually beneficial partnership. Dogs are natural pack hunters, so they work well with human beings as a team. In the past, such a relationship was practical and reciprocal. The animals served a useful function for early humans. In effect, people gained a reliable natural alarm system. The dogs, in return, received shelter and mammalian affection from their companions and likely greater and more consistent amounts of food. However, cats have never served such a useful function. They were neither sentinels nor good team players. Aside from reducing the number of vermin in the immediate area, their service was limited. According to the narrator of *The Cat Inside*, cats in fact have remarkably little to offer human beings. The storyteller simply claims, "The cat offers itself" (10). While the cat would seem to offer itself unconditionally, the speaker does not always show full and unqualified acceptance of animals.

He receives a great deal from the creatures—and on occasion even more than he provides or is willing to acknowledge. While there are poignant moments in *The Cat Inside* where the speaker attempts to use the text as a medium to teach respect for animals, the writing is not characterized by total selflessness. The narrator does not see animals as a commodity, per se, but they do serve as what Burroughs called "sensitive screens" for emotions in *The Cat Inside* (*Word Virus* 506). The protagonist sees animals as sources of company and emotional warmth, and he describes the experiences. The text therefore functions as a canvas for the narrator's emotions. The reflections on relationships with cats, while touching, also show the lonesomeness the narrator experiences.

There are glimpses into other areas of animal contact in *The Cat Inside*. One such experience involves a mysterious encounter with a lone gray cat. The storyteller relates an incident occurring after a long winter: "As spring came I glimpsed occasionally a gray cat shadow and put out food, which disappeared, but I could never get close" (19). He wants to approach the animal, but it keeps its distance and avoids direct contact. He does not force himself on the creature, and the animal remains hidden. In this particular case, the narrator's relationship with the animal is limited to infrequent glances and thus never approaches the close bond he shares with other creatures. At other points in the text, the narrator sees himself as an important addition to animal lives. In one example, he explains how (in his eyes) cats acknowledge his special role:

> At the far end of the porch was the first gray cat and beside him was a big white cat I'd never seen before. Now the white cat starts towards me, rubbing himself against the table, slow, tentative. . . . Clearly the gray cat had brought him along. (21)

Did the gray cat see the narrator as a protector for "plaintive lost spirits" (13)? While such an event may not seem particularly unusual or out of the ordinary, in the narrator's universe such an incident carries deep significance: "The white cat symbolizes the silvery moon" (31). While the white cat has cosmic significance to the narrator, the observation does not fully accept the cat's natural context, which is much more ordinary and plain than cosmic.

An emergent sense of advanced animal ethics involves an even deeper engagement with animals. Malamud suggests that a fifth condition includes not only knowing animals (incompletely) but also learning about them and learning how animal lives connect to human lives. This implies developing what Malamud calls "a culturally and ecologically complex, problematized vision of what an animal means" (45). The reflections on the origins of the cat species in the narrative, and the creative descriptions of their sometimes fantastic evolution, fit this condition well. In *The Cat Inside*, the speaker meditates on the long, mysterious relationship between cats and their human allies. He traces this connection back to the Egyptian cult of the animal other.

In exploring the ways in which humans resemble cats, and how the animals at times resemble humans, the narrator problematizes the distinction between human and animal. Michael Lundblad points out just "how difficult it has become to maintain easy distinctions between 'the human' and 'the animal'" (496). Jacques Derrida and Marie-Louise Mallet say likewise and claim the "catch-all concept" of the animal is wholly unfitting, emphasizing

> the infinite space that separates the lizard from the dog, the protozoan from the dolphin, the shark from the lamb, the parrot from the chimpanzee, the camel from the eagle, the squirrel from the tiger, the elephant from the cat, the ant from the silkworm or the hedgehog from the echidna. (34)

The familiar distinctions between humans and nonhuman creatures no longer apply or, even more profoundly, never really did.

If one questions the old distinctions, one can also question the proposition that cats are the antithesis of human beings. The narrator questions this notion. Here the choice of the term "breed" is crucial (51), since it reverses the typical use of the expression, thus further breaking down the distinctions between human and animal. The speaker describes his bond with his cat companions as so strong that he sometimes feels as though he is actually part cat. He wholly embraces the idea and suggests that people should accept such a union between humans and other animals.[8] In imagining possibilities of animal merging, the author acknowledges that humans are part of the larger animal world, to the point of envisioning trans-species hybridity. As in other Burroughs texts, numerous chimera creatures are introduced and described in detail in *The Cat Inside*. The speaker also depicts human and cat hybridization. He warns. "You can't hide from your white cat because your white cat hides with you" (31). In the narrator's world, the cat is an animal familiar—a supernatural and psychic cosmic companion.

Another aspect to meeting Malamud's fifth condition is to embellish the space where humans and animals make contact (45). By exploring the imagined mythological history of cats, and by exaggerating the points of contact between himself and the animals, the narrator once again problematizes the cat by locating the story in the imaginary space between human and animal. The narrator adorns the text as a way to explore the place in which he connects with the animals. Such textual adornment also serves to improve the writing style of what might otherwise appear to be rather mundane episodic descriptions of ordinary cat lives. Such descriptions are not limited to *The Cat Inside*. In *The Western Lands*, too, the narrator embellishes the zones of contact between humans and cats and even makes a supernatural link:

> [T]he Deercat [is] half deer and half cat. The grass-eater and the flesh-eater are united in this spirit. It is a bright green color with the head and horns of a deer and the claws of a cat. It can climb trees and run with great speed. It can eat flesh or grass at will. (242)

Numerous instances in *The Cat Inside* also show the use of embellishment to enlarge the space where animals exist. The narrator describes possible previous cat species that are strange and aesthetically alluring. The scenes are imaginative, colorful, dramatic, and certainly embellished:

> A cat that is bright electric blue, giving off a faint smell of ozone . . . aquatic cats with webbed feet [. . .] delicate, thin, lightboned swamp cats with large, flat paws—they can skim over quicksand and mud with incredible speed . . . tiny lemur cats with huge eyes . . . a scarlet, orange and green cat with reptile skin, a long, sinewy neck and poison fangs. (11)

In this reflection, an attempt is made to show that the cat species is both ancient and diverse in origin. The speaker refers to cat traditions that go back eons. Furthermore, he describes intriguing, exaggerated feline defense systems. The reader is warned, "[T]wo steps and you fall on your face . . . skunk cats with a deadly spray that kills . . . cats with poison claws" (11).

Another account involves a dreamlike vision of a miniature reindeer. The narrator explains seeing "a little green reindeer about the size of the cat . . . this was a totem animal vision" (17). Such forays into detailed animal dreams are common in Burroughs' late writing and suggest the need for humans to reinvent their relationships with animals. Elizabeth Atwood Lawrence writes that as "humankind moves farther and farther from our roots in nature, we seem to cling more tenaciously to our ancient bond with other living beings" (47). Certainly, by putting words to paper, by recording deep concerns about the plight of animals and the environment, Burroughs uses literature to teach people about animals and their importance to continued human existence. Ultimately, the narrator of *The Cat Inside* believes in "the curative power of animals" (West 36). Such a belief explains much about the narrative's consideration of animal issues and, in the larger sense, the connections between humans and the natural world. While Anspaugh sees autobiographical self-pity in *The Cat Inside*, I propose that far more interesting are the ways in which the novella achieves, in part, the animalistic "ecocritical aesthetic" for which Malamud's model strives.

While Malamud's criteria are a useful way to study some of the ways in which a literary text engages with issues of animality, the approach admittedly has its limits. Malamud's model is certainly not the only way to examine human-nonhuman interactions in a literary text, and other ecocritics are working on the problems of human-animal representations in various media. This chapter should thus be considered just a part of the discussion. Malamud shows how one can systematically scan a work of literature for evidence of animal awareness. Moreover, this chapter illustrates how Malamud's method, which until now has been used only in the analysis of ecopoetry, can deal with other forms of literature such as *The Cat Inside*, which are considered outside the nature-writing genre. Furthermore, even if Malamud's model cannot fully deal with issues involving animal hybridity in Burroughs' work, this might be attributed to the originality of Burroughs' writing rather than any limitation of the model. Burroughs' writing about chimera creatures is one way to "queer" old distinctions, complicate long-standing human-animal assumptions, and generate fascinating new questions.[9]

Even more interesting is how researchers can try to deal with the lengthy and lurid descriptions of "nonhuman/interspecies sexual activity" that occur frequently throughout the writer's other works (Murphy "Random Insect Doom" 229). Such sexual events can be seen simply as an affirmation of interspecies affection and love, or they might be viewed as more heinous events and yet further examples of human domination and oppression over nonhuman animals. Such scenes once again blur the old distinctions of what it means to be human and what it means to be an animal. Using literature to challenge and decondition us from our inherent anthropomorphic tendencies is the best way William Burroughs' rich animal world contributes to ecocriticism. Through the imaginative force of literature, Burroughs problematizes the animal and makes us rethink our common assumptions about things we take for granted.

Broader Environmental Concerns

Other elements of *The Cat Inside* are also relevant to an ecocritical discussion of the text. In the novella, the narrator expresses a deepening concern about species depletion. He discusses the problems faced by various animal species, some of which are endangered. The speaker directly addresses what can be called "nature fatigue" at the hands of human beings and warns the reader:

> The magical medium is being bulldozed away. . . . The angels are leaving all the alcoves everywhere, the medium in which Unicorns, Bigfoot, Green Deer exist growing always thinner, like the rain forests and the creatures that live and breathe in them. (18)

Not only does the narrator deal with the fate of real animals under threat by humans, but he also considers the fate of fantastic creatures in a time of unparalleled environmental destruction. For Burroughs, it can be said that the death of the environment heralds the death of human imagination, and this shows the extent to which he is a pastoral writer.

William Burroughs exhibits empathy for animals and deep apprehension about the destruction of the rainforests throughout his later work (Lotringer 772). This concern certainly resonates in *The Cat Inside*, where the narrator reveals a deep anxiety about the fate of lemurs. Although the novella mostly deals with human relationships with felines, the speaker directly addresses the issue of endangered lemurs. In his mind, he hears the warning cries of "bat cats" and lemurs (*Cat Inside* 13). He appreciates the gravity of animal endangerment and considers the future of such animals in what he sees as a time of crisis: "There will be fewer and fewer exotic, beautiful animals. The Mexican hairless cat is already extinct" (13). The storyteller reflects mournfully on the ecological state of the planet. While animals naturally become extinct over time, there can be no doubt that exploding human populations have contributed much to extinction over the centuries. The narrator of *The Cat Inside* acknowledges the dangers that animals face in a world where the forces of conservation are nearly always trumped by the forces of the free market, a key association that becomes even stronger in *Ghost of Chance*.

The human pressures on the ecosystem are also acknowledged in the story, and it is suggested that further extinctions are likely to occur on a massive scale. In *The Cat Inside*, the speaker refers to a number of doomed animal species: "I've eulogized the fennec fox. The red fox, the silver fox, the bat-eared fox of Africa . . . all beautiful" (62). His mournful advocacy echoes the sentiment expressed by animal activist Elizabeth Costello, who points out that in the end, endangered and extinct animals will "have only their silence left with which to confront us" (qtd. in Huggan 711). In another section from *The Cat Inside*, the speaker describes the ability to sense the sadness of creatures doomed to extinction: "The cry I heard . . . was a sad, plaintive voice of lost spirits, the grief that comes from knowing you are the last of your kind" (89). The narrator is optimistic for a better balance in the future, but he is adamant that the window for action is temporary: "A hope. A chance. The chance lost" (89). Many of Burroughs' narratives warn that it is imperative to reconsider the values of modern human civilization at once if a better balance is to be found.

Lawrence Buell pictures ecocriticism as an ideological struggle in the "spirit of environmental praxis" (*Environmental Imagination* 430). According to this view, ecocritics ought to become advocates of the natural world. In *The Cat Inside*, the narrator accomplishes this by describing the place where animals thrive in nature as a "magical medium" (18). Now this enchantment remains only in a few isolated pockets, and even those areas are shrinking every year. In protesting against this state of affairs, the narrator speaks with an environmentalist voice. The author's personal concern with the state of contemporary environmental affairs is expressed in his other works as well. In *Last Words* (2000), Burroughs suggests that the late twentieth century was the beginning of the time "[w]hen whales and seals and elephants weep" (30). Such a disheartening reflection on the environment is also present in *The Cat Inside*. The narrator explains how his visions of ecological destruction filled him with dread and a need to share his deep concern (32). He goes on to propose that the current environmental situation is so dire that supernatural intervention is necessary (32). Such attention to looming disaster is common throughout Burroughs' work, from his earliest publications to his final apocalyptic narratives. This disaster was found in the early experimental forms the author used, which later morphed into a more thematic representation of disaster in his mature writing.

The narrative also contemplates, on a wider scale, the effects of a ruined world for the future of both animals and humans. When the speaker of *The Cat Inside* thinks about the environmental state of the planet and the mistreatment of animals, he feels a deep foreboding (82). It is at this point that the narratological difference between writer and narrator becomes ambiguous once again. Not only does the storyteller consider the destruction of the environment and numerous animal species in the text, but he also reflects on a time in the not too distant future, an ominous time, when humans will face extinction at their own hands. He describes the period long after humans will have disappeared as the time after books (45). The text captures the emptiness and solitude of the last human life. The speaker writes of "an aching, wrenching sadness. This is grief without witness. Last human crying. . . . The chance was there for an enchanted moment. The chance was lost" (89). The narrator goes on to imagine the struggle of the last human being: "Nuclear winter. . . . An old man in a shack . . . huddles under torn comforters, blankets full of holes, and dirty rugs with his cats" (81). A connection is made between human self-destructive habits and the ultimate failure of the human species. This collapse, in his view, will culminate in some profound disaster.

The Cat Inside refers to the possibility of a nuclear catastrophe in several places. The narrator even insists that "the cat is a messenger . . . to confront the horror of thermonuclear devastation" (32). In a vision, the speaker sees the land of the dead. It is not a distant or foreign place. As he sees it, this could be any one of a hundred cities in the modern United States. The speaker describes the chemical stench of an ecosystem in total collapse. He imagines the "reek of boiling sewage, coal gas and burning plastics . . . oil patches . . . roller coasters and Ferris wheels overgrown with rank weeds and vines" (6). In *The Cat Inside*, a postindustrial wasteland of stinking garbage and thick smoke is seen as a prophecy. This observation of industrial culture as careless, contaminated, and unhealthy echoes what Glotfelty and Fromm have described as "a postindustrial culture defined by its waste" (front matter).

In dealing with broader environmental concerns and issuing tormented warnings in apocalyptic mode, Burroughs' novella ultimately exceeds mere animal advocacy. The book on cats appeals to the cat inside all of us in that it is a powerful plea to conserve resources and protect the environment, on which humankind depends both for its long-term physical survival and for the larger workings of the environmental imagination. However, at the same time, *The Cat Inside* may not be the author's fullest contribution to the present ecocritical discussion. Animals remain a potent symbol of environmental concern in Burroughs' late work, certainly, and the author's gift for representing apocalyptic potentialities is especially haunting and fascinating to consider within the context of ecocriticism.

7.

A Blackness Too Pure: The Elegy of Ecophagy in *Ghost of Chance*

> The black monkey creature is in front of him, and he looks into its eyes, completely black. It is singing a black song, a harsh melody of blackness too pure to survive in time.
>
> —William Burroughs, *Ghost of Chance*

Ghost of Chance appeared very late in Burroughs' career, just six years before his death. The Library Fellows of the Whitney Museum of American Art first published the story as a special limited edition in 1991. This was thirty-two years after the initial publication of *Naked Lunch*. In 1995, High Risk Books released a hardcover edition of *Ghost of Chance*. After Burroughs died in 1997, a paperback edition was made available to the wider public. The book is too short to really be considered a novel. The question of genre is necessarily complex. But since the present chapter is interested in other questions, and because of the negative association of the term novelette, *Ghost of Chance* will be referred to as a novella here, as the text is intermediate in length and focuses on a series of events with a final twist (Baldick 233). Surprising is that so little critical attention has been given to *Ghost of Chance*.

Until now, no researchers have seriously examined Burroughs' writing strategies in the creation of *Ghost of Chance*. The present chapter thus seeks to provide the novella with much-needed scholarly recognition and at the same time tries to show how Burroughs' use of apocalyptic writing strategies contributes to a powerful ecological narrative. The novella never attained the notorious status of many of Burroughs' earlier novels. Literary reviewers who have examined the book usually comment on what appears to be the author's emergent environmental turn, a point with which I agree.[1] A brief review of the limited criticism and the green imagery of the narrative can assist in determining whether the thematic elements of the novella fit in the general context of current environmental writing. After an initial ecological incursion, the chapter probes deeper into the text to detect the rhetorical strategies the author employs. I suggest that in *Ghost of Chance*, Burroughs employs apocalyptic rhetoric (as envisioned by Stephen O'Leary) to communicate anxieties about the continued destruction of the environment.

Ghost of Chance is loosely based on an apparent eighteenth-century French and English attempt to create a new society in the wilderness of Madagascar. It is a similar situation to that presented in Burroughs' earlier *Cities of the Red Night*, a narrative about a health-care emergency as well as self-government and autonomous communities. In *Cities*, it is also pointed out that the modern condition is simply unsustainable. An unknown character maintains, "My point is very simple. The whole human position is no longer tenable" (25). In the same text, weapons of mass destruction are seen as the ultimate destroyer of the environment:

> I remember a dream of my childhood. I am in a beautiful garden. As I reach out to touch the flowers they wither under my hands. A nightmare feeling of foreboding and desolation comes over me as a great mushroom-shaped cloud darkens the earth. (*Cities* 332)

Cities is concerned with questions of sustainable governing systems as well as human existence in a post-apocalyptic setting. In this sense, *Ghost of Chance* exhibits thematic continuity from the first book of the *Cities* trilogy. *Ghost of Chance* is a fictional alternative historical account of the endeavor to construct a libertarian state by a group of reformed pirates. Just as Europeans sought refuge in the New World, Captain Mission seeks sanctuary for his comrades from the pressures of modernizing human society. The parallels with *Cities of the Red Night* are striking in this sense.

The emphasis in the settlement in *Ghost of Chance* is on self-government and release from social, sexual, and religious oppression. More important, the group attempts to build a more sustainable society. Captain Mission and his supporters do find a sense of balance between civilization and nature for a few brief pages, before things fall apart. Inhabitants of the community initially try to limit their footprint on the ecosystem. The animals and plants in Madagascar are described as particularly delicate and vulnerable, and people take care not to harvest too much of the vegetation. At the start of the narrative, as the initial scene is set, the natural beauty of Madagascar is highlighted. The narrative attempts to articulate the tranquillity, diversity, and majestic scale of the natural kingdom in such a unique place, as well as the fragile balance between people and the environment. The speaker describes "[g]iant ferns and palms, bulbous tamarind trees, vines and bushes" (*Ghost of Chance* 15). In this distant outpost, far from the emerging industrial cities of the Western world, life thrives, and Captain Mission reaches a personal epiphany, "the sudden, intolerable knowing that everything is alive" (3).

By taking the reader back to an imaginary place outside the context of the Industrial Revolution, the narrative provides yet another opportunity to fix things before they break. The manipulation of time, or the media tape of history, is a recurring theme throughout Burroughs' writing. His narratives often struggle with the problem of trying to unwind the clock to prevent present undesirable circumstances. However, the author's narratives never seem quite able to fully restore the real potential of humanity. This can be considered evidence of a degree of pessimism for the human condition, a view that is also revealed in the final book of the *Cities* trilogy, *The Western Lands*. At the same time, such pessimism works to garner sympathy from the reader, since the *Ghost of Chance* narrative ends with hope for humanity.

The notion of an island sanctuary for both humans and animals is intriguing in the context of an ecological evaluation of the narrative. By relating the uniqueness of the ecosystem of the island, the narrative engages in both "conservationist" and "ecological" discourse (Reed, "Toward" 148–49). The discussion of the unique ecosystem of the island can work to make the reader think about and appreciate the natural world. Moreover, the initial scenes in *Ghost of Chance* are "ecological" in their consideration of the specific bioregion of Madagascar (Reed). An additional concern is whether *Ghost of Chance* proposes the need for some kind of sanctuary for living creatures. Such a proposition is common in Burroughs' writing over the course of his career and reveals a deepening sense of environmental praxis. Some of the more activist ecocritical theorists believe the practice of eco-conscious writing involves the vigorous defense of environmentalist goals.[2] *Ghost of Chance* does this in part by suggesting there is a genuine need to reinvent human civilization to prevent accidental or intentional suicide. As shown at the beginning of the narrative, the newly arrived migrants are efficient and use local resources to keep a sense of balance between nature and modernity, in the elusive (and impossible) condition Leo Marx describes as the "middle landscape" (31). Useful technologies such as vaccines are made available to all in the remote island community. However, villagers take special care not to rely too much on technology, to prevent living "with less and less wild spark, the priceless ingredient" (*Ghost of Chance* 19). No large structures exist that one would typically expect to find in a developed society. Instead, the settlers construct dwellings from clay bricks that they produce. Others live in ancient cave dwellings of those who have come before. Some people even occupy hollow trees.

The protagonist of the narrative is a judicious man named Captain Mission, and the early pages are filled with an omniscient narrator's rich descriptions of Madagascar's unique ecosystem. Captain Mission is a former naval pirate turned benevolent leader of what would seem to be an upstart, ideologically inspired ecovillage. The speaker provides a wider shot of the distinctive ecosystem of Madagascar and attributes its biodiversity to its breaking off from Africa millions of years earlier. An attempt is made to contextualize the geology of the island before its separation from the African continent:

> When attached to Africa, Madagascar was the ultimate landmass, sticking out like a disorderly tumor cut by a rift of future contours. . . . The rift was a mile across in places, and in others narrowed to a few hundred feet. It was an area of explosive change and contrast, swept by violent electrical storms, incredibly fertile in places, entirely barren in others. (16)

The island is recognized as a distinctive ecosystem, and at the same time it functions as a window into the biological history of the entire planet. The narrator contemplates the moment when Madagascar split from the African continent:

> Separated by a curtain of fire. Like a vast festive ship launched with fireworks, the great red island moved majestically out to sea, leaving a gaping wound in the earth's side, bleeding lava, and spurting noxious gases. It has lain moored in enchanted calm for a hundred sixty million years. (16)

The island's remoteness, tranquility, and natural wonder initially attract Captain Mission and his small band of apparently rehabilitated pirates. The group had previously roamed the world, living outside of state legal systems in search of a new home where they could establish an improved civilization. In the early parts of the novella, the remoteness of Madagascar seems to suit their purposes well.

After the reader is introduced to the unique geography of the setting, Captain Mission begins to explore the wide area in an effort to learn about the animals that inhabit the island. He moves through the thick vegetation with the aid of a cutlass: "A moment of arrested motion, then a bush, a stone, a log moved, as a tribe of ring-tailed cat lemurs appeared, parading back and forth around each other, tails quivering above their heads" (3). The fragility of the numerous animal species, including lemurs, is also highlighted. The narrator directly addresses the issue of extinction in *Ghost of Chance*. This is done not only by describing the very real problem of vanishing lemur species but also by reflecting on other creatures that have become extinct because of human pressure. The speaker even imagines the end of entire animal species: "The last Tasmanian wolf limps through a blue twilight, one leg shattered by a hunter's bullet. As do the almosts, the might-have-beens, who had one chance in a billion and lost" (18). In the text, the suggestion is also made that people should reflect on animal extinctions to become more mindful of the human impact on the natural world. This will in turn force people to reassess their future on this planet. The narrator believes that such reassessment can be accomplished by forcing people to witness the pain and sadness of animal extinction. By reassessing the human position, it is argued, one can breathe new life into real animals in danger of extinction, while at the same time summoning the essence of the huge number of creatures that have already disappeared. The issue of animal extinction is explored at length in the course of the narrative, exhibiting what Reed calls evidence of "biocentric/deep ecological" discourse ("Toward" 148–49).

Other sections of the novella attempt to show the ways in which humans can breach the human-nonhuman dichotomy by bonding emotionally with nonhuman creatures. The speaker attempts to convey the affection and warmth of the animals located in Madagascar: "The creatures were trusting and gentle and open to human affection" (11). Captain Mission also takes pleasure in watching the shifting shapes glide through the treetops (4). The text describes in detail the island's great variety of different lemur species, all of which seem to recognize the protagonist as a sympathetic and benign human being. The speaker announces the presence of a strange small creature: "[H]e saw an animal that looked at first like a small deer. The animal came to his outstretched hand, and he saw that it had no horns" (5). The narrator further details the splendor of the unusual creature: "[Its] ears were large, flaring forward, the eyes limpid amber, in which the pupil floated like a glittering jewel, changing color with shifts of the light: obsidian, emerald, ruby, opal, amethyst, diamond" (5).

Over time, Captain Mission becomes personally invested in the lives of the animals on the island. His compassion and sympathy for the creatures grow as the narrative unfolds. Mission develops a particularly close relationship with a specific lemur he has named Ghost. The lemur becomes the constant animal companion to the central character and later functions as sacrificial victim and trigger for the apocalyptic events that follow. This section, while powerful, reflects a move toward biocentrism via human anthropocentrism. In other words, the emotional bonding between humans and lemurs demonstrates a point of slippage into what can be considered mainstream environmental attitudes, since it shows that animals can have utility to humans as a source of emotional warmth. *Ghost of Chance* thus shows a human need for animals.

The balance in the narrative starts to shift with Mission's alienation from the human community and begins to prefigure the approaching apocalyptic events. Captain Mission eventually decides to move away from the human settlement because of his feelings of estrangement as well as his strong desire to become more acquainted with the nonhuman primates that inhabit the island. His goal is to learn more about the lemurs that live deep in the forest. This is where his emotional connection to Ghost develops, and for a brief moment, a modern human mind links to an animal that has millions of years of solitary primate wisdom. His bond with the lemur is so intense that Captain Mission even expresses a sincere longing to be physically transformed into a lemur. He is basically fascinated with the ancient qualities of the creature and desires to link to their ancient knowledge:[3]

> The Lemur People are older than Homo Sap, much older. They date back one hundred sixty million years, to the time when Madagascar split off from the mainland of Africa. Their way of thinking and feeling is basically different from ours, not oriented toward time and sequence and causality. They find these concepts repugnant and difficult to understand. (15)

In another section of the narrative, Captain Mission observes the feeding practice of the lemurs and again reflects on the special temporal situation on the island that has allowed these creatures to develop over ages:

> Tiny mouse lemurs stole out of the roots and niches and holes in the ancient tree and frisked around the room, falling on insects with little squeals. . . . They had been doing this for millions of years. The twitching tail, the trembling ears mark the passage of centuries. (14)

The enduring nature of the animals that inhabit the unusual island is conveyed to the reader. Gradually, less emphasis is placed on the rich biodiversity of the setting, and the narrative zooms in on the beauty and simplicity of lemur lives. Then, slowly, the account begins to prefigure the coming doom, and the tone becomes more harried and ominous. These building tensions are chronicled in the form of fragmentary dream episodes, which retain a sense of the fragmentary aesthetic embedded in Burroughs' early experimental writing.

Captain Mission begins to have recurring nightmares foretelling the imminent human slaughter of the lemurs and other creatures on the island, as well as the dark aftermath such an occurrence will have for all plant and animal species. When relating a particular dream encounter between Captain Mission and a lemur deer, the narrator states, "Slowly the animal raised one paw and touched his [Mission's] face, stirring memories of the ancient betrayal. . . . For the deer ghost there was no time" (5). At another point in the text, the speaker depicts the defenselessness of a particular group of lemurs that reside in an open area:

> [H]e had located a troop of the larger lemurs. These lemurs were too big and heavy to be comfortable in arboreal conditions and lived mostly on the land, in an area of grass and scrub where the forest thinned out, a mile from his campsite. Ideal grazing land. (11)

It is difficult to imagine how such docile creatures, in the open and with no significant defenses, could protect themselves against human aggression. Because of the island's unique ecosystem, and above all the lack of natural predators, the grazing lemurs are presented as especially exposed. Mission understands this, and visions of impending slaughter grip him completely.

As foreshadowed in the opening pages, humans do eventually turn on the animals living on the island, in a sort of replication of the fall of man.

In the case of this particular narrative, the human fall occurs by breaking open what is called the Museum of Lost Species, an ancient Pandora's box containing the world's deadliest microbial and viral diseases. The act of opening the repository initially seems to infect the humans with a sort of primitive bloodlust, based to some extent on an extreme obsession with the profit motive. As a result, most of the people living on the island indiscriminately destroy all the creatures, with no regard for animal beauty or the consequences such actions have for human survival. The speaker takes great care in documenting the painful deaths of various animals and cites greed as a major cause of human-generated suffering. The narrator explains the fate of passenger pigeons: "Falling out of the trees like rain. You can sell all you can shoot. Good prices too" (38). He goes on to elucidate the wider scope of human carnage in this place: "The last deer lemur falls to a hunter's arrow. Passenger pigeons rain on the plates of fat bankers and politicians with their gold watch chains and gold fillings. The humans belch out the last passenger pigeon" (18). Donna Haraway argues a major cause for the current environmental crisis is the "hypercapitalist accumulation of wealth, the turning of the ecosystem into a planetary apparatus of production" (qtd. in Braidotti 529). The scenario played out in *Ghost of Chance* suggests the result of such an unsustainable system. The novella discusses the end result of capitalism and implies that it is time to develop a better system, showing once again how the author looked to the past for ideas to change the present.

Unsurprisingly, the lemurs on the island share a fate similar to that of the passenger pigeons, and even Mission's companion, Ghost, becomes a victim. The speaker describes the moment Mission finds his dying animal companion:

> Ghost is pinned under a heavy stone. He [Captain Mission] pries the stone aside and gathers the dying lemur in his arms, knowing that Ghost has been there waiting for him. The lemur puts a slow paw up to his face with a sad, weak cry. The paw drops. (*Ghost of Chance* 21)

This is the pivotal moment, the point in the narrative when human beings are inescapably doomed. The speaker laments the lost opportunity for the upstart community and the lemurs that inhabit the island: "Mission knows that a chance that occurs only once in a hundred sixty million years has been lost forever" (21). Just as *The Cat Inside* reveals what Malamud calls a sense of the "ecocritical aesthetic" (45), *Ghost of Chance* too issues a call to mobilize supporters on behalf of the environment and animals. This is particularly apparent near the end of the novella, when the narrator makes an impassioned plea for readers to donate money to animal causes, as well as continue to comprehend the depth and seriousness of anthropogenic environmental destruction. This direct action as a tactic at the same time reveals a contradiction between Burroughs' broader seeming pessimism and the practical step of seeking aid for charities, which shows a latent optimism. The speaker asks for donations to a university primate center that tries to prevent real lemur extinctions: "The Duke University Primate Center needs financial support from concerned individuals. Write to DUPC, Duke University, Durham, North Carolina 27706" (*Ghost of Chance* 58).[4] The center breeds endangered lemurs in captivity and thus preserves different lemur species in what can be called a semiwild state.

At the same time, the narrative links global environmental problems, the supposed war on drugs, and the movement to create an international governmental control apparatus. The storyteller warns, "To distract their charges [the voting public] from the problems of overpopulation, resource depletion, deforestation, pandemic pollution of water, land, and sky, they inaugurated a war against drugs" (29–30). This is another instance in which a narrative by Burroughs slips into accusatory form, which perhaps does not aid the environmental movement. Here again a good deal of paranoia is revealed, and this is rather deflating since the narrative otherwise legitimately dramatizes the environmental dangers facing humans and animals. However, paranoia is not always necessarily negative and certainly remains an essential component to apocalyptic thinking. Paranoia can also work to exploit common fears to generate conditions for social renewal. Nonetheless, the speaker retains some hope and optimism for the possibility of recovery for humanity and for the creatures that survive the onslaught of violence and disease as chronicled in the narrative. Thus the title of the text, *Ghost of* [*a*] *Chance*, is given substance.

Reviewers of *Ghost of Chance* discuss the environmental turn in the late writing of Burroughs. Jim Dwyer describes the text's ethical dimension as "powerful moral brew" (91). Isobel Shirlaw writes that the novella effectively communicates "the frightening reality that mankind is destroying a multitude of species" (23). Other reviewers argue that Burroughs has moved philosophically in the direction of politically engaged writing. Florian Vetsch asserts, "Mit *Ghost of Chance* ist Burroughs jedenfalls ein brandaktuelles, wundersam komponiertes Alterswerk gelungen, ein verwuchert glühendes Plädoyer für die Formenvielfalt der Natur" (Writing *Ghost of Chance*, Burroughs accomplished a red-hot topical, wondrously composed mature work, a raw passionate plea for nature's diversity of shapes) (45). While ideology saturated Burroughs' writing throughout his long and distinguished career, his late work seems particularly rooted in environmental engagement. Literary reviewers recognize this to some degree, although this book shows that such a turn was not late and began in Burroughs' early experimental writing. One value of this study is that it shows this environmental turn was not a sudden development.

Still other critics focus on the openness of the text and the changing language of Burroughs' writing. Will Self contends that *Ghost of Chance* is ultimately a narrative of hope written to salvage the humanity that Burroughs believes modern civilization has lost. Self thinks "it is clear early on that the generative force for the narrative (such as it is) comes from the author's own preoccupations with global environmental catastrophe" (para. 9). Dwyer even suggests that Burroughs' narrative is "one of his most accessible and finest books" (91). Others propose that his distinctive use of language is particularly suited to environmental writing. According to Guy Mannes-Abbott, "While Burroughs makes dreams uniquely productive, the language of ecology seems as if constructed for him" (48). Existing reviews consistently link narrator and writer, and there does appear to be the possibility of some overlap between author and speaker of *Ghost of Chance*. This once again shows the ways in which the author plays with conventional reader expectations. Burroughs cared about environmental issues, but we can never be totally sure whether he is the speaker, given his tendency to undermine conventions and defy expectations.

While many evaluations of *Ghost of Chance* are positive, some are noticeably less enthusiastic. However, it is noteworthy that even the most negative assessments acknowledge the politically driven ecoconsciousness manifest in the text. Joachim Kalka concedes the narrative's political engagement but also links the writer's ecological vision to pure paranoia (36). The most negative reviews of the novella employ the familiar ad hominem attacks against Burroughs that have taken place since his earliest publications. While Kalka seems to recognize the conservationist drive to Burroughs' late work, he also derides the author for apparently being artless. He decries, "Das senile

Murren und Räuspern, das Auskramen alter Zwangsvorstellungen, das giftige, das dumme, das banale Geschwätz, die hysterische Sektenpredigt. . . . Hier jedoch erscheint es nicht als Strategie, als literarische Form, sondern als kunstlose, bare Albernheit" (The senile grumbling and coughing, the digging-up of old obsessions, the poisonous, the stupid, the banal chatter, the hysterical evangelical sermon. . . . Here, however, it does not appear as a strategy, as a literary form, but as an artless, bare foolishness) (36). Although this particular reviewer pulls no punches in his criticisms of Burroughs, he does stumble across one thorny issue and cautions, "Der Autor haßt die Menschheit . . . die Menschheit zerstört den Regenwald" (The author hates humanity . . . mankind destroys the rainforest) (36). Kalka believes the author hates humanity, based on the narrative of *Ghost of Chance*. The reviewer here clearly sees the author as narrator, which is a troublesome issue and blurs the distinction between author and narrator completely. This is a key issue and once again shows that reading Burroughs is not a straightforward affair. One can never be sure whether the narrator is the writer or whether the narrative is autobiographical or is autobiographical fiction.

Other evaluations of the novella suggest that *Ghost of Chance* contains not a message of optimism, but rather one of deep introspection and ultimately of melancholy and alienation. There are points in the text at which the speaker veers close to misanthropy. Shirlaw holds that Burroughs attempts to comprehend the animal world and that the novella shows how "[i]n the wooden mirror man and ape are grotesquely merged into one" (23). She also believes that "*Ghost of Chance* is alienating. Burroughs seeks to retrieve the irrevocable, the futility of which leaves the novella with a sadness bordering on elegy" (23). Even though there is no agreement about the ultimate success of the narrative, those familiar with *Ghost of Chance* generally recognize a solemn turn in the author's late writing. Contrary to Kalka's claim that *Ghost of Chance* employs no real strategy or literary form, this chapter subsequently attempts to better identify the complex combination of rhetorical techniques the writer used to deliver such a somber message of environmental urgency.

Apocalyptic Environmental Writing

Over the decades, the writers of the Beat Generation used apocalyptic imagery as a way to emphasize the need for what they considered positive social change. While Ginsberg's "Howl" does not attempt to communicate the need for ecological restoration directly, the poem does use the representation of Moloch to dramatize the threats facing human beings in an increasingly industrial and urban age. Other Beat writers also attempted to convey the need for a fundamental rethinking of industrial values in the texts they produced. For example, Gregory Corso's influential poem "Bomb" in *The Happy Birthday of Death* admonishes readers to consider the profound hazards of global atomic war.

Burroughs too relied on apocalyptic writing as a strategy throughout his career and most certainly in his most provocative novels. Other texts by the author suggest that science can ignite war, plague, and famine, and this would seem to echo some of the foundational texts of ecocriticism. In *The Ticket That Exploded*, development of human tools of violence is acknowledged: "Modern man has advanced from the stone ax to nuclear weapons in ten thousand years" (50). In *Cities of the Red Night*, the narrative involves a health-care emergency. In the same text, weapons of mass destruction are seen as the ultimate destroyer of the environment: "I have blown a hole in time with a firecracker. Let others step through. Into what bigger and bigger firecrackers? Better weapons led to better and better weapons, until the earth is a grenade with the fuse burning" (287). Such an emphasis on great ecological calamities is also present in *The Four Horsemen of the Apocalypse*. The speaker warns the reader about the development and possible use of chemical germ agents on a massive scale against human populations. The disturbing and apocalyptic scenarios of manufactured pandemics that strip the earth of life are documented:

> We now have substances which could be introduced into the water supply, or even in gaseous form into the enemy air, that have no effect unless it is withdrawn. And then a battery of crippling symptoms would develop, reducing the enemy to complete impotence. There are certain metabolic illnesses in which the subject is unable to absorb certain essential vitamins and minerals no matter how much he ingests. In fact, it is not far-fetched to conceive of inducing metabolic changes that would make the absorption of any nutriments impossible: no matter how much he eats the person would die of starvation. . . . In other words, we have a permanent change. . . . The age-old dream of a selective pestilence is now within the reach of modern technology. (13)

In other narratives, a connection is made to conservative political policies as a source of ruin. In a short piece entitled "Quick Fix," the narrator laments that in his view, the political right of America will destroy civilization in an effort to finally rid the world of what remains of Native American resistance: "Conservative factions is [*sic*] set on nuclear war / as a solution to the Indian personality." In *The Western Lands*, doom takes the form of governmental agents that have not only the tools to wreck the world but also the unique and damning power to kill souls: "This awesome power to destroy souls forever is now vested in farsighted and responsible men in the State Department, the CIA, and the Pentagon" (9).

In much of Burroughs' work, apocalyptic writing serves, as Jeffrey Nealon puts it, to "demonstrate the role of inhuman systems, substances, economies, drives, and practices" (qtd. in Berman 946). Barbara Rose finds that apocalyptic strategies emphasize a need to move to an ideological clean slate in Burroughs' texts (97). This is true of *Ghost of Chance*, where, after the final judgment and near annihilation of human civilization, people return to their humble origins to begin anew.[5] Such a wiping of the slate works to echo not only apocalyptic thinking but also religious beliefs. Apocalyptic strategies can do far more than simply express disapproval of a given culture's unsustainable practices. Jonathan Schell maintains, "[M]aybe only by descending into this hell in imagination now [can we ever] hope to escape descending into it in reality" (5). Apocalyptic writing strategies can help reframe society in an attempt to endorse or impose forms of cultural renewal.

Apocalyptic writing was a natural development of late twentieth-century fears, and perhaps unsurprisingly, publications from the period often emphasize ecological ruin. Jimmie Killingsworth and Jacqueline Palmer believe apocalyptic rhetoric challenges the dominant view in industrialized cultures of science as a universal remedy for human problems, and they propose that apocalyptic writing works as "a kind of rhetorical and ideological counterweight to the scientific worldview" (24). The semipermanent state of looming catastrophe that developed as a product of mid-twentieth-century Cold War science, militarism, and resulting hysteria certainly fed into apocalyptic views in art. The devastating danger and effects of nuclear war and ecophagy—the entire collapse and consumption of an entire ecosystem—are quite similar. Both would result in inconceivable human suffering and social disorder. Greg Garrard admits, "The unimaginable threat of nuclear weapons, like a rocketing population, is an ample stimulus to apocalyptic thinking" (*Ecocriticism* 2004, 102). James Berger further argues that apocalyptic writing revolves around nuclear or ecological suicide, particularly in the modern context.[6] Peter von Ziegesar holds that "an apocalypse is only one of several alternative universes that appear plausible in the post–cold war era" and that a "collective image of a scorched planet" is a permanent and powerful image in the human mind (297). Apocalyptic writing remains an influential force in art and can work toward many of the same goals as environmental writing. *Ghost of Chance* suggests that by symbolically forcing humanity to begin anew, real humans can develop a deeper appreciation and awareness of their relationship with the environment.

At the same time, invoking the final doom can certainly promote fear. Apocalyptic writing can effectively dramatize the devastating effects that humans are having on the planet. The core Beat Generation writers were not particularly interested in mainstream forms of environmentalism, with the exception of perhaps Ginsberg, McClure, and Snyder. However, of major concern for Beat writers were the effects of modernization and the prospect of deep social rupture. While Beat Generation authors believed the primary goal of the movement was the attainment of higher consciousness in the manner of the transcendentalists, the invocation of doom was also an essential ingredient to their writing.

The invocation of apocalypse not only is common in the work of the Beat writers, including Burroughs, but also is a key ingredient in Western culture. After all, in the context of Judeo-Christian culture, a final day of reckoning is invariably tied to scripture. Apocalypse is understandably one of the most easily recognizable and historically significant rhetorical tools available to writers. All major religious texts in the Judeo-Christian tradition draw heavily on such imagery, so the notion of doom is frequently rooted in the cultural memory of Western cultures. Hardly surprising is that such a powerfully ingrained cultural concept would filter through the texts of William Burroughs. In *Ghost of Chance*, the narrative exploits the cultural memory of apocalypse in a number of ways to communicate what is essentially an environmental message.

Weaving Destruction

Stephen O'Leary identifies three characteristics of apocalyptic rhetoric: "time, evil, and authority" (20). Lawrence Buell suggests that O'Leary's model is particularly relevant to studies of contemporary literature (*Environmental Imagination* 306). Buell links O'Leary's three features of apocalyptic rhetoric directly to environmental writing in a short discussion of George Perkins Marsh's *Man and Nature; or, Physical Geography as Modified by Human Action* (1965). However, Buell does not offer any additional analyses or readings of any texts within this framework. Up until now, no serious study has coupled O'Leary's features of apocalyptic rhetoric with a thorough ecocritical examination of a literary text. Such an assessment of *Ghost of Chance* can be instructive in helping establish the connections between apocalyptic rhetoric and environmental writing in the context of William Burroughs.

A primary characteristic of apocalyptic writing involves what Buell identifies as the concept of "time as epochal" (*Environmental Imagination* 306). Although Burroughs does not rely on the notion of time nearly as much as he relies on apocalyptic imagery, *Ghost of Chance* does include a number of references to time as an enduring agent of ecological change. The speaker presents time as a colossal force that will ultimately work against humankind. In the initial passages of *Ghost of Chance*, the pace of life is slow and people do not feel the constant rush of modern life. Burroughs makes an effort to show that time operates differently on the island than in the rest of the world. Lengthy musings on geological change over hundreds of millions of years reinforce the notion of time as a persistent instrument of geological and biological change. In several places, the text even suggests that time is a purely human burden. The narrator reminds the reader, "Time is a human affliction; not a human invention but a prison. So what is the meaning of one hundred sixty million years without time? And what does time mean to foraging lemurs?" (*Ghost of Chance* 16–17). He also suggests that time is a restriction for "[t]he time-bound, the tethered, like the tethered goose that will forever resent its bondage" (13). At several points in the narrative, the reader is reminded that humans have an astonishingly short attention span and that time is always the victor.

Near the beginning of the novella, the reader is made aware of the brief balance between the people of the settlement and the animals that inhabit the surrounding area. A single act of violence disrupts that balance. At a certain point, Captain Mission senses imminent danger and an unidentifiable evil presence. He seeks out the source of his anxiety: "He knew at once that he was too late, that something was horribly wrong. No one would meet his eye. Then he saw Bradley Martin, standing over a dying lemur" (5). In an act of ignorance, Bradley had shot the lemur for stealing a mango. Mission covers the dead lemur with a tarp, determined to take the animal's dead body into the jungle the next morning with the intention of eulogizing the creature. Bradley's killing of the lemur is sad, needless, and mistaken, and it is the first real mark of wickedness in the narrative. His deed, though perhaps not evil, begins to tie humans to acts of malevolence. The setting of the narrative also gradually begins to shift from a lush and thriving landscape to one of blackness and indeterminate uneasiness and fear. This shift highlights the division between humans and the animals that inhabit the island.

Other incidents in the text also dramatize wicked human deeds. The speaker points out that the animals on the island are largely "untouched by the evil that flows in and fills Homo Sap as he picks up a weapon—now *he* has the advantage" (17; emphasis in original). The narrator later describes another brutal animal killing by a human being: "A lemur frisks up to a bestial settler, who with an ugly snarl slashes it with his machete and leaves it to bleed to death" (38). The narrative suggests the killing of this particular creature is unethical. Stephen O'Leary suggests that evil represents what he calls "[t]he prospect of cultural death," which he says is "most readily understood through the symbolism of evil, for the negation of communal ideals comes about either through the actions of a demonic Other or through the living community's own moral failure" (32). Such an explanation is particularly apt in considering the heinous acts committed against the animals and the environment in *Ghost of Chance*. The depraved acts the narrator describes suggest that the attempt to rebuild human society has failed and that the upstart state is morally ruined.

There are places in the text where the speaker actually calls humans evil: "'The evil and armed draw near.' Homo Sap with his weapons, his time, his insatiable greed, and ignorance so hideous it can never see its own face" (*Ghost of Chance* 17). Evil saturates the text. The narrator proposes that humans, or at least some humans, kill animals purely for pleasure:

> There were of course species that became extinct before man, but Homo Sap added a twist. He has killed to eat, but he has also killed for pleasure, to be sure. Moreover, he has killed for the sheer ugliness of the thing. The Thing inside him. The Ugly Spirit who found a worthy vessel in Homo Sap, the Ugly Animal. (48)

This shows a real contradiction in the text, as it suggests that humans are evil even though Captain Mission is portrayed as a moral man. The narrator also argues that simple bloodlust is another unique component to the human disposition and details acts of desperate cannibalism (53), one of the few ultimate taboos that exist across nearly all human cultures. In such a spoiled environment, Captain Mission senses doom all around him. He even sees signs of evil in his nightmares: "He dreamed that there were dead lemurs scattered through the settlement, and woke up at dawn with tears streaming down his face" (7).

At other points in the narrative, the storyteller makes use of the allegorical representation of evil in the form of the aforementioned Pandora's box of carnage and misery. The Museum of Lost Species functions as a potent symbol of evil after the fall of man in the text. Essentially, the museum is a depository of the earth's extinct animals, diseases, and viruses and contains actual living specimens, many of which were thought to have gone extinct. After the museum is unlocked by the evil acts of human beings, a number of prophesied plagues are unleashed on both humanity and the animals that inhabit the earth. The infections subsequently escape from the ancient storeroom to destroy nearly all life. The narrator details the initial cracking open of the repository: "THE ARCH HAS been blown to fragments . . . the torn roots like broken hands spilling stone and rubble" (21). The reader is told to "[r]emember the cave contains also all extinct diseases, the Seven Plagues of Egypt . . . all contained in the mold of man. Once the mold is shattered, all of the plagues are released" (22).

While Captain Mission is tricked into going to sea to defend the colony against an apparent planned attack by rogue pirates, the other people crack open the depository and begin the indiscriminate slaughter of the helpless creatures on the island. When Mission returns to the island, he senses the deception and proceeds to the settlement with haste: "He made his way past the carnage on the land and through the jungle to the ancient structure [and] saw that the settlement was now a burnt-out ruin, with nothing left but the smell of ashes and death" (21). The immoral inhabitants thus gain an advantage over Captain Mission, who is presented as the honorable man of the narrative. And in this case, the moral man is powerless when faced with unyielding evil.

The allegory of evil is represented through the human act of breaking open the museum, as well as the various diseases that later infect and destroy the living creatures of the island and then the world. For example, the Spider Fever acts in a way that is similar to the bubonic plague. The effects of the illness are described to the reader:

> [The disease] is transmitted by a small red spider. . . . The subject feels an intense burning itch at the site. The itch quickly spreads. . . . Glands in the armpits and groin swell and finally burst open. . . . The disease then spreads to the internal organs, resulting in massive hemorrhages and suffocation from swelling in the throat and lungs. Death usually occurs within twenty-four hours of infection. (44–45)

Ghost of Chance is filled with countless descriptions of shocking diseases. One unnamed and particularly fatal malady spreads from the African mainland to Europe and later to North America. The narrator explains that the victims' "veins filled not with blood but with a yellow-green ichor that gave off a horrible stench" (33). In addition, tens of millions of human beings quickly succumb to what is called the Christ Sickness. The bulk of such descriptions of disease emphasize the initial evil acts that open the Museum of Lost Species, though the sheer volume of such passages becomes repetitive. The recurrence of the explanations of how the various diseases affect humans also strengthens the apocalyptic drive to the narrative.

Disease is even described as being contained in the earth itself, and the text suggests that such diseases work to oppose human evil as a sort of neutralizing agent. This poses the even more crucial question of where evil originates. Burroughs' narratives at times reveal a misanthropic polemic, though the evil in *Ghost of Chance* affects not only humans; a number of illnesses appear that destroy animals as well:

> There are also animal diseases: anthrax, aftosa, malignant distempers, and other viral illnesses. Starting in Madagascar, the cattle of the world were virtually annihilated. Sheep fared little better, decimated by a variation of the visna virus. . . . Dogs and cats . . . died by the millions. (44)

Diseases also wait for the chosen moment to resurface. The narrator recounts, "Ravenous diseases lurk in dust and straw, mist and swamps and fossilized rock" (47). One particular sickness that emerges from the depository affects only human beings and is called the Roots, entwining and eventually consuming the victim. There are other examples of latent diseases waiting to act as a moral cleansing agent. Not altogether surprising is that the book relies heavily on apocalyptic rhetoric and includes abundant descriptions of, and ruminations on, pathogens. While the evil acts of humans unseal the Museum of Lost Species, the various illnesses also seem to counter human evil. Strangely, though the diseases detailed in the narrative are unleashed by evil acts, the numerous descriptions can work toward the aims of environmental activism, since infection here counters the environmentally destructive behavior exhibited by people in the novella.

The narrative depends on the repetitive metaphor of infection to force people to reexamine their own values. O'Leary points out that the recurring connection of disease and sin works "to overwhelm the reader's consciousness with an awareness of the extent of cosmic pollution" (129). This is particularly appropriate in the context of *Ghost of Chance*, since a good portion of the text involves frequent and lengthy musings on various infections after the fall of humanity. O'Leary also points out that in apocalyptic writing, the recurrent images of disease, pollution, and death guide readers to trepidation, and the scope of evil forces them to consider alternative paths to redemption (129). The narrator of *Ghost of Chance* is obsessed with the consuming qualities of infections and the potent imagery of evil that the disease metaphor provides. Disease often functions as a metaphor for social collapse in the works of Burroughs. Even the author's early books, such as *Naked Lunch*, depict the dangers of latent diseases just waiting to spring forth to ravage humanity. In *Ghost of Chance*, disease works as an image of evil after humans seal their destiny through their various wicked deeds. The anxiety the narrative causes and the link to moral collapse the allegory of disease provides may move the reader to reconsider his or her position. Thus the reader can essentially "turn back the clock" to make things right before they go bad, though it is important to note that reconsidering individual actions is not the same as the species making a complete turnaround. However, at the individual level, this is one of the ways in which the text works in the spirit of environmental praxis.

The final key to O'Leary's three characteristics of apocalyptic writing is what Buell calls a "sense of irrefutable authority" (*Environmental Imagination* 306). While the need to convey the urgency of environmental problems is important, to be truly persuasive a narrative must also be believable. Although a fictional alternative history of the effort to create a new society in Madagascar can be interesting to read, it does not by itself lend much credibility to the environmentalist argument. Burroughs might have been aware of this and tried to compensate by attempting to insert what he saw as authority into the text. What is unclear is whether the effort was conscious and if Burroughs actually believed more authority was needed to bolster the case for ecological restoration. In any case, the reader can never be certain whether the use of anecdotal evidence and additional footnotes was a real attempt to bring credibility to the narrative or simply a tactic to mock academic writing. This once again illustrates how Burroughs tries to undermine power. What is clear is that the writer attempts to insert authority into the text in a number of ways.

In *Ghost of Chance*, the final judgment of humanity draws heavily on Christian parable. The narrative exploits the potent symbolism of the Four Horsemen of the Apocalypse throughout. Burroughs relies on such deeply rooted cultural knowledge to reinforce the credibility of the book and therefore the narrator's sense of authority. Several instances in the text rely on Christian allegory. In one instance, the speaker explains the ability of Christ to heal only those with faith. He exploits the image of the savior/healer: "With the fingers of his right hand he touches the wound [of a believer], which knits and seals under his touch. Not even a scar remains" (23). An attempt is later made to use ancient beliefs to bring authority to the narrative, while at the same time disparaging Christian dogma. The image of the healer is exploited for the purposes of the narrative, but the speaker also criticizes the duplicity of healing only those with faith. The narrator points out that Christ does not heal suffering animals such as lemurs and cats, which can be considered to be sentient and therefore as deserving of therapeutic healing as human beings.

Subsequently in the novella, in a pseudoscholarly exposition, the speaker traces the origins of the current ecological crisis to the rise of Christianity over pantheism. In the narrative, the Four Horsemen of the Apocalypse travel through the urban and rural areas of the world. They seek to wipe out all peoples that have not already been killed by the revived primordial diseases. While the narrative draws on biblical motifs, at the same time it lampoons the notion of forgiveness inherent in Christian faith. The narrator warns:

> The teachings of Christ read like biological suicide. Shall the deer seek out the leopard and offer its throat to its fangs? Shall fish impale

> themselves on hooks and leap into nets? No animal species could survive by seeking out and loving its enemies. (26)

What follows is a suggestion that the ultimate mission of Jesus was to induce countless millions of human beings into accepting a colossal lie (28). Such an antagonistic position borders on religious intolerance.

Another means used to reinforce the larger argument is to introduce copious footnotes and sometimes-confusing references. A fragment of one such footnote should help provide an impression of the general content of the inserted references. The following note is incorporated into a larger footnote in a section of the novella detailing Mission's mourning of the lemur killed by the misguided character Bradley:

> Those who have heard voices from the nondominant brain hemisphere remark on the absolute authority of the voice. They know they are hearing the Truth. The fact that no evidence is adduced and that the voice may be talking utter nonsense is irrelevant. That is what Truth is. And Truth has nothing to do with facts. Those who manipulate Truth to their advantage, the people of the Big Lie, are careful to shun facts. In fact nothing is more deeply offensive to such people than the concept of fact. To adduce fact in your defense is to rule yourself out of court. (7–8)

It is debatable whether the attempt to imitate scholarly writing, through the use of copious footnotes and citations, is successful. Will Self insists:

> The lively and idiosyncratic footnotes to this text are hideously unpalatable—not so much politically as existentially uncorrect, receiving an ethical lecture from Burroughs being something in the manner of a category mistake. But seen as another experimental bloom on the neuronic culture it makes perfect sense. (12)

Given Burroughs' penchant for black comedy, he could have employed this tactic to lampoon academic writing and the presumed authority such writing provides a text. While the narrative seemingly tries to ridicule the scholarly apparatus, at the same time it relies on the academic convention of footnotes to strengthen the credibility of the narrative. By drawing on religious allegory and by using cross-references in an effort to imitate scholarly writing, the narrative strains to inject a sense of authority in *Ghost of Chance*.

The Brink of Human Imagination

Ghost of Chance explores the result of human overconsumption of natural resources and extreme violence against nonhuman creatures. The narrative puts forward that a milder form of human existence would be preferable to present systems of human social organization. One of Burroughs' most emotive works, *Ghost of Chance* is a mournful reflection on the current environmental crisis. Lawrence Buell cautions that "nature as an ideological screen becomes unfruitful if it is used to portray the green world as nothing more than projective fantasy or social allegory" (*Environmental Imagination* 36). But the use of apocalyptic writing strategies in *Ghost of Chance* contributes to an uncommon text in the context of Burroughs' wider writing, which should be considered in any serious discussion of late twentieth-century American environmental writing.

Afterword

To what extent can Burroughs' texts be evaluated within an ecocritical framework? The answer to this question is deeply complex and requires much consideration and discussion, as the previous chapters try to show. I believe this book steers the critical reception of Burroughs' writing into a new direction entirely. Since the 1970s, postmodern studies into Burroughs, the postmodern aspects of his books, his cut-up narrative strategy, and his views of subjectivity and the human body have been exhaustive. In the age of environmental upheaval, though, such views need updating. Burroughs is often seen as an example of twentieth-century postmodern writing, and therefore the contemporary environmental relevance of his work frequently goes unrecognized. The focus of this book is on texts that exist far outside of the nature-writing genre. It exposes not only the growth of ecocritical scholarship, which is very important, but also the fact that experimental writing demands much more attention in the context of increasing environmental awareness. If Burroughs' work is packed with environmental potential, then his position in the context of American letters must surely shift. A number of crucial themes that work through the chapters of this book, when considered as a whole, fundamentally change our views about one of the most important American literary outlaws.

As discussed in the second chapter, the Modern Toxic Human in *Naked Lunch* functions as an alternative form of modern human ecological identification, which has implications for how we think about ecology and its connection to disability studies. Elizabeth Wheeler, who has written on the links between ecocriticism and disability studies, asks an important question: "Whose body will be exemplary?" (554). Her question is laden with significance. The long-term effects of chemicals on the human body physically and psychically alter the human, creating what I call the Modern Toxic condition. While we might recognize at some level that altered forms of human consciousness, including that of the impaired, exists, the assumption that able-bodiedness is the default state of human consciousness is one-sided and demands rethinking. Serenella Iovino asserts:

> Issues such as madness or disability, for example, radically challenge and provoke the very idea of being human, regardless of social contexts, race, religion, or ethnicity. Madness and disability create in fact a "wilderness zone" inside the civilized or "tame" area of humanity-as-normality. By showing that the Other is not only nature (as the other-than-human), madness and disability introduce a radical fracture in the traditional taxonomy of the human subject. The human itself can become the Other, the human alien. (55)

Ultimately, the addict, as one example of the Modern Toxic Human, expresses the contemporary struggle in modern cultures between our bodies and the very trappings of our modernity. Important is that *Naked Lunch* ultimately functions as a form of ecological advocacy on behalf of the contaminated. This antitoxic advocacy intersects the present discussion of both environmental justice and disability studies. Matthew Cella believes a critical approach to literature that considers both diminished states of able-bodiedness and place can be very fruitful. He stresses that "[d]isability studies [. . .] recasts disability as something created by discriminatory social, political, and economic practices and environments" (578). If this is true, one might say that Burroughs accomplishes much more than simply relating the disorganized and painful thoughts of an addict seeking recovery. He effectively opens the door to acknowledging the many cultural and social factors that contribute to how we think about disability and the human body.

The third chapter of this book is important in showing that early cut-ups from *Minutes to Go* and *The Yage Letters* can be considered proto-ecological writing forms. The modification of Harriet Tarlo's methods for the analysis of found text practices in experimental ecopoetry shows that experimental aesthetic forms are also rich material for ecocritical analysis. The slight recalibration of Tarlo's method allows for the investigation of texts outside the nature-writing genre that use found text. This allows us to better understand aesthetic practices in which the source texts are uncertain or even impossible to ever precisely identify. Such a development suggests that other experimental forms that have thus far been neglected can benefit from serious ecocritical consideration. For example, what might future ecocritical studies suggest about altar poetry, assemblage, ASCII art, concrete poetry, glorious plagiarism, L=A=N=G=U=A=G=E poetry, or guerrilla semiotics? One can even imagine the possibility of extending ecocritical perspectives to texts written in runes. While many first-wave studies of American texts focus on such issues as thematic environmental activism, experimental methods such as Burroughs' early cut-ups represent a form of guerrilla writing that eschews both conventional ways of writing and, more important, conventional ways of reading. In other words, Burroughs accomplishes much more with his diminutive early cut-ups than only aesthetic experimentation, though that remains important. The method of creation itself forces us to reconsider the incredibly complex materiality of the text.

Chapter 4 builds on previous scholarship on the *Nova* series by showing the ways in which radically experimental aesthetic forms can be analyzed in an eco-Dada context. While the commodification and repurposing of source texts can be traced to some degree in Burroughs' early cut-up experiments, the *Nova* trilogy represents an exponential explosion of the careful embryonic cut-up experiments carried out at the Beat Hotel in Paris starting in 1959. The suggestion of the existence of a Dada ecopoetics forces us to recognize the continued relevance of Dada one hundred years on. More recent neo-Dada forms reveal trash aesthetics as rich compost for creative rebirth that goes beyond just human agency. Jed Rasula sees such recycling as one method to continually reimagine the creativity possibilities of aesthetics: "[R]epurposing and recycling [of existing material is] a strategic means of breaking the stranglehold of 'originality' and uniqueness that continues to offer misleading models of human agency" ("Bringing In the Trash" 22). This chapter is important since it shows how what we consider some of the most experimental writing forms can benefit from a perspective that not only recognizes and adulates the historical avant-garde but does so in the context of modern environmental concerns. What is most significant about this chapter is that a theoretical framework previously applied only to Dada-era works is extended to more recent work. Moreover, the theory is pushed even further through the examination of an experimental film in a transcultural context. So essentially, this chapter advances a working Dada ecopoetics of books, movies, and moving images.

Chapter 5 engages the pastoral as found in the *Red Night* trilogy. In the latter phase of Burroughs' career, he moved away from the radical fragmentary aesthetic strategies of the cut-up to more linear narratives and accessible content. The *Red Night* series is particularly interesting in the context of ecocriticism, since it deals with larger questions of sustainable forms of social organization. Leo Marx's conceptions of the sentimental and complex pastorals are particularly relevant in highlighting the many ways Burroughs' trilogy builds on the potential of America past. Burroughs' strategies effectively navigate the peculiar and often contradictory relationship between historical notions of American liberty and the search for a place open to reinvention of a better society.

In the end, the past cannot be restored, and the *Red Night* project, while broad in both scope and ambition, simply cannot create a retroactive utopia. Moreover, the series reveals not only the limits of language but also the capacity for literature to effect change in the real world. One can only wonder what the study of other Beat texts in the context of the pastoral can tell us about the deeply complex links between the pastoral and the environment, as well as the transnational connections that reveal human cultural responses to environmental pressures.

Chapter 6 discusses to what extent an "ecocritical aesthetic" (Malamud 45) can be found in *The Cat Inside*. This chapter builds on previous ones and extends an existing theoretical approach that previously has been limited to poetry. Furthermore, it suggests several specific new insights about Burroughs' writing. Important is that this chapter corrects the limited scholarship on *The Cat Inside* by revealing how the narrative engages animals in a number of ways, including documenting the real hurt animals experience, raising philosophical considerations of animal death rituals as human entertainment, and encouraging a positive view of the aesthetic beauty of many animal species. Also significant is that the speaker of the narrative repeatedly challenges anthropocentric thinking by continually recognizing nonhuman contexts. Another notable component to engagement with animals is the interpretation of colorful dream visions involving animals. In the end, this chapter accepts the infeasibility of ever fully being able to deal with Burroughs' frequent descriptions of animal hybridity, monsters, and cross-species sexual activity. But this limitation does not mean Randy

Malamud's model is unsuccessful in providing new insights into animals in literary texts—on the contrary. The book on cats is a powerful prayer for both the reduction of ecological damage and respect for nonhuman creatures. This is crucial in understanding Burroughs' wider work, as well as his late shift toward environmental praxis.

Chapter 7 considers features of apocalyptic rhetoric as a strategy to convey concerns about environmental destruction. Of all Burroughs' many publications, *Ghost of Chance* is perhaps the most open to a thematic environmental reading. The narrative goes beyond knee-jerk environmentalism by raising much deeper philosophical considerations, such as the human presence on the earth. Significant in the context of ecocriticism is that the narrative centers on an island sanctuary, which at first suggests that conventional forms of conservation may be an answer to the many ecological threats humans and animals face. However, the narrative quickly questions such a rosy and naïve environmental activism by delving deep into much more serious ecological concerns. Stephen O'Leary's concepts of "time, evil, and authority" (20) as rhetorical devices to drive home the urgency of apocalyptic concerns are discussed at length. The narrative addresses the issue of extinction directly and reflects on other creatures that have become extinct because of human pressures. This chapter suggests that apocalypticism is particularly suited to dramatizing the consequences of continued environmental destruction. If this is true, it is understandable that writers use apocalyptic writing to convey ecological concerns. Also important is that this chapter addresses a very late publication by the author that has been largely ignored in the critical discourse and offers a new view on the writer.

The wider implications of *The Green Ghost* are directly important to an entire philosophical and aesthetic movement that remains far too neglected in ecocritical circles, that of the Beat Generation. Yet to suggest that no one has considered the Beat writers in an ecocritical context would be incorrect.[1] Allen Ginsberg, Gary Snyder, Jack Kerouac, and Michael McClure have all, to varying degrees, been acknowledged for the nature awareness shown in their creative work. However, if the connection between the Beat Generation writers and environmentalism is so obvious, and the group's resistance to industrial culture so clear, then it is indeed surprising that so little ecocritical research has been carried out on the tremendous body of cultural texts by Beat Generation artists. I believe this book will legitimately help open up a wider ecocritical discussion of Beat artists. *The Green Ghost* suggests that William Burroughs is relevant to environmental discourse, but this study is just a beginning; the other core members of the group clearly need more attention. Many open questions remain unanswered about the Beat Generation, and those working in the environmental humanities might be able to complement the large body of research on the group.

Surprising is that ecocritics have so far largely overlooked Jack Kerouac. His *On the Road* reveals a longing for a more pastoral America and fascination with the other. The book describes moments of contact with a number of colorful characters, including Native Americans, African Americans, cowboys, farmers, and the rural folk Kerouac thought represented a pure form of human being. It would be interesting to consider Kerouac's character and world creation in the context of ecocriticism. The author wrote at length about longing for a mythical natural location of human spiritual abundance. Thomas Newhouse reminds us that *On the Road* "moves away from areas that are systematically stifling—from east to west, from civilized to primitive—and it is within more remote environments that primal connection and strangeness are seen as promising vehicles to psychic and spiritual recovery" (*Beat Generation*, 58). The book employs a rich use of vernacular language that is far less formal than the language found in Kerouac's earlier work, *The Town and the City*. The language of *On the Road* is accessible, even if at times unrefined, with a conversational and informal tone. Interestingly, punctuation remains a distinctive feature throughout. The abundant use of comma splices and ellipses accentuates the literal horizontal movement through the novel, thus giving the reader the impression of moving rapidly through the text:

> Out we jumped in the warm, mad night, hearing a wild tenorman bawling horn across the way, going "EE- YAH! EE- YAH! EE- YAH!" and hands clapping to the beat and folks yelling, "Go, go, go!" Dean was already racing across the street with his thumb in the air, yelling, "Blow, man, blow!" A bunch of colored men in Saturday-night suits were whooping it up in front. (197)

Ecocritics might study bop prosody as extemporaneous literary technique. In other words, how might bop prosody function to transport the reader from a civilized state to a more primitive condition, from the sophisticated urban to the rural past? Other questions also need answering.

Allen Ginsberg's work appears visibly open to ecological perspectives, but his most important poem remains a powerful aesthetic response to the arrival of atomic culture. Current interest in queer ecology might bring much insight to the writer. There are a number of ways that ecocritics might think about the intersection of queer ecology and poetry. For example, we might take another look at Ginsberg's poetry while considering complex "interrelations among sexualities, natures, gender identities, . . . bodies," and place (Mortimer-Sandilands, para. 34). The apocalyptic sense of much of Ginsberg's work might also be considered using theoretical models of the apocalypse. It would be exciting to consider the monstrous power of an industrially advanced but spiritually drained nation, as imaged in "Howl." Ginsberg declares, "Moloch! Solitude! Filth! Ugliness! Ashcans and unob- / tainable dollars! Children screaming under the / stairways!" (*Howl and Other Poems* 21). Ann Charters believes that the image of Moloch confronts the reader with the apocalyptic realities of an insane age:

> ["Howl"] describes and rejects the Moloch of society which confounds and suppresses individual experience and forces the individual to consider himself mad if he does not reject his own deepest senses . . . criticism of society is that "Society" is merciless. (217)

Such a dystopian vision of modern life swerves toward the apocalyptic. "Howl" remains perhaps the most important single literary creation in the Beat canon, and it would be very interesting for ecocritics to reread this poem, and others written by Ginsberg, using ecocritical models.

Scholarship on other writers affiliated with the Beat Generation would benefit from further reconsideration. For example, Gary Snyder holds a special place in Beat lore and is recognized for his powerful ecological vision,[2] though more ecocritical work on this writer might challenge stereotypical views of the Beats as hedonists who also happened to write. Whereas most other Beat Generation writers came from urban backgrounds, Snyder's rural experience and sense for nature informed his writing deeply. However, Greg Garrard pokes fun at what he apparently sees as unbalanced ecocritical interest on Snyder. While celebrating the arrival of a special issue of the *Journal of Ecocriticism* dealing with ecopoetics and the avant-garde, Garrard remarks, apparently in jest, that "not a single one" of the articles was written on Gary Snyder ("Ecocriticism" 64). If ecocriticism really matters, then more engagement with a wide spectrum of writers, including Gary Snyder, would seem necessary.

However, this is not the first time that Garrard has knocked Snyder and the Beat Generation. In his 2004 edition of *Ecocriticism*, Garrard repeats a common notion that a main component to Snyder's poetry involves a degree of "Beat Generation hedonism" (84). Such an observation is problematic for two reasons. First, it ignores the fascinating deep connections between the Beat Generation and the transcendentalist movement, which needs much further research if American ecocritics are to better understand the Beats' nature-intellectual origins. Second, Garrard's remark betrays his unfamiliarity with the wider work of the Beat Generation. Even more alarming is another observation Garrard made about Snyder in the 2004 edition, which he repeated in the book's second edition in 2012. He complains, "Much of Snyder's poetry is marred by earnest ecopieties and hectoring propaganda" (*Ecocriticism* 2004, 82; 2012, 90). But the fact that such a predominant ecocritic lacks a basic understanding of the Beat Generation is also an opportunity to correct a long-standing inaccuracy about the generative impulse of Beat works. In other words, ecocriticism really needs to reconsider the work of Gary Snyder and countless other Beats, men and women of many races who all shared an eternal longing, poetic voice, and beatific sense of humility that created a recipe for incredible art.

It is hoped that *The Green Ghost* is a modest contribution to scholarship on both William Burroughs and the ever-evolving environmental humanities, as it seeks to uncover the striking ecological aspects in the writing of this prolific author. The real novelty of this book is its ecological focus on a writer whose environmental significance is so counterintuitive. Burroughs is often connected to twentieth-century American thinking, but this book strives to show that his writing remains relevant. Ecocritics need to ultimately wrestle with American authors beyond those writing from within the nature-writing genre. If everything is really linked to everything else, then it would seem that no literary text, indeed no artistic production, really lies outside the range of ecocriticism. *The Green Ghost* shows that many ecocritical concepts are relevant to writers on the aesthetic fringe. At the same time, this study confirms that Burroughs remains an enigma.

NOTES

WORKS CITED

INDEX

NOTES

1. Introduction

1. See also Bucher; “Burroughs Anniversary”; Colloff; Grauerholz, “Queer Utopia,” “Late Work,” and “Epilogue.”
2. See Douglas; Harris, “Cold War Correspondents.”
3. See Beiles et al.; Burroughs and Gysin; Weinreich; Watters; Harris, “Response to John Watters”; Loranger; Miles, *Beat Hotel*; Tietchen; Houen; Campbell-Johnston; Collins; Harris, “Cutting Up the Corpse.”
4. See Ehrenstein; Ayers; Weir; Grauerholz, “Queer Utopia”; Harris, “Can You See a Virus?” and *William Burroughs*; Russell; Sondergard; Schneiderman and Walsh; Paton.
5. See Knickerbocker; Perrin; Whitaker; Weinstone; Mortenson; Brodie and Redfield; Johnston; Tsai; Doyle, *Darwin's Pharmacy.*
6. Jennie Skerl argues, “The Beats can be an accessible ‘port of entry’ to illuminating the culture wars and the theory wars, as well as understanding the problematics of canonicity, periodization, and the modernism/postmodernism debate” (“Introduction: Unspeakable Visions” 4). She refers to Murphy, who points out Burroughs' “ambiguous relationship to modernism and postmodernism” (qtd. in Skerl 5).
7. See also Nusbaum.
8. See also Suiter, who ponders the developing nature awareness of not just Kerouac but also Gary Snyder and Phillip Whalen as they worked as fire lookouts in the North Cascades in the 1950s.
9. See Ginsberg, “A Definition of the Beat Generation.” He discusses, among many other issues, the group's contribution to a wider “spread of ecological consciousness” and the “notion of a fresh planet” (52). Ginsberg expressly mentions the contributions of both Gary Snyder and Michael McClure to this shared vision.

10. The canonization of Thoreau also suggests the essential American is an individualist.
11. See also Slotkin.
12. Annie Oakley is a rare exception and remains one of the few nineteenth-century female sharpshooters to capture the American imagination.
13. See also Lyon; Bartlett; Blanchard; Arnold et al.; Aldred; Hobson; Suiter; Wapner; Cohen; Garrard, *Ecocriticism* (2004); Hart and Slovic; Morrell.

2. Burning Bones: The Limits of Material Culture and the Toxic Human in Naked Lunch

1. See also Algren; Mandel.
2. *Naked Lunch* also includes other moments of environmental reflection. In an early scene, the reader sees "swamps and garbage heaps, alligators crawling around in broken bottles and tin cans . . . islands of rubbish" (*Naked Lunch: Restored* 13). Within a larger section employing off-color humor and a parody of the grotesque human body, the reader is presented with a fleeting moment of antithetical splendor:

> Pictures of men and women, boys and girls, animals, fish, birds, the copulating rhythm of the universe flows through the room, a great blue tide of life. Vibrating, soundless hum of deep forest—sudden quiet of cities when the junky cops. A moment of stillness and wonder. (69)

3. Mutable Forms: The Proto-ecology of Early Cut-ups from Minutes to Go *and* The Yage Letters

1. See also Lydenberg, *Word Cultures* 48–49.
2. Gregory Corso dissents in *Minutes to Go*, deploring what he calls "uninspired machine-poetry" (63).
3. See Harris, "Response to John Watters."
4. See also Slovic.
5. Consider the Hindu deity Hanuman, a subject of contemporary veneration.
6. Burroughs thought the cut-up method helped uncover ideological subtexts. Contemporary English poet Frances Presley also believes writing practices that involve found text can help restructure "texts and extract their sub-texts" (qtd. in Tarlo, "Recycles" 116).
7. The history of the US Centers for Disease Control and its forerunners can be traced to at least 1921. The Communicable Disease Center was established in Atlanta in 1946 (National Archives and Records Administration).

8. For example, in a 2001 article published in the *Guardian*, Duncan Campbell reports that the Federal Bureau of Investigation discovered the US military was actively "producing anthrax in a powdered form suitable for use as a weapon," possibly in violation of numerous international treaties (paras. 1–2).
9. The "London conference" might refer to the Seventh International Congress of Cancer Research held in London in July 1958. More than two thousand scientists attended the meeting ("World Cancer Group to Meet in London").
10. Lydenberg posits that the "power of metonymy" Burroughs begins to employ in the mosaic of *Naked Lunch* reaches its most radical use in subsequent cut-ups (*Word Cultures* 33).
11. Medical conspiracy theories demonstrate both the fear of disease and suspicion of authorities. A 2005 study published in the *Journal of Acquired Immune Deficiency Syndromes* showed nearly 48 percent of blacks surveyed believed "HIV is a man-made virus" (Bogart and Thorburn 215). While such a view may seem exceptionally paranoid, there are historical reasons for such distrust. The Tuskegee syphilis study represents just one instance in which public health workers infected unknowing members of the public with a deadly disease. In the case of the Tuskegee study, hundreds of blacks were infected with syphilis. Many never received medical treatment and subsequently died.

4. A Land of Grass without Mirrors: The Dada Ecopoetics of Moving Images in William Burroughs' Nova Express *and Věra Chytilová's* Sedmikrásky *(*Daisies*)*

1. See also Gammel and Zelazo.
2. See also Baldwin's 2000 reading.
3. See also Gifford.
4. See also Eagle, Sélavy, LeVasseur, and Talbot for a wider discussion of Dada characteristics present in the film.
5. See also Frank; Parvulescu.
6. See also Sélavy.
7. For a detailed discussion of the complex statistical theory behind Cinemetrics, see http://www.cinemetrics.lv.

5. The Retroactive Pastoral: Comic Dark Ecology, Deep Green Resistance, and the Romantic Plastic Indian in the Red Night *Trilogy*

1. The Anthropocene is a neologism suggesting humans have created a new geological age that began during the Industrial Revolution, when humans began adding significant amounts of carbon to the earth's atmosphere. The essential

meaning of the Anthropocene is that humans have fundamentally changed the geology of the planet, and evidence of human activities will be found in both the fossil and geological records for ages to come.

2. Thomas Malthus suggests something very similar to warn humans about the rising problem of overpopulation, detailing what he sees as the inevitable consequences of an ever increasing human population:

> The power of population is so superior to the power of the earth to produce subsistence for man, that premature death must in some shape or other visit the human race. The vices of mankind are active and able ministers of depopulation. They are the precursors in the great army of destruction, and often finish the dreadful work themselves. But should they fail in this war of extermination, sickly seasons, epidemics, pestilence, and plague advance in terrific array, and sweep off their thousands and tens of thousands. Should success be still incomplete, gigantic inevitable famine stalks in the rear, and with one mighty blow levels the population with the food of the world. (72–73)

   See also Ehrlich.

3. See McBay, Keith, and Jensen. Essentially, their provocative manifesto argues that a violent worldwide eco-insurgency is the only plausible method to prevent a global slide to ecocide.
4. Consider the role of firearms to members of contemporary American survivalist militias, who, even as they reject many aspects of industrial society, rely on firearms as an artifact of their independence from federal government.
5. I am aware of the real problems of using such a politically loaded term such as Indian in the context of this project. However, given the historical context of the Beat Generation and the period in which they wrote, the use of the term Indian here is at times more accurate than politically correct substitutes such as Native American or Amerindian in use in the contemporary vernacular.
6. Cormac McCarthy's powerful novel *The Road* (2006) is a recent illustration of apocalypse gripping the contemporary human imagination.

6. Terrestrial Creatures: Problematizing the Animal and Empathizing the Human in The Cat Inside

1. The violent cat episode appears in the 1977 version of *Junky.*
2. When Burroughs was a child, he struggled with his sexual orientation. He was deemed a juvenile delinquent and was consequently sent to summer camp in New Mexico, no doubt to help toughen him up and teach him how to become a real man (*Word Virus* front matter). While this study is not primarily interested in biographical questions, I acknowledge that there are often points of intersection.

3. The speaker attempts to show a link between the geographic area where the camp is located and more profound tragedies, pointing out that Los Alamos was also where the atomic bomb was developed (*Cat Inside* 14).
4. The issue of blood-sport rituals remains a focus of animal studies scholarship, as well as an important issue to ecocritical scholars. For an intriguing article that touches on blood-sport hobbies involving animals, see McHugh.
5. Anspaugh argues that this is not really about cats, but instead about the death of Joan Vollmer (141).
6. This point was emphasized at the July 2012 "Minding Animals Conference" held at Utrecht University in the Netherlands. It was generally agreed among participants that there is a seeming conflict between allowing humans to be human, and thus to project a naturally anthropomorphized view of animals, and the desire to appreciate the essential differences between human and nonhuman creatures. Attendees decided that this issue might not be as problematic as one might first assume, since one can conceivably both recognize human sensibilities and at the same time consider the concerns of other nonhuman creatures. Such a view would echo the utilitarian view of Bentham.
7. Throughout his career, Burroughs' narratives rely on emotion and melancholy. *Queer* is more concerned with homosexual human relationships than environmental concerns, but the episodes described are also quite sentimental and emotional. See also Grauerholz, "Queer Utopia." These publications emphasize a significant issue, since sentimentality and emotion do not fit Burroughs' commonly understood maverick image.
8. In a special study circle on animal studies and queer communities at the 2012 "Minding Animals Conference," participants discussed how queer perspectives force us to question our most basic assumptions in a world that remains largely anthropocentric, Eurocentric, and heteronormative. See also Mortimer-Sandilands. Greg Garrard offers a dissenting view and sees queer ecology as a problem since, according to him, "the queer commitment to transgression seems to outweigh concerns about conservation" ("How Queer Is Green?" 77).
9. Una Chaudhuri's keynote lecture at the Species, Space, and the Imagination of the Global Conference of the Association for the Study of Literature and Environment (ASLE) at Indiana University in June 2011 discussed the ways in which queer perspectives can teach ecocriticism to further "breech boundaries and confuse states."

7. A Blackness Too Pure: The Elegy of Ecophagy in Ghost of Chance

1. See the reviews by Dwyer; Mannes-Abbott; Self; Seed; Shirlaw; Guilbert; Kalka; and Vetsch.
2. See Adams; Adamson; Estok; and Gaard.

3. Lemurs are frequently personified throughout the narrative, thus projecting an anthropomorphic view.
4. Affiliated with Duke University, the research institute is now called the Duke Lemur Center. Its mission statement is to advance "science, scholarship, and biological conservation through interdisciplinary research on lemurs. By engaging scientists, students and the public in new discoveries and global awareness, the Center promotes a deeper appreciation of biodiversity and an understanding of the power of scientific discovery" (Duke Lemur Center).
5. Richard Dellamora commonly sees in the writing of Burroughs "the possibility of a cosmic conflict between the powers of the Angel of Darkness and of the Sons of Light" (147).
6. Berger contends that we are waiting for an ending that might have already happened and that we essentially live in a post-apocalyptic world (38). Brian Massumi also maintains, "What society looks toward is no longer a return to the promised land but a general disaster that is already upon us, woven into the fabric of day-to-day life" (11).

Afterword

1. For example, I co-organized, along with Franca Bellarsi, a panel called "Fractured Ecopoetics from the Beat Underground" at the June 2015 Association for the Study of Literature and Environment Conference at the University of Idaho. Papers discussed both canonical and fringe Beat writers in an environmental context. Consider also the "Ecocritical Readings of the Beats" panels at the Fourth European Beat Studies Network Conference at the Université Libre de Bruxelles, Belgium, in October 2015.
2. See Tovey; Suiter; Rod Phillips; and Lyon.

WORKS CITED

Adams, Carol. *The Sexual Politics of Meat: A Feminist-Vegetarian Critical Theory.* New York: Continuum, 1990. Print.

Adamson, Joni. "Environmental Justice and Third Wave Ecocritical Approaches to Literature and Film." *Ecozon@* 1.1 (2010): 11–16. Web. 13 Dec. 2015.

Adamson, Joni, and Scott Slovic. "The Shoulders We Stand On: An Introduction to Ethnicity and Ecocriticism." *MELUS* 34.2 (2009): 5–20. Print.

Aldred, Lisa. "Plastic Shamans and Astroturf Sun Dances: New Age Commercialization of Native American Spirituality." *American Indian Quarterly* 24.3 (2000): 329–52. Print.

Algren, Nelson. *The Man with the Golden Arm.* Garden City: Doubleday, 1949. Print.

Allister, Mark Christopher, ed. *Eco-Man: New Perspectives on Masculinity and Nature.* Charlottesville: UP of Virginia, 2004. Print.

Anspaugh, Kelly. "The Black Cat Inside: Burroughs as Unredeemed Confessant." *Genre* 34.1 (2001): 125–48. Print.

Arnold, Jean, et al. "Forum on Literatures of the Environment." *PMLA* 114.5 (1999): 1089–1104. Print.

Ayers, David. "The Long Last Goodbye: Control and Resistance in the Work of William Burroughs." *Journal of American Studies* 27.2 (1993): 223–37. Print.

Baldick, Chris. *The Oxford Dictionary of Literary Terms.* Oxford: Oxford UP, 2004. Print.

Baldwin, Douglas G. "'Word Begets Image and Image Is Virus': Undermining Language and Film in the Works of William S. Burroughs." *College Literature* 27.1 (2000): 63–83. Print.

Bartlett, Lee. *The Beats: Essays in Criticism.* Jefferson: McFarland, 1981. Print.

Bass, Patricia. "On Daisies: Does It Matter." *East European Film Bulletin.* 1 Apr. 2013. Web. 25 Aug. 2014.

Baumbach, Jonathan. "Joe the Dead Seeks Immortality." *New York Times.* New York Times, 3 Jan. 1988. Web. 12 Feb. 2011.

Beiles, Sinclair, et al. *Minutes to Go.* San Francisco: City Lights Books, 1960. Print.

Bekoff, Marc. *The Emotional Lives of Animals: A Leading Scientist Explores Animal Joy, Sorrow, and Empathy—and Why They Matter.* Novato: New World Library, 2007. Print.

Bellarsi, Franca. "'Alien Hieroglyphs of Eternity' and 'Cold Pastorals': Allen Ginsberg's 'Siesta in Xbalba' and John Keats's Great Odes." *Comparative American Studies* 11.3 (2013): 243–364. Print.

———. "The Challenges of Nature and Ecology." *Comparative American Studies* 7.2 (2009): 71–84. Print.

———. "Eleven Windows into Post-Pastoral Exploration." *Journal of Ecocriticism* 1.2 (2009): 1–10. Print.

———. "William S. Burroughs's Art: The Search for a Language that Counters Power." *Voices of Power: Cooperation and Conflict in English Language and Literatures.* Ed. Marc Maufort and Jean Pierre van Noppen. Liege: Belgian Association of Anglicists in Higher Education, 1997. 45–56. Print.

Benjamin, Walter. "The Work of Art in the Age of Mechanical Reproduction." *Art in Modern Culture: An Anthology of Critical Texts.* Ed. Francis Frascina and Jonathan Harris. London: Icon Editions, 1992. 297–307. Print.

Bentham, Jeremy. *An Introduction to the Principles of Morals and Legislation.* Oxford: Clarendon Press, 1907. Print.

Berger, James. *After the End: Representations of Post-Apocalypse.* Minneapolis: U of Minnesota P, 1999. Print.

Berman, Jessica. "No Consensus on Ethics: New Work in Ethical Criticism." *Modern Fiction Studies* 46.4 (2000): 941–48. Print.

Blanchard, Bob. "A Voice in the Wilderness." *The Progressive* 59.11 (1995): 28–32. Print.

Bogart, Laura M., and Sheryl Thorburn. "Are HIV/AIDS Conspiracy Beliefs a Barrier to HIV Prevention among African Americans?" *Journal of Acquired Immune Deficiency Syndromes* 38.2 (2005): 213–18. Print.

Bolton, Micheal Sean. *Mosaic of Juxtaposition: William S. Burroughs' Narrative Revolution.* Postmodern Studies 51. Amsterdam: Editions Rodopi, 2014. Print.

Braidotti, Rosi. "Animals, Anomalies, and Inorganic Others." *PMLA* 124.2 (2009): 526–32. Print.

Brodie, Janet Farrell, and Marc Redfield. *High Anxieties: Cultural Studies in Addiction.* Berkeley: U of California P, 2002. Print.

Broyard, Anatole. "Books of the Times." Rev. of *The Place of Dead Roads,* by William S. Burroughs. *New York Times.* New York Times, 15 Feb. 1984. Web. 12 Feb. 2011.

Bryan, Jeff. “William Burroughs and His Faith in X.” *West Virginia U Philological Papers* 32 (1986): 79–89. Print.

Bucher, François. “Burroughs’s Tree.” *Review of Contemporary Fiction* 4.1 (1984): 131–34. Print.

Buell, Lawrence. *The Environmental Imagination: Thoreau, Nature Writing, and the Formation of American Culture*. Cambridge: Belknap-Harvard UP, 1995. Print.

———. *The Future of Environmental Criticism: Environmental Crisis and Literary Imagination*. Blackwell Manifestos. Malden: Blackwell, 2005. Print.

———. “Toxic Discourse.” *Critical Inquiry* 24.3 (1998): 639–65. Print.

Burroughs, William S. *The Adding Machine: Collected Essays*. London: Calder, 1985. Print.

———. *Blade Runner*. Berkeley: Blue Wind, 1979. Print.

———. *The Burroughs File*. San Francisco: City Lights, 1984. Print.

———. *The Cat Inside*. New York: Viking, 1992. Print.

———. *Cities of the Red Night*. New York: Holt, 1981. Print.

———. *Exterminator!* 1973. Harmondsworth: Penguin, 1979. Print.

———. *The Four Horsemen of the Apocalypse*. 3rd ed. Bonn: Hartmut Bremer, 1996. Print.

———. *Ghost of Chance*. 1991. London: Serpent’s Tail, 1995. Print.

———. *Junkie: Confessions of an Unredeemed Drug Addict*. New York: Ace Books, 1953. Print.

———. *Junky*. New York: Penguin, 1977. Print.

———. *Junky: The Definitive Text of “Junk.”* 50th Anniversary ed. Ed. Oliver Harris. New York: Penguin, 2003. Print.

———. *Last Words: The Final Journals of William S. Burroughs*. Ed. James Grauerholz. New York: Grove, 2000. Print.

———. *My Education: A Book of Dreams*. New York: Viking, 1995. Print.

———. *The Naked Lunch*. Paris: Olympia, 1959. Print.

———. *Naked Lunch: The Restored Text*. Ed. James Grauerholz and Barry Miles. New York: Grove, 2001. Print.

———. *Nova Express*. New York: Grove, 1964. Print.

———. *The Place of Dead Roads*. New York: Holt, 1983. Print.

———. *Queer*. New York: Viking, 1985. Print.

. “Quick Fix.” N.p., 1 Aug. 1999. Web. 9 Sept. 2010. <http://www.textfiles.com/stories/quickfix>.

———. *The Soft Machine*. Paris: Olympia, 1961. Print.

———. *The Ticket That Exploded*. Paris: Olympia, 1962. Print.

———. “The War Universe.” Interviews with Raymond Foye. *Grand Street* 37 (1991): 92–108. Print.

———. *The Western Lands*. New York: Viking Penguin, 1987. Print.

———. *The Wild Boys: A Book of the Dead*. New York: Grove, 1971. Print.

———. *Word Virus: The William S. Burroughs Reader.* Ed. James Grauerholz and Ira Silverberg. New York: Grove, 1998. Print.

Burroughs, William S., and Allen Ginsberg. *The Yage Letters.* San Francisco: City Lights, 1963. Print.

———. *The Yage Letters: Redux.* Ed. Oliver Harris. San Francisco: City Lights, 2006. Print.

Burroughs, William S., and James Grauerholz. *Interzone.* New York: Viking, 1989. Print.

Burroughs, William S., and Brion Gysin. *The Third Mind.* New York: Viking, 1978. Print.

Burroughs, William S., and Oliver Harris. *The Letters of William S. Burroughs: 1945–1959.* New York: Viking, 1993. Print.

———. *Nova Express: The Restored Text.* New York: Grove/Atlantic, 2014. Print.

———. *The Soft Machine: The Restored Text.* New York: Grove/Atlantic, 2014. Print.

———. *The Ticket That Exploded: The Restored Text.* New York: Grove/Atlantic, 2014. Print.

"Burroughs Anniversary." Narr. Linda Wertheimer. *All Things Considered.* National Public Radio. Rec. 3 Aug. 1998. Radio.

Campbell, Duncan. "FBI Uncovers US Military Production of Anthrax Powder." *Guardian.* Guardian News and Media Limited, 14 Dec. 2001. Web. 8 Nov. 2012.

Campbell-Johnston, Rachel. "In the Sights of a Revolutionary 'Gun Nut.'" *Times* 24 Aug. 2005: W1. Print.

Caulfield, Emily. "Self-Realization and Destructive Feminism in New Wave Cinema." *Film Matters* 1.4 (2011): 27–31. Print.

Cella, Matthew J. C. "The Ecosomatic Paradigm in Literature: Merging Disability Studies and Ecocriticism." *Interdisciplinary Studies in Literature and Environment* 20.3 (2013): 574–96. Print.

Charters, Ann. *Beat Down to Your Soul: What Was the Beat Generation? Poems, Essays, Memoirs, Notes, Protests, Attacks, and Apologies—from the Beat Explosion That Rocked the World.* New York: Penguin, 2001. Print.

Chaudhuri, Una. "Theatre of Species." ASLE Conference: Species, Space, and the Imagination of the Global. Indiana University, Bloomington. 22 June 2011. Keynote Address.

Chytilová, Věra. *Sedmikrásky.* Video recording. Second Run, London, 2009.

Clouzot, Claire. Rev. of *Daisies*, dir. Věra Chytilová. *Film Quarterly* 21.3 (1968): 35–37. Print.

Cohen, Michael P. "Blues in the Green: Ecocriticism under Critique." *Environmental History* 9.1 (2004): 9–36. Print.

Collins, Karen. "Dead Channel Surfing: The Commonalities between Cyberpunk Literature and Industrial Music." *Popular Music* 24.2 (2005): 165–78. Print.

Colloff, Pamela. "Looking for Bill." *Texas Monthly* 1 Oct. 2001: 38, 40, 44, 46, 48. Print.

Corso, Gregory. *Gregory Corso: Writings from Unmuzzled Ox Magazine*. New York: Unmuzzled Ox Foundation, 1981. Print.

———. *The Happy Birthday of Death*. New York: New Directions, 1960. Print.

Coughran, Chris. "Sub-Versions of Pastoral: Nature, Satire and the Subject of Ecology." *Journal of Ecocriticism* 2.2 (2010): 14–29.

Dellamora, Richard. *Postmodern Apocalypse: Theory and Cultural Practice at the End*. New Cultural Studies. Philadelphia: U of Pennsylvania P, 1995. Print.

Der, Donovan. Rev. of *Daisies* (1966), dir. Věra Chytilová. *Bonjour Tristesse Foreign Indie & Cult Cinema*. 2012. Web. 12 Aug. 2014.

Derrida, Jacques, and Marie-Louise Mallet. *The Animal That Therefore I Am*. New York: Fordham UP, 2008. Print.

Dolan, Frederick M. "The Poetics of Postmodern Subversion: The Politics of Writing in William S. Burroughs's *The Western Lands*." *Contemporary Literature* 32.4 (1991): 534–51. Print.

Douglas, Ann. "Periodizing the American Century: Modernism, Postmodernism, and Postcolonialism in the Cold War Context." *Modernism/modernity* 5.3 (1998): 71–98. Print.

Doyle, Richard M. *Darwin's Pharmacy: Sex, Plants, and the Evolution of the Noösphere*. Seattle: U of Washington P, 2011. Print.

———. "Naked Life: William S. Burroughs, Bioscientist." *Naked Lunch @ 50: Anniversary Essays*. Ed. Oliver Harris and Ian MacFadyen. Carbondale: Southern Illinois UP, 2009. 238–49. Print.

Duke Lemur Center. "Mission Statement." *Duke Lemur Center*. Duke Lemur Center, n.d. Web. 2 Aug. 2012.

Dwyer, Jim. "Book Reviews: Fiction." *Library Journal* 15 Sept. 1995: 91. Print.

Eagle, Herbert. "Dada and Structuralism in Chytilova's *Daisies*." *Cross Currents* 10 (1991): 223–34. Print.

Ehrenstein, David. "Burroughs on Tear Gas, Queers, *Naked Lunch* and the Ginsberg Affair." *The Advocate* 581 (1991): 38–43. Print.

Ehrlich, Paul R. *The Population Bomb*. New York: Sierra Club–Ballantine, 1968. Print.

Ellis, R. J. "'They . . . Took Their Time over the Coming': The Postwar British/Beat, 1957–1965." *The Transnational Beat Generation*. Ed. Nancy M. Grace and Jennie Skerl. New York: Palgrave Macmillan, 2012. 145–64. Print.

Estok, Simon. "Theory from the Fringes: Animals, Ecocriticism, Shakespeare." *Mosaic* 40 (2007): 61–78. Print.

Forcer, Stephen. "The Importance of Talking Nonsense: Tzara, Ideology, and Dada in the 21st Century." *Dada and Its Legacies*. Ed. Elza Adamowicz and Eric Robertson. Amsterdam: Rodopi, 2013. 263–74. Print.

Frank, Alison. "Formal Innovation and Feminist Freedom." *Cineaction* 81 (2010): 46–49. Print.

Freeman, Mary Eleanor Wilkins. *Understudies*. New York: Harper, 1901. Print.

Gaard, Greta. "Hiking without a Map: Reflections on Teaching Ecofeminist Literary Criticism." *Interdisciplinary Studies in Literature and Environment* 3.1 (1996): 155–82. Print.

Gammel, Irene, and John Wrighton. "'Arabesque Grotesque': Toward a Theory of Dada Ecopoetics." *Interdisciplinary Studies in Literature and Environment* 20.4 (2013): 1–22. Print.

Gammel Irene, and Suzanne Zelazo. "'Harpsichords Metallic Howl—': The Baroness Elsa von Freytag-Loringhoven's Sound Poetry." *Modernism/modernity* 18.2 (2011): 255–71. *Project MUSE*. Web. 27 June 2014.

Garrard, Greg. "Ecocriticism." *The Year's Work in Critical and Cultural Theory* 19.1 (2011): 46–82. Print.

———. *Ecocriticism: The New Critical Idiom*. New York: Routledge, 2004. Print.

———. *Ecocriticism: The New Critical Idiom*. 2nd ed. New York: Routledge, 2012. Print.

———. "How Queer Is Green?" *Configurations* 18.1 (2011): 73–96. Print.

Geertz, Armin W. *The Invention of Prophecy: Continuity and Meaning in Hopi Indian Religion*. Berkeley: U of California P, 1994. Print.

Gifford, Terry. *Pastoral: The New Critical Idiom*. New York: Routledge, 1999. Print.

Ginsberg, Allen. "A Definition of the Beat Generation." *Friction* 1.2–3 (1982): 50–52. Print.

———. *Howl and Other Poems*. San Francisco: City Lights, 1956. Print.

Gioia, Dana. "Can Poetry Matter?" *Atlantic Monthly* 267.5 (1991): 94–106. Print.

Glotfelty, Cheryll, and Harold Fromm, eds. *The Ecocriticism Reader: Landmarks in Literary Ecology*. Athens: U of Georgia P, 1996. Print.

Grace, Nancy M., and Jennie Skerl, eds. *The Transnational Beat Generation*. New York: Palgrave Macmillan, 2012. Print.

Grattan, Sean. "A Grenade with the Fuse Lit: William S. Burroughs and Retroactive Utopias in *Cities of the Red Night*." *Utopian Studies* 21.1 (2010): 118–38. Print.

Grauerholz, James. "Epilogue." *Word Virus: The William Burroughs Reader*. Ed. James Grauerholz and Ira Silverberg. London: Flamingo, 1998. 526–30. Print.

———. "Late Work." *Word Virus: The William Burroughs Reader*. Ed. James Grauerholz and Ira Silverberg. London: Flamingo, 1998. 501–3. Print.

———. "Queer Utopia." *Word Virus: The William Burroughs Reader*. Ed. James Grauerholz and Ira Silverberg. London: Flamingo, 1998. 357–62. Print.

Guilbert, Georges-Claude. Rev. of *Ghost of Chance*, by William S. Burroughs. *Cercles: Revue Pluridisciplinaire du Monde Anglophone* 2003: n. pag. Web. 19 June 2008. <http://www.cercles.com/review/r10/burroughs.html>.

Gysin, Brion. "Cut-ups: A Project for Disastrous Success." *Evergreen Review* 32 (1964): 56–61. Print.

Hames, Peter. *Daisies (Sedmikrásky)* Insert. Second Run DVD, 1 June 2009. Print.

Harris, Oliver. "'Burroughs Is a Poet Too, Really': The Poetics of *Minutes to Go.*" *Edinburgh Review.* Ed. Ronald Turnbull. Edinburgh: Edinburgh Centre for the History of Ideas in Scotland, 2004. 24–36. Print.

———. "Can You See a Virus? The Queer Cold War of William Burroughs." *Journal of American Studies* 33.2 (1999): 243–66. Print.

———. "Cold War Correspondents: Ginsberg, Kerouac, Cassady, and the Political Economy of Beat Letters." *Twentieth Century Literature* 46.2 (2000): 171–92. Print.

———. "Cutting Up the Corpse." *The Exquisite Corpse: Chance and Collaboration in Surrealism's Parlor Game.* Ed. Kanta Kochhar-Lindgren, Davis Schneiderman, and Tom Denlinger. Lincoln: U of Nebraska P, 2009. 82–103. Print.

———. "From Dr. Mabuse to Doc Benway: The Myths and Manuscripts of *Naked Lunch.*" *Naked Lunch* @ 50. Columbia University, New York. 9 Oct. 2009. Keynote Address.

———. "Not Burroughs' Final Fix: Materializing *The Yage Letters.*" *Postmodern Culture: An Electronic Journal of Interdisciplinary Criticism* 16.2 (2006): n. pag. Web. 3 Jan. 2012.

———. "A Response to John Watters, 'The Control Machine: Myth in *The Soft Machine* of W. S. Burroughs.'" *Connotations* 6.3 (1996): 337–53. Print.

———. *William Burroughs and the Secret of Fascination.* Carbondale: Southern Illinois UP, 2003. Print.

Harris, Oliver, and Ian MacFadyen, eds. *Naked Lunch @ 50: Anniversary Essays.* Carbondale: Southern Illinois UP, 2009. Print.

Hart, George, and Scott Slovic. *Literature and the Environment.* Exploring Social Issues through Literature. Westport, CT.: Greenwood Press, 2004. Print.

Heise, Ursula K. "The Android and the Animal." *PMLA* 124.2 (2009): 503–10. Print.

———. *Sense of Place and Sense of Planet: The Environmental Imagination of the Global.* Oxford: Oxford UP, 2008. Print.

Hobson, Geary. "The Rise of the White Shaman: Twenty-Five Years Later." *Studies in American Indian Literatures* 14.2 (2002): 1–11. Print.

Honeywell, SJ [Steve]. "Tune In, Turn On, Czech Out." *1001Plus.* Blogger, 19 May 2013. Web. 11 June 2014.

Houen, Alex. "Novel Spaces and Taking Place(s) in the Wake of September 11." *Studies in the Novel* 36 (2004): 419–37. Print.

Hoving, Isabel. "On the Absence of Nature: Writing on Nature and Ecocriticism in the Netherlands." *Ecozon@* 1.1 (2010): 167–73. Web. 15 Dec. 2015.

Huggan, Graham. "'Greening' Postcolonialism: Ecocritical Perspectives." *Modern Fiction Studies* 50.3 (2004): 701–33. Print.

Iovino, Serenella. "The Human Alien. Otherness, Humanism, and the Future of Ecocriticism." *Ecozon@* 1.1 (2010): 53–61. Web. 14 Dec. 2015.

Jameson, Fredric, and Paik Nak-chung. "South Korea as Social Space: Fredric Jameson interviewed by Paik Nak-chung, Seoul, 28 October 1989." *Global/Local: Cultural Production and the Transnational Imaginary.* Ed. Rob Wilson and Wimal Dissanayake. Durham: Duke UP, 1996. 348–71. Print.

Johnson, Kelli Lyon. "Writing Deeper Maps: Mapmaking, Local Indigenous Knowledges, and Literary Nationalism in Native Women's Writing." *Studies in American Indian Literatures* 19.4 (2007): 103–21. Print.

Johnston, Allan. "Consumption, Addiction, Vision, Energy: Political Economies and Utopian Visions in the Writings of the Beat Generation." *College Literature* 32.2 (2005): 103–26. Print.

Jones, Clydefro. Rev. of *Daisies (Sedmikrásky)* DVD. *The Digital Fix.* Poisonous Monkey Ltd., 10 June 2009 Web. 11 June 2014.

Kalka, Joachim. "Die Ganze Affenbande Brüllt: Überflüssige Hassesmüh: Ein Spätwerk von William Burroughs." *Frankfurter Allgemeine Zeitung* 4 Dec. 2003: 36. Print.

Kerouac, Jack. *On the Road.* New York: Penguin, 1991. Print.

Kerridge, Richard. "Climate Change and Contemporary Modernist Poetry." *Poetry and Public Language.* Ed. Tony Lopez and Anthony Caleshu. Exeter: Shearsman Books, 2007. 131–48. Print.

Kerridge, Richard, and Neil Sammells. *Writing the Environment: Ecocriticism and Literature.* New York: Zed, 1998. Print.

Killingsworth, M. Jimmie, and Jacqueline S. Palmer. "Millennial Ecology: The Apocalyptic Narrative from Silent Spring to Global Warming." *Green Culture: Environmental Rhetoric in Contemporary America.* Ed. Carl G. Herndl and Stuart C. Brown. Madison: U of Wisconsin P, 1996. 21–45. Print.

Knickerbocker, Conrad. "Interview: William S. Burroughs, *The Art of Fiction No. 36.*" *Paris Review* 35 (1965): 13–49. Print.

Knight, Peter. "Everything Is Connected: Underworld's Secret History of Paranoia." *Modern Fiction Studies* 45.3 (1999): 811–36. Print.

Lane, Véronique. "The Parting of Burroughs and Kerouac: The French Backstory to the First Beat Novel, from Rimbaud to Poetic Realist Cinema." *Comparative American Studies* 11.3 (2013): 265–79. Print.

Langeteig, Kendra. "*Horror Autotoxicus* in the *Red Night* Trilogy: Ironic Fruits of Burroughs's Terminal Vision." *Configurations* 5.1 (1997): 135–69. Print.

Lardas, John. *The Bop Apocalypse: The Religious Visions of Kerouac, Ginsberg, and Burroughs.* Urbana: U of Illinois P, 2001. Print.

Lawrence, Elizabeth Atwood. "Seeing in Nature What Is Ours: Poetry and the Human-Animal Bond." *Journal of American Culture* 17.4 (1994): 47–53. Print.

LeVasseur, Andrea. Rev. of *Daisies* (1967), dir. Věra Chytilová. *Allmovie.* All Media Network, LLC. Web. 13 Aug 2014. <http://www.allmovie.com/movie/daisies-v88453>.

Lim, Bliss Cua. "Dolls in Fragments: *Daisies* as Feminist Allegory." *Camera Obscura: A Journal of Feminism, Culture, and Media Studies* 16.47 (2001): 37–77. Print.

Lopez, Tony. "Restricted Zone (Slight Return)." *Jacket* 4 (1998): n. pag. Web. 25 Aug 2014.

Loranger, Carol. "'This Book Spill Off the Page in All Directions': What Is the Text of *Naked Lunch?*" *Postmodern Culture* 10.1 (1999): n. pag. *Project MUSE*. Web. 13 May 2011. <http://muse.jhu.edu/journals/postmodern_culture/v010/10.1loranger.html>.

Lotringer, Sylvère, ed. *Burroughs Live: The Collected Interviews of William S. Burroughs, 1960–1997.* Los Angeles: Semiotext(e), 2001. Print.

Lundblad, Michael. "From Animal to Animality Studies." *PMLA* 124.2 (2009): 496–502.

Lydenberg, Robin. "El Hombre Invisible." *William S. Burroughs at the Front: Critical Reception, 1959–1989.* Ed. Jennie Skerl and Robin Lydenberg. Carbondale: Southern Illinois UP, 1991. 233–37. Print.

———. *Word Cultures: Radical Theory and Practice in William S. Burroughs' Fiction.* Urbana: U of Illinois P, 1987. Print.

Lydenberg, Robin, and Jennie Skerl. "Points of Intersection: An Overview of William S. Burroughs and His Critics." *William S. Burroughs at the Front: Critical Reception, 1959–1989.* Ed. Jennie Skerl and Robin Lydenberg. Carbondale: Southern Illinois UP, 1991. 3–15. Print.

Lyon, Thomas J. "The Ecological Vision of Gary Snyder." *Kansas Quarterly* 2.2 (1970): 117–24. Print.

Mackay, Polina, and Chad Weidner. "The Beat Generation and Europe." *Comparative American Studies* 11.3 (2013): 221–26. Print.

Madan, Sangeeta, and Pankaj Madan. *Global Encyclopaedia of Environmental Science, Technology and Management.* New Delhi: Global Vision Publishing House, 2009. Print.

Malamud, Randy. *Poetic Animals and Animal Souls.* New York: Palgrave, 2003. Print.

Malthus, Thomas. *An Essay on the Principle of Population; or, A View of Its Past and Present Effect on Human Happiness.* London: T. Bensley, 1806. Print.

Mandel, George. *Flee the Angry Strangers.* Berkeley: Thunder's Mouth Press, 2004. Print.

Mannes-Abbott, Guy. "The Beats Go On." *New Statesman & Society* 8.376 (1995): 47–48. *Academic Search Elite.* Web. 19 June 2008.

Martino, John R. "'Remember I Was the Movies': The Cinematic Prose of William S. Burroughs." Diss. West Virginia U, 2000. Print.

Marx, Leo. *The Machine in the Garden: Technology and the Pastoral Ideal in America.* New York: Oxford UP, 2000. Print.

Massumi, Brian. *The Politics of Everyday Fear.* Minneapolis: U of Minnesota P, 1993. Print.

McBay, Aric, Lierre Keith, and Derrick Jensen. *Deep Green Resistance: Strategy to Save the Planet.* New York: Seven Stories Press, 2011. Print.

McCarthy, Cormac. *The Road.* New York: Alfred A. Knopf, 2006. Print.

McClure, Michael. "Peyote Poem." *The Portable Beat Reader.* Ed. Ann Charters. New York: Penguin, 1992. 265–73. Print.

McHugh, Susan. "Literary Animal Agents." *PMLA* 124.2 (2009): 487–95. Print.

Meisel, Paul. "Gunslinger in a Time Warp." *New York Times* 19 Feb. 1984: 8–9. Print.

Miles, Barry. *The Beat Hotel: Ginsberg, Burroughs, and Corso in Paris, 1958–1963.* New York: Grove Press, 2000. Print.

———. *William Burroughs: El Hombre Invisible: A Portrait.* New York: Hyperion, 1993. Print.

Morgan, Ted. *Literary Outlaw: The Life and Times of William S. Burroughs.* London: Pimlico, 1988. Print.

Morrell, John J. "Summers in the Skagit: Gary Snyder, Jack Kerouac, and the Language of the Lookout." The Beat Generation Symposium. Beat Studies Association. Columbia College, Chicago, 11 Oct. 2008. Conference Paper.

Morris, R. B. "I Am No Doctor." *Naked Lunch @ 50: Anniversary Essays.* Ed. Oliver Harris and Ian MacFadyen. Carbondale: Southern Illinois UP, 2009. 107–13. Print.

Mortenson, Erik. "Xmas Junkies: Debasement and Redemption in the Work of William S. Burroughs and David Foster Wallace." *Dionysos: The Literature and Addiction TriQuarterly* 9 (1999): 37–46. Print.

Mortimer-Sandilands, Catriona. "Unnatural Passions? Towards a Queer Ecology." *Invisible Culture* 9 (2005): n. pag. Web. 5 Mar. 2012.

Morton, Timothy. "Dark Ecology." Ecology without Nature. Fifteenth Annual Activating the Medium Festival, San Francisco. 2012. Talk.

———. *The Ecological Thought.* Cambridge: Harvard UP, 2010. Print.

———. *Ecology without Nature: Rethinking Environmental Aesthetics.* Cambridge: Harvard UP, 2007. Print.

Mottram, Eric. *William Burroughs: The Algebra of Need.* 1971. Critical Appraisals. London: Boyars, 1977. Print.

Murphy, Timothy S. "Intersection Points: Teaching William Burroughs's *Naked Lunch.*" *College Literature* 27.1 (2000): 84–102. Print.

———. "Random Insect Doom: The Pulp Science Fiction of *Naked Lunch.*" *Naked Lunch @ 50: Anniversary Essays.* Ed. Oliver Harris and Ian MacFadyen. Carbondale: Southern Illinois UP, 2009. 223–32. Print.

———. *Wising Up the Marks: The Amodern William Burroughs.* Berkeley: U of California P, 1997. Print.

Nagel, Thomas. "What Is It Like to Be a Bat?" *Philosophical Review* 83.4 (1974): 435–50. Print.

Nasrin, Mohsen. "*Daisies (Sedmikrasky)* (1966, Czechoslovakia) Directed by: Vera Chytilova." *Cinemetrics*. 18 July 2013. Web. 25 Aug. 2014.

National Archives and Records Administration. *Records of the Centers for Disease Control and Prevention*. U.S. National Archives and Records Administration. 19 Oct. 2011. Web. 8 Apr. 2012.

Newhouse, Thomas. *The Beat Generation and the Popular Novel in the United States, 1945–1970*. Jefferson: McFarland, 2000. Print.

———. "Subcultures: The Underground in American Fiction, 1945–1970." Diss. State U of New York at Buffalo, 1993. Print.

Nusbaum, Arthur S. "Kerouac Meets Burroughs *On the Road*." *Third Mind Books*. Third Mind Books, 10 Feb. 2010. Web. 4 Oct. 2012.

Odier, Daniel. *The Job: Interviews with William S. Burroughs*. New York: Penguin, 1989. Print.

Oerlemans, Onno Dag. "'The Meanest Thing That Feels': Anthropomorphizing Animals in Romanticism." *Mosaic* 27.1 (1994): 1–32. Print.

O'Leary, Stephen D. *Arguing the Apocalypse: A Theory of Millennial Rhetoric*. New York: Oxford UP, 1994. Print.

Osman, Jena. "Is Poetry the News? The Poethics of the Found Text." *Jacket* 32 (2007): n. pag. Web. 31 May 2013.

Pacini, Peggy. "Satori in Paris: Deconstructing the French Connection or the Legend's Satori." *Comparative American Studies* 11.3 (2013): 290–99. Print.

Parvulescu, Anca. "'So We Will Go Bad': Cheekiness, Laughter, Film." *Camera Obscura: A Journal of Feminism, Culture, and Media Studies* 21.62 (2006): 144–67. Print.

Passaro, Vince. "The Forgotten Killer." *Harper's Magazine* 296.1775 (1998): 71–76. *Academic Search Premier*. Web. 13 Oct. 2015.

Paton, Fiona. "Monstrous Rhetoric: *Naked Lunch*, National Insecurity, and the Gothic Fifties." *Texas Studies in Literature and Language* 52.1 (2010): 48–69. *Project MUSE*. Web. 7 Nov. 2012. <http://muse.jhu.edu/journals/texas_studies_in_literature_and_language/v052/52.1.paton.html>.

Perrin, Stephen. "Hero and Heroin: Opiate Use and Sexual Identity." *Dionysos: The Literature and Addiction TriQuarterly* 4.3 (1993): 25–29. Print.

Phillips, Dana. "Ecocriticism, Literary Theory, and the Truth of Ecology." *New Literary History* 30.3 (1999): 577–602. Print.

———. *The Truth of Ecology: Nature, Culture, and Literature in America*. Oxford: Oxford UP, 2003. Print.

Phillips, Rod. *"Forest Beatniks" and "Urban Thoreaus": Gary Snyder, Jack Kerouac, Lew Welch, and Michael McClure*. New York: P. Lang, 2000. Print.

Punday, Daniel. "Narrative after Deconstruction: Structure and the Negative Poetics of William Burroughs's *Cities of the Red Night*." *Style* 29.1 (1995): 36–57. *Academic Search Elite*. Web. 19 Jan. 2011.

Rasula, Jed. "Bringing In the Trash: The Cultural Ecology of Dada." *Green Letters* 18.1 (2014): 22–35. Print.

———. *This Compost: Ecological Imperatives in American Poetry*. Athens: U of Georgia P, 2002. Print.

Reed, T. V. "Toward an Environmental Justice Ecocriticism." Ed. Joni Adamson, Mei Evans, and Rachel Stein. *The Environmental Justice Reader: Politics, Poetics, & Pedagogy*. Tucson: U of Arizona P, 2002. 145–62. Print.

———. "Toxic Colonialism, Environmental Justice, and Native Resistance in Silko's Almanac of the Dead." *MELUS: The Journal of the Society for the Study of the Multi-Ethnic Literature of the United States* 34.2 (2009): 25–42. Print.

Robinson, Edward S. *Shift Linguals: Cut-up Narratives from William S. Burroughs to the Present*. Amsterdam: Rodopi, 2011. Print.

Rose, Barbara. "Cultural Paranoia, Conspiracy Plots, and the American Ideology: William Burroughs's *Cities of the Red Night*." *Canadian Review of American Studies* 29.2 (1999): 89–111. Print.

Russell, Jamie. *Queer Burroughs*. New York: Palgrave, 2001. Print.

Schell, Jonathan. *The Fate of the Earth*. New York: Knopf, 1982. Print.

Schneiderman, Davis, and Philip Walsh. *Retaking the Universe: William S. Burroughs in the Age of Globalization*. London: Pluto Press, 2004. Print.

Seed, David. "William S. Burroughs *Ghost of Chance*." *Review of Contemporary Fiction* 16.1 (1996): 150. Print.

Sélavy, Virginie. Rev. of *Daisies*, dir. Věra Chytilová. *Electric Sheep*. 4 June 2009. Web. 25 Aug. 2014.

Self, Will "Strange Cats." 1995. *Guardian*. Guardian News and Media Limited, 14 Aug. 1995. Web. 10 Oct. 2003.

Shelley, Percy Bysshe. "Lines." *Posthumous Poems*. London: John and Henry L. Hunt, 1824. Print.

Shirlaw, Isobel. Rev. of *Ghost of Chance*, by William S. Burroughs. *Times Literary Supplement* 15 Nov. 2002: 22–23. Print.

Skerl, Jennie. "The Book, the Movie, the Legend: *Naked Lunch* at 50." *Naked Lunch @ 50: Anniversary Essays*. Ed. Oliver Harris and Ian MacFadyen. Carbondale: Southern Illinois UP, 2009. 167–76. Print.

———. "Introduction: The Twenty-Fifth Anniversary Edition of *Naked Lunch*." *Naked Lunch*. By William S. Burroughs. New York City: Grove, 1984. v–xix. Print.

———. "Introduction: The Unspeakable Visions of the Individual in Academe." *College Literature* 27.1 (2000): 1–7. Print.

———. *William S. Burroughs*. Twayne's United States Authors Series. Boston: Twayne, 1985. Print.

Slotkin, Richard. *Regeneration through Violence: The Mythology of the American Frontier, 1600–1860*. Middletown: Wesleyan UP, 1973. Print.

Slovic, Scott. *Nature and the Environment*. Critical Insights. Ipswich: Salem Press, 2013. Print.

Sondergard, Sid. "Unable to Queer the Deal: William S. Burroughs's Negotiations with 'Eugene Allerton.'" *Critique* 44.2 (2003): 144–56. Print.

Soukup, Katarina. "Banquet of Profanities: Food and Subversion in Věra Chytilová's *Daisies*." *Tessera* 24 (1998): 38–52. Print.

Stephenson, Gregory. *The Daybreak Boys: Essays on the Literature of the Beat Generation*. Carbondale: Southern Illinois UP, 1990. Print.

Sterritt, David. "Revision, Prevision, and the Aura of Improvisatory Art." *Journal of Aesthetics & Art Criticism* 58.2 (2000): 163–72. Print.

Strickman, Daniel, Stephen P. Frances, and Mustapha Debboun. *Prevention of Bug Bites, Stings, and Disease*. Oxford: Oxford UP, 2009. Print.

Suiter, John. *Poets on the Peaks: Gary Snyder, Philip Whalen and Jack Kerouac in the North Cascades*. New York: Counterpoint, 2002. Print.

Sullivan, Heather. "Unbalanced Nature, Unbounded Bodies, and Unlimited Technology: Ecocriticism and Karen Traviss." *Bulletin of Science, Technology and Society* 30.4 (2010): 274–84. Print.

Talbot, Rob. "Sedmikrásky—Věra Chytilová, Czechoslovakia 1966." Rev. of *Daisies*. *Cult and World Cinema Connection*. 5 Jan. 2013. Web. 3 Aug. 2014. <http://robtalbotcultandworld.blogspot.cz/2013/01/daisies-1966.html?q=daisies>.

Tarlo, Harriet. *Ground Aslant: An Anthology of Radical Landscape Poetry*. Exeter: Shearsman Books, 2011. Print.

———. "Radical Landscapes: Experiment and Environment in Contemporary Poetry." *Jacket* 32 (2007): n. pag. Web. 14 Aug. 2014.

———. "Recycles: The Eco-Ethical Poetics of Found Text in Contemporary Poetry." *Journal of Ecocriticism* 1.2 (2009): 114–30. Print.

Thompson, Bill. Rev. of *Sedmikrásky* (*Daisies*, 1966), dir. Věra Chytilová. *Bill's Movie Emporium*. WordPress, 17 Dec. 2013. Web. 25 Aug. 2014.

Thoreau, Henry David. *Resistance to Civil Government*. Project Gutenberg. 3 May 2011. Web. 10 Aug. 2012.

———. "Walking." *The Thoreau Reader*. Iowa State University Department of English, n.d. Web. 4 Mar. 2009.

———. *Writings of Thoreau*. The Internet Archive, n.d. Web. 8 Nov. 2012.

Tietchen, Todd. "Language out of Language: Excavating the Roots of Culture Jamming and Postmodern Activism from William S. Burroughs' *Nova* Trilogy." *Discourse* 23.3 (2001): 107–29. Print.

Todorov, Tzvetan. *The Poetics of Prose*. Ithaca: Cornell UP, 1977. Print.

Tovey, Paige. "The Measured Chaos of Gary Snyder's Post-Romantic Poetic Form." *Romantic Presences in the Twentieth Century*. Ed. Mark Sandy. Amsterdam: Ashgate, 2012. 73–88. Print.

Tsai, Jen-chieh. "From Need to Needle: 'The Cult of Addiction' in William Burroughs's *Junky*." *NTU Studies in Language and Literature* 16 (2006): 1–24. Print.

Tsivian, Yuri. "Cinemetrics, Part of the Humanities' Cyberinfrastructure." *Digital Tools in Media Studies*. Ed. Michael Ross, Manfred Grauer, and Bernd Freisleben. Bielefeld, Germany: Transaction Publishers, 2009. 93–100. Print.

Tzara, Tristan. *Seven Dada Manifestos and Lampisteries*. Trans. Barbara Wright. London: John Calder, 1977. Print.

Vance, Linda. "Beyond Just-So Stories: Narrative, Animals, and Ethics." *Animals and Women: Feminist Theoretical Explorations*. Ed. Carol J. Adams and Josephine Donovan. Durham: Duke UP, 1995. 163–91. Print.

Van der Bent, Jaap. "Beating Them to It? The Vienna Group and the Beat Generation." *The Transnational Beat Generation*. Ed. Nancy M. Grace and Jennie Skerl. New York: Palgrave Macmillan, 2012. 165–78. Print.

Vetsch, Florian. "Nur den Hauch einer Chance." *Neue Zürcher Zeitung* 12 Feb. 2003: 45. Print.

Von Ziegesar, Peter. "After Armageddon: Apocalyptic Art since the Seventies: Tactics of Survival in a Postnuclear Planet." *The Year 2000: Essays on the End*. Ed. Charles B. Strozier and Michael Flynn. New York: NYUP, 1997. 284–99. Print.

Wald, Priscilla. *Contagious: Cultures, Carriers, and the Outbreak Narrative*. Durham: Duke UP, 2008. Print.

Wapner, Paul. "Leftist Criticism of 'Nature': Environmental Protection in a Postmodern Age." *Dissent* 50.1 (2003): 71–75. Print.

Watson, Steven. *The Birth of the Beat Generation: Visionaries, Rebels, and Hipsters, 1944–1960*. New York: Pantheon, 1995. Print.

Watters, John G. "The Control Machine: Myth in *The Soft Machine* of W. S. Burroughs." *Connotations* 5.2–3 (1995): 284–303. Print.

Weinreich, Regina. "The Dynamic Déjà Vu of William Burroughs." *Review of Contemporary Fiction* 4.1 (1984): 55–58. Print.

Weinstone, Ann. "Welcome to the Pharmacy: Addiction, Transcendence, and Virtual Reality." *Diacritics* 27.3 (1997): 77–89. Print.

Weir, John. "The 10 Most Hated Books." *Advocate* 24 June 1997: 91. Print.

Wells, Ryan. "Girls Gone Wild!" *Cinespect* 5 July 2012 Web. 11 June 2014.

West, Nathanael. *Miss Lonelyhearts & the Day of the Locust*. New York: New Directions, 2009. Print.

Weston, L. K. Rev. of *Daisies/Sedimkrásky* DVD. *Cine Outsider*. 2009. Web. 12 June 2014.

Wheeler, Elizabeth A. "Don't Climb Every Mountain." *Interdisciplinary Studies in Literature and Environment* 20.3 (2013): 553–73. Print.

Whitaker, Steven. "Burroughs and De Quincey: Two Tasters of 'The Divine Luxuries.'" *Dionysos: The Literature and Addiction TriQuarterly* 4.3 (1993): 9–11. Print.

White, Lynn, Jr. "The Historical Roots of Our Ecologic Crisis." *The Ecocriticism Reader: Landmarks in Literary Ecology.* Ed. Cheryll Glotfelty and Harold Fromm. Athens: U of Georgia P, 1996. 3–14. Print.

Wolfe, Cary. *Animal Rites: American Culture, the Discourse of Species, and Posthumanist Theory.* Chicago: University of Chicago Press, 2003. Print.

"World Cancer Group to Meet in London; 50 Soviet Specialists Listed to Attend." *New York Times* 4 July 1958: 4. Print.

INDEX

CHAD WEIDNER teaches English and film at University College Roosevelt, Utrecht University, in the Netherlands. He has published on ecocriticism, experimental aesthetics, Dadaist film, Burroughs, and other Beat writers.